I0754910

PRIVACY'S DEFENDER

The MIT Press's publishing mission benefits from the generosity of our donors, including Sally Yu.

PRIVACY'S DEFENDER

MY THIRTY-YEAR FIGHT AGAINST DIGITAL SURVEILLANCE

CINDY COHN

THE MIT PRESS CAMBRIDGE, MASSACHUSETTS LONDON, ENGLAND

The MIT Press
Massachusetts Institute of Technology
77 Massachusetts Avenue
Cambridge, MA 02139
mitpress.mit.edu

The MIT Press would like to thank the anonymous peer reviewers who provided comments on drafts of this book. The generous work of academic experts is essential for establishing the authority and quality of our publications. We acknowledge with gratitude the contributions of these otherwise uncredited readers.

This book was set in ITC Stone and Avenir by New Best-set Typesetters Ltd. Printed and bound in the United States of America.

Library of Congress Cataloging-in-Publication Data is available.

ISBN: 978-0-262-05124-8

10 9 8 7 6 5 4 3

EU Authorised Representative: Easy Access System Europe, Mustamäe tee 50, 10621 Tallinn, Estonia | Email: gpsr.requests@easproject.com

To all the Fighting EFFers, past, present, and future,
and
Patrick, Steven, KC, and the Ladle,
and
and all the four-leggeds,
Chimpy, Samedi, Dimanche, Sadie, Cosmo, Buffy, Willow, Kodiak,
McKinley, Denali, and Whitney

In this increasingly electronic age, we are all required in our everyday lives to rely on modern technology to communicate with each other. This reliance on electronic communication, however, has brought with it a dramatic diminution in our ability to communicate privately. . . . Whether we are surveilled by our governments, by criminals or by our neighbors, it is fair to say that never has our ability to shield our affairs from prying eyes been at such a low ebb.

—Judge Betty Fletcher, *Bernstein v. Department of Justice,* May 6, 1999

This capability at any time could be turned around on the American people, and no American would have any privacy left, such is the capability to monitor everything: telephone conversations, telegrams, it doesn't matter. There would be no place to hide. The technological capacity that the intelligence community has given the government could enable it to impose total tyranny . . . and we must see to it that this agency and all agencies that possess this technology operate within the law and under proper supervision, so that we never cross over that abyss. That is the abyss from which there is no return.

—Senator Frank Church, *Meet the Press,* August 17, 1975

CONTENTS

PREFACE AND ACKNOWLEDGMENTS ix

INTRODUCTION 1

1 **FREEING CRYPTOGRAPHY: *BERNSTEIN V. DEPARTMENT OF JUSTICE*** 11

2 **NATIONAL SECURITY AGENCY SPYING: *HEPTING* AND *JEWEL*** 79

3 **NATIONAL SECURITY LETTERS: THE ALPHABET CASES** 169

CONCLUSION 203

LIST OF ABBREVIATIONS 211
NOTES 213
INDEX 225

PREFACE AND ACKNOWLEDGMENTS

While this book is true to my memories, it's still a memoir, not a history. I have re-created conversations, and provide my impressions of other people's positions and reactions based on what I recall. The stories should be interpreted that way rather than as exact quotes or objective truths. I have changed many of the names of people who are not already publicly known, including my birth family, friends, and exes. I have left out some pieces of my personal life where I thought they would be more hurtful than helpful or not sufficiently relevant to the larger story. Finally, I am certain that I have forgotten or overlooked many important moments and people along the way. My apologies to anyone who I've accidentally slighted or written out of this extremely personal set of stories. All mistakes are my own.

Another caveat. The Electronic Frontier Foundation (EFF) has done much more work than the stories I tell here. We helped ensure that the First and Fourth Amendments apply online, although there's more work to be done on each. We helped set a high bar for attempts to unmask anonymous speakers in online forums to stop intimidation by litigation. We have consistently supported section 230, a law that protects the intermediaries that everyone needs in order to speak and share information online. While the focus of this book is governmental attacks on privacy, we have argued against the current surveillance business model and for a comprehensive consumer privacy law since long before concerns about surveillance capitalism became front-page news.

There's more. We also established that bloggers are journalists and subject to journalist shield laws. We fought against the early, insecure electronic voting machines that had no way to audit or recount votes. We started a patent-busting project that for over a decade fought to eliminate stupid patents—a phrase coined by the investor Mark Cuban, who also financially supported that work.

EFF, along with our friend Aaron Swartz, helped lead the charge against two proposed laws called SOPA/PIPA that would have created a "blacklist" of censored websites based on accusations of copyright infringement. We pushed back on copyright bullies, including defending a mom who received a takedown because she posted a video of her toddler dancing to a Prince song.

Our Coders' Rights Project has helped countless security researchers conduct and publish their work, thereby aiding all of us to have a more secure digital world. We have long defended free and open-source coding and coders. We keep pushing back on the overbroad application of computer crime laws. EFF helped encrypt the web as a part of the Let's Encrypt project. We built Privacy Badger to help users protect themselves against online tracking and surveillance capitalism.

As well, we stood up for digital privacy beyond the Fourth Amendment—pushing back against government use of facial recognition tools, automated license plate readers, ubiquitous cameras, and the exploding surveillance dystopia at or near the US southern border as part of our Street-Level Surveillance work.

And that's just the start.

There are other books to be written about all of this other work and more. I hope others will tell those stories because they are important. By choosing to focus on these three governmental, national security-based privacy fights, I in no way mean to diminish all of that work, or the fearless fighters at EFF who continue to do it.

Thanks to EFF staff and board of directors, who agreed with me that these stories needed to be told, trusted me to do so, and have supported me from this initial idea to its completion. Special thanks to Shari Steele and Pam Samuelson, who have been my champions and heroes throughout the past thirty-odd years.

My appreciation to the unflappable Madeleine Mulkern for her expert help wrangling this text as well as several sets of EFF interns who helped with the research and cite checking, especially Katie Farr and Nick Delehanty.

Thanks also to Rebecca Jeschke for the original suggestion to write a book, Cory Doctorow and Dave Maass for reading early proposals, and Jennifer Lynch for handling the legal side for EFF along with Michael Wolfe. Heartfelt gratitude to Bruce Schneier for his enthusiastic initial reading of my proposal and connecting me to the MIT Press. Thanks to Gita Manaktala and the MIT Press for taking a chance on me, and Elaine Elinson for supportive editing.

This book would not exist without Rainey Reitman, who signed on to make sure that I would actually write it even as I continued serving as EFF's executive director. As anyone who has ever worked with Rainey can attest, she is a force of nature. Rainey never let me slide away from the book for too long, and served as a coach, thought partner, enthusiastic first reader, and strong editor. Her thoughtfulness, careful reading, and inspirational ideas are reflected throughout the book. I'm eternally grateful.

Finally, my deep and ongoing thanks to John Gilmore. John had the vision to help found and steer EFF for its first thirty years, and took a chance on a young, female, nontechnical lawyer to handle one of the most important early cases involving privacy and the internet. Even when we have disagreed—and we have definitely disagreed—John has never wavered in his support of me or in his commitment to preserving privacy.

INTRODUCTION

CYPHERPUNK DRESS-UP DAY

As I rounded the corner from the elevator on the nineteenth floor of the federal building in San Francisco, I could see that the crew that gathered in front of Judge Marilyn Hall Patel's courtroom was definitely not your normal courthouse fare. Standing and even sitting on the majestic marble floors were well over thirty people. Mostly pale white men in their thirties, with longish, stringy hair, they were uniformly scruffy and awkwardly dressed in suits and ties. They all seemed to be in outfits that their mothers had picked out for them for a family wedding.

Or maybe I was just projecting. I was thirty-two years old, worried about my hair, and wore a suit that my mother picked out for me from the Denver department store where she worked.

They may have been a motley bunch, but they warmed my heart. They were there to show support for me as I argued a case called *Bernstein v. Department of Justice*.

It may not have looked like it, but it was obvious to me and that crew gathered on a cool San Francisco morning in September 1996 that what happened in that courtroom would be crucial to the future of the internet. How Judge Patel ruled would play a major role in determining whether people would have privacy online.

I must have seemed nervous because my cocounsel Jim Wheaton looked over at me. He touched my elbow and said quietly, "You're in your mother's arms."

With that, I pulled open the heavy wooden doors and walked into the courtroom.

PRIVACY ISN'T WHAT YOU THINK IT IS

Privacy isn't what most people think it is, at least not entirely.

It's not a secret coat of anonymity you throw on before doing something embarrassing. It's not about keeping your passwords safe or your sex life hidden. It's not even about freedom of the mind.

Yes, all of those are pieces of privacy, but they aren't the whole thing. Privacy scholar Daniel Solove has done more than anyone else to try to enumerate all the pieces of privacy, and he rightly articulated it as including freedom of thought, control over one's body, solitude in one's home, control over personal information, freedom from surveillance, protection of one's reputation, and protection from searches and interrogations. But Professor Solove also pointed out that it's far more helpful to talk about what privacy is "for" rather than what privacy "is."[1]

For individuals like you and me, privacy is fundamentally *for* control—for giving us control over who can know what we do, where we do it, and who we do it with. In that way it is fundamental to our individual safety, dignity, and human rights.

But here's the broader, less talked about thing that privacy is for—one that has animated my work for thirty years: privacy is a check on power.

Privacy limits the power of individuals over each other. It limits the power of governments over us. It also limits the power of corporations over us. Privacy allows people to protect themselves while creating a space to think, connect, communicate, share, and most critically, organize for change.

Put another way, privacy is important to *each* of us individually, but it is important for *all* of us too. Safeguarding privacy is part of safeguarding a free, open, democratic society that supports everyone's rights and liberties.

The protection that privacy gives isn't just theoretical. At EFF, we've worked with people who have suffered harassment, assault, arrest, torture, and disappearances facilitated by surveillance of their online accounts or devices. Some are domestic violence victims trying to escape their abusers, others are members of disfavored minority or marginalized groups, and still others are activists, journalists, or lawyers.

The range of people at risk from their digital footprints is wide and growing. In 2023, a mother in Nebraska went to jail for discussing an abortion with her daughter using Facebook Messenger after Facebook was required to turn those messages over to law enforcement.[2] Text messages between friends were used as the basis for a lawsuit against them in Texas for helping one of them seek an abortion.[3] The issue of reproductive freedom in the United States after the Supreme Court struck down the federal right to abortion has awakened many people in the United States to this truth that members of marginalized groups, human right defenders, and journalists have known for years: the lack of privacy can be very, very dangerous.

Privacy's historical importance in checking power is clear once you start looking. In the civil rights era, the Supreme Court expressly recognized the connection between privacy, the First Amendment, and dissent by rejecting an Alabama law that required the NAACP to reveal its membership lists to a hostile state government. Separately, and just within my lifetime, we've moved from a situation in which privacy was necessary for the safety of those discussing the idea that gay people should have the right to love and marry who they choose, to this right being vindicated in the Supreme Court. Most people remember the public parts of those fights for justice—the protests, lawsuits, and congressional debates—but each of those fights required privacy in order to get started as well as to resist brutal backlashes from governments and other opponents.

Privacy was also critical to the founding of the United States. Thomas Jefferson, John Adams, James Madison, and others needed to have many private conversations to create the conditions under which they could check the power of their colonial rulers. Some even used an encryption method developed by Jefferson as they plotted and carried out a revolution over great physical distances. This is like thousands of other activists for freedom and justice around the world who have needed privacy to help them organize.[4] It is no accident that controlling and surveilling how citizens communicate is consistently one of the first moves of a dictatorship, or that finding ways to avoid that surveillance is a key step for freedom movements.

The digital era presents new challenges for privacy. This is something the founders of my organization, the Electronic Frontier Foundation (EFF), saw in 1990. Some of these challenges are technical and others are legal. Technically it is much easier to surveil thousands or even millions of people digitally, especially since all of our digital communications and activities pass through a series of third-party service providers. Legally, the law still treats the noncontent parts of our communications—called metadata, as I'll discuss more later—as deserving of less privacy protection, even though the collection and analysis of metadata is an extremely powerful way to spy on us. Worse, both of these challenges have been supercharged by the online surveillance business models that emerged in the early 2000s and have become ubiquitous.

While I care deeply about personal privacy, this public purpose of checking power is why standing up for privacy has been my life's work. Over the years I've taken on the intelligence community, Federal Bureau of Investigation (FBI), and the tech and telecom giants, each time to try to protect and enhance the check on power that privacy can provide.

Because if we can do that, we can create the space necessary to push the needle online toward human rights, freedom, and democracy. But if we fail, we face what the digital world could easily become: the most repressive, controlling, and authoritarian space ever created. We could end up with what US senator Frank Church in 1975 called "total tyranny," and what more recently National Security Agency (NSA) whistleblower Edward Snowden called "turnkey totalitarianism."[5]

NATIONAL SECURITY TALISMAN

One of the frustrating things about fighting these fights from the 1990s onward has been how often I've felt like Cassandra—issuing warnings about the dangers of unchecked surveillance and incursions into privacy that were consistently ignored or brushed off. I've tried to convince high-ranking national security officials that even if they would never misuse the awesome spy powers they were amassing, a future set of government officials might not be as honorable. This hubris, belief in their own goodness and the power of norms led multiple administrations to resist efforts to reform the excesses of the post-9/11 spying, despite a growing mountain of evidence of gross mistakes and abuses. As you'll see in the rest of this book, national security has become a talisman that can be held up to reduce the checks and balances built into our Constitution and laws.

In early 2025, the second Trump administration summarily fired many of those same national security professionals and has stripped some of their security clearances. The Trump government seems not only uninterested in observing the stated norms of the previous administrations but also hell-bent on publicly blowing past them. It has repeatedly deployed and expanded the national security talisman. It is no surprise that one of the first things that the second Trump administration did was seize control of the giant government agency databases that contain personal information about tens of millions of people in the United States. I fear we are at, if not over, the abyss before tyranny that Senator Church warned about.

THIS BOOK

I've framed this book as a memoir because I don't just want to make an argument in favor of digital privacy. I'm a practitioner, not a journalist or academic. I want to bring you with me into the actual work of protecting privacy, especially in the courts. This frontline work is how privacy actually gets protected, and my goal is to pull back the curtain so that you can see not just what we did but how we did it, and how it felt along the way.

This book contains stories about three sets of lawsuits I've handled trying to protect and extend the right to privacy in the digital age.

The first story is about my fight in the 1990s to free up the science of encryption from US government regulation that effectively blocked internet users from obtaining security and privacy.

The second one arises out of a set of cases that started in 2005, but really reach back to the government's secret response to the 9/11 attacks in 2001. Through these cases, I tried to stop the NSA from dragnet spying on the internet, which it did by piggybacking on the networks run by the telecommunications giants AT&T and Verizon. The NSA spying cases finally ended at the Supreme Court in 2022.

The third story is about the cases we brought to scale back a kind of governmental subpoena called National Security Letters (NSLs), which had been supercharged by the USA Patriot Act in 2001. NSLs allowed the FBI to require various companies to provide metadata about their customers and then gagged them from ever telling anyone what had happened. Those cases started in 2011 and ended in 2022, so the second and third set of stories overlap in time.

While these three sets of cases are now all in the past, they help set the frame for some of the issues we confront today and will continue to face regardless of the specifics of the technology. Protecting the publication of information and the separation of powers, closely scrutinizing national security claims and ensuring transparency in government will all remain vital to preserving our human rights. The legal arguments and strategies may shift, but protecting privacy will remain a critical part of protecting people against power, whether the mechanisms for spying are based in artificial intelligence, drones, nanotechnologies, neurotechnologies, or something entirely new.

In between the court cases, I'll talk about the ways that my personal life intertwined with and was enriched by this work. Because a life standing up for privacy—or whatever value grabs your heart and won't let go—isn't just about the work. Privacy is both a personal and public right, and my fights for it have included both sides too.

PRIVACY, REALLY?

Now I know what you're thinking: How quaint to talk about privacy right now! Wasn't it declared dead a long time ago, leaving us in a sea of cameras, logs, cookies, and pixels that have trapped us in a modern panopticon? And haven't the titanic companies surpassed the government as a threat to our privacy?

Let me start by dismantling the false choice often embedded in these questions: that some sort of separation exists between private, corporate surveillance and governmental surveillance such that we have the luxury of choosing which one we care about more. We don't. It's a mistake to not see how the intelligence agencies and law enforcement rely on the data that companies collect about us.[6] All the stories I'll tell here arise from the government's piggybacking on private data collection and handling. And the government's interest in ongoing access to that corporate data is one of the things blocking comprehensive privacy legislation. The truth is that too much corporate power to spy on us and too much government power to spy on us are each a threat individually, and they combine for a truly toxic mix. Ultimately, they undermine our ability to check either source of power over us.

And what about the other old saw: that privacy and security are on some sort of teeter-totter, such that if we give up some of our privacy, we'll get more security? I'm still waiting for the evidence that this is true. There is a widespread belief—fueled by law enforcement and the intelligence agencies—that somehow we can surveil ourselves to safety. But if that were true, we'd see increased security in places where we have more surveillance, like the plethora of cameras in city neighborhoods across the country where low-income and marginalized people live. These places already have much more surveillance than suburban and country locations without becoming demonstrably safer—especially for the people who live there.

Another example of more surveillance without more security is police-worn body cameras. These cameras were sold to the public as a way to reduce police violence and ensure truth in prosecutions. But in part due to the power dynamics that allow most police to control what gets recorded, review the recordings before giving their statements, or outright deny or delay release to the public or victims, we haven't seen a sea change in police accountability (much less police behavior) from the millions of taxpayer dollars spent on these cameras.[7]

I believe that over time, privacy and security are mutually reinforcing. This is especially the case with encryption, where the same techniques that offer privacy also provide security and protection from criminals, stalkers, and spies.

Yet it's also true that privacy can be controversial and even subversive, as in the case of the founders of the United States. The right to privacy can protect our ability to disobey—including disobeying criminal laws that are reasonable and justified as well as those that are oppressive. There is an old saying that one man's terrorist is another man's freedom fighter. Privacy protects them both.

In theory, privacy can make it more difficult for governments to locate and identify wrongdoers. Yet people often envision a "ticking time bomb" scenario that comes out of movies and TV, seeing privacy as a barrier to stopping malicious actors who are just about to do terrible things. But what makes exciting television isn't really how law enforcement or the intelligence community do their work. Real police and intelligence work happen during a timespan that almost always leaves more than enough time to seek a warrant or other judicial review to minimize mistakes and avoid misuse. And both mistakes and misuse happen far more often than we see on TV.

Fights about digital surveillance also tend to assume that it is the only tool in the governmental toolbox, ignoring more widely used techniques like old-fashioned physical surveillance, convincing one participant of an encrypted or secret conversation to provide access, or infiltrating criminal or terrorist networks. Moreover, TV almost never shows you the reality that having collected so much information, the ability to sort through it all for what matters becomes its own problem. When you're looking for a needle in a haystack—and even today terrorist attacks are still that rare and unpredictable—adding more hay to the pile can make the job harder, not easier.

In my thirty years of these fights, the government consistently exaggerates the risks—calling the use of encryption "going dark" and making apocalyptic predictions that never seem to come true.[8] We regularly find out that claims of mass surveillance actually playing a key role in solving terrorist attacks or serious crimes are overblown, if not flat-out lies. For the likely hundreds of millions of innocent people whose communications were subject to the NSA's mass surveillance that I discuss in the second set of stories in this book, and the hundreds of thousands of people impacted by NSLs that I explore in the third set of stories, fewer than 550 individuals in the United States were convicted of terrorism in total in the fifteen years between 2001 and 2016.[9]

While stopping even one horrific attack is important, these techniques just haven't been shown to do so, especially inside the United States. At the same time, misuse and abuse have been consistent, including incidents of government officials tracking their exes and lovers, deemed "love intelligence" or "LOVEINT" by the NSA.[10] Various US inspector general reports show just how sloppy the government is with our privacy, even with rules that are extremely loose. I suspect much more is not yet visible to the public. At some point we should demand that the benefits be weighed honestly against the costs. Those costs include lost liberty and trust of those communities targeted. More practically, those costs include a tremendous amount of taxpayer money and other resources that could have been put toward strategies that would actually make us safer.

But for the purposes of this book, I'll concede that for both law enforcement and the intelligence communities, their jobs solving crimes and listening to spies or potential terrorists could be easier if no one had privacy—with no pesky warrant requirements and communications just sitting on the open wire so that they are easy to tap into, collect, and analyze.

The question isn't whether privacy always protects conversations that are good. It doesn't, any more than free speech always protects ideas we agree with or due process always protects the innocent. Instead, the question of protecting privacy is about what kind of a society we want to live in: one that protects human dignity along with the ability for society to change and self-govern, or one that makes the job of law enforcement and spies a little easier while putting us all at greater risk not only from our own governments but from foreign governments and criminals too.

This assertion—that people need privacy and security so we should build and protect the tools that give it to them as well as require limits on law enforcement's powers to surveil them even if it sometimes makes law enforcement's job harder—seems straightforward and even banal. But the path to making it happen has been anything but. We've been at it for over thirty years now and we're still fighting.

At times this has puzzled me, and at other times I kind of understand it, but mostly it just infuriates me. That's a long way of saying that for any number of reasons—from small, individual dignity to the protection of democracy and self-government—I strongly disagree with the former CEO of Sun Microsystems that privacy is something we just need to "get over."[11] I hope by the end of this book that you'll agree.

I AM TRYING TO RECRUIT YOU

Cards on the table: I'm trying to recruit you. That's why I included so much of my personal story here, including when and how I have found support in dark times. Of course, if I convince you to join the digital rights movement, I'll be overjoyed. But I hope that these stories help inspire you to jump into whatever righteous cause calls to you. We need lawyers for digital rights, but we also need coders, artists, marketers, scientists and economists. And we need all of those and more for issues far afield from the internet too, yet that still contribute to a better, more just world. Regardless of the context, I hope to inspire you to dedicate some of your life to making the world a better place, in whatever way best suits you. If you do, surprising and interesting things can also happen in your personal life. At least they did in mine.

I have another reason for writing down these stories. I have noticed something about the narratives that tend to dominate the history of the first two decades of broad public internet use. The central tales seemed to be about the handful of predominantly white men who built businesses out of new technologies—with names like Steve Jobs, Bill Gates, Sergey Brin, Eric Schmidt, and Jeff Bezos, and then following them, Mark Zuckerberg, Jack Dorsey, Sam Altman, Elon Musk, and Tim Cook.

Not that these aren't important stories, but they paint a pretty narrow portrait of what were incredibly rich times. They feed a false sense that businesses were all that mattered in the early internet. These narratives overlook people like me, along with the hackers who built the networks and protocols that support privacy, and the cypherpunks (sometimes the same people) who publicly pushed for both the law and technology to support digital privacy from the earliest days of the internet. We had a large, colorful, and eclectic posse working to embed privacy into the law and technology of this new digital world. While we didn't always win, our work helped make things better. I'm hoping that by sharing these stories, I'll help make the history of the first two decades of the public internet a little more complete.

1

FREEING CRYPTOGRAPHY: *BERNSTEIN V. DEPARTMENT OF JUSTICE*

MATH = PRIVACY AND SECURITY?

When I walked into the San Francisco courtroom on that September day, I was a lawyer representing Daniel Bernstein, a math PhD student who was studying at the University of California at Berkeley. Dan specialized in cryptography, also called encryption. Cryptography works by scrambling information so that it can only be accessed by someone with a kind of key, keeping it secret from anyone who doesn't have that key.

The facts of the case were undisputed: Bernstein wanted to publish some cryptographic computer code and an academic paper in an online public forum called sci.crypt. Cryptographers and security experts used the forum to share and develop ideas about cryptography. The government forbade Bernstein from publishing his work without first applying for a license, and given the kind of encryption Bernstein wanted to publish, the license would not be granted.

The case may have seemed like it was about computers, math, or science, but it was also about privacy, confidentiality, security, and the right to free speech.

How did encryption, an ancient science of applied math, become so critical to our privacy and security online? It's because scrambling digital communications and data so that they can only be unscrambled by others with a digital key ends up being one of the only ways we can control who has access to the information we create, store, and share on digital systems.

Put another way, an internet without encryption is one without trust at its most basic level. We cannot trust that we know who we're talking to, where we're navigating to, or that our messages were not altered in transit. Without that trust, so many things that we rely on the internet for just wouldn't have developed.

In the 1990s before encryption became widely available, no communication on the internet—whether intimate, professional, or ideological—could happen without fear of exposure, fraud, and interruption. The same is true of sales for everything from airplane tickets to office supplies to groceries. Everything we buy or sell online relies on encryption to protect those transactions. Online banking, investing, and services like Zelle and Venmo that let us send money to friends, buy from small businesses, or donate to a good cause all rely on encryption too. Without encryption we could not have end-to-end secure messaging through software like Signal, WhatsApp, or Apple's iMessage. Only a fool would put confidential business plans or trade secrets into an email or cloud storage before encryption became ubiquitous.

While we didn't have handheld mobile devices in the 1990s, other than some clunky and expensive ones, encryption was a necessary element for those to become trustworthy tools too. Without encryption of your data, if your phone or computer was stolen or lost, anyone who had physical custody could have easy access to your entire life. In all likelihood, they could also thoroughly impersonate you. That password, finger, or face you use to unlock your phone or computer gives a lot of protection that just wouldn't exist if encryption had remained highly restricted.

But wait, there's more. Encryption helps ensure that when we think we're at our bank's website, we can trust that we actually are, instead of at some fake site that has hijacked our device, browser, or network. Without encryption, we couldn't trust that when we go to our local government website, we're actually getting the government's information about weather and other emergencies, where to get services or where to vote. The list goes on.

Don't get me wrong; we still have tremendous security and privacy problems on the internet today, and still need more trust. Criminal and state-sponsored hacking, data breaches, identity theft, and other attacks on our networks continue to be dangerous as well as costly problems. We're nowhere near the security needed to vote with a secret ballot online. Biometric identifiers create their own issues. But without encryption, it would be much, much worse. It's fair to say that if we had not freed encryption, the internet would be a much less useful and much less important place than it has become. It could easily have stayed the tool and plaything of a few elite hackers, scientists, and governments that it was in the 1990s.

When we started this case, the US government was actively blocking the deployment of strong encryption tools. The Department of Justice criminally investigated a Colorado man named Philip Zimmermann for creating and publishing a strong encryption program for use by anyone called PGP.[1] PGP is short for pretty good privacy. The name is an homage to the claim of "Powdermilk Biscuits," the fictitious sponsor of public radio's *A Prairie Home Companion*, to be "pretty good" for everyone. In this it nods both to the Midwestern gift of understatement and the idea of making cryptography available to all. PGP was widely used by human rights activists and journalists, yet Zimmermann faced a multiyear fight for his freedom for offering this basic privacy tool.

And it wasn't just Zimmermann. Cryptographic academics, businessperson, scientists, and developers all faced governmental threats. The US government was serious that it viewed encryption as a weapon.

SOFTWARE CAPABLE OF MAINTAINING SECRECY

The specific rules we were challenging in court that September day, and that were critical to blocking the development of encryption for all the uses I named above, were, somewhat strangely, export restrictions. The US Munitions List is a giant list of all the things that no one can export from the United States without a license. This includes things like rocket launchers, grenades, and chemical weapons. In the early 1990s it also included encryption software, specifically "software capable of maintaining secrecy."

The regulations define "export" as making something available to foreigners abroad, so publishing anything on the public internet qualifies as an export since foreigners always potentially have access. That's how a grad student publishing a computer program from Berkeley, California on an internet newsgroup still ran afoul of the export regulations.

This export restriction may have made sense in a time where secret codes were predominantly a military tool. After all, the breaking of Nazi encryption by the Enigma device—led by legendary scientist Alan Turing and accomplished by a crew of women code breakers at Bletchley Park near London—is rightly credited as critical to the Allied victory in World War II.[2]

But the fact that in the 1990s encryption software remained categorized as a munition meant that it remained a serious criminal offense to share the information as well as develop and distribute the tools that would help protect us, even as the developing internet made digital security and privacy more critical to more people than ever.

HOW DID A NICE IOWA GIRL LIKE YOU COME TO SUE THE NSA?

So how did I become the person walking into court that day? At one point a reporter asked me that, not so subtly pointing out my gender along with my Midwestern childhood. While the phrasing was a little belittling, in some ways it probably does start from my beginning.

I grew up in a small town in central Iowa, but I wasn't born there. I was born in Detroit and had been adopted at birth. My parents had always treated my adoption as my special story. When the call came that I had been born, they jumped into their yellow station wagon with fake wood siding and headed east to Michigan to pick me up. Along the way, they dropped off my eight-year-old brother Steven with my aunt and uncle who were living on a naval station in Chicago since my uncle was in the navy. While my brother was waiting for my parents to return, he colored and cut out paper baby bottles and taped them to the ceiling of their ranch house.

According to my mother, their station wagon didn't have a license plate for some reason, so it was illegal to drive it across state lines. This gave the story a tiny bit of outlaw flavor. My mother said that she urged my father to drive under the speed limit, despite their hurry, since she was afraid of getting stopped by the police while crossing from Iowa through Illinois, to Michigan and back. The implication was that he didn't listen to her because he was so eager to meet me. I loved the story since that was about as "outlaw" as my Midwestern parents ever got.

When they returned, they told their friends to meet at their house for a surprise, but didn't tell them what it was. There had been all sorts of speculation that it was a new car or refrigerator. Then the punch line came: "They drove up with a baby girl with the biggest brown eyes we'd ever seen!"

In addition to my older brother, my mother got pregnant again four years after they adopted me. That was my little sister. I was the adopted one yet also the middle child. I looked like my parents, so much so that we'd play games and have people guess which one of us was adopted. They'd usually pick my blond sister or redheaded brother rather than me, the brunette like my parents.

I was a daddy's girl, crawling into his lap when he got home after work as he settled into his brown tweed easy chair with a blended whiskey. On the weekends we went camping as a family, over the years moving from a tent to a pop-up camper to a small motor home. Dad loved to fish, so we camped near lakes and reservoirs. At the end of those days, we often had fresh walleye, crappie, or catfish for dinner. Dad and I were Minnesota Vikings fans, in the days of Fran Tarkington, Chuck Foreman, and Ahmad Rashad.

Even so, I always felt that in some critical ways, I didn't quite fit in. I couldn't shake the feeling that I could be abandoned or exiled at any time.

That vulnerable feeling was fed by what happened when I was about eight. I woke one morning and my mother was gone. A family friend was in the kitchen making breakfast for my brother, sister, and me. She told us that our mom had gone to the hospital, but that we still needed to go to school. I later learned that my mother had developed bipolar disorder, and the illness led her to hear voices as well as act paranoid and erratic. I had seen that myself. Just before she was taken away, she had come into my bedroom in the middle of the night. She did not seem like herself at all and had angrily demanded that I make my bed. It was confusing and scary. My father came in to get her and told me to go back to sleep.

We kids numbly went to school as we were told. By the time we came home, my father was there. He sat us at the kitchen counter and told us that our mom would be gone for a while, and that we could not visit or call her. I don't remember much about that time, just being scared that she wouldn't come back.

In a way, she didn't. When she returned home a month or so later, she was quite a different person. She had undergone shock treatments and was on the heavy medication called lithium that was the norm for what was labeled a "nervous breakdown" in the 1970s. She was slower, less able to think, and her emotions were flattened in ways that were obvious, even to us kids. But she also wasn't manic anymore and didn't act strangely.

I adapted to losing her and getting her back by working hard to not be any trouble. I started thinking of myself as her caretaker and protector as well as the protector of my little sister. I got good grades and was responsible. I worked hard to be perfect on the outside. I even chased popularity since she wanted me to be a cheerleader. Inside I always felt like it could all go away at any time if I didn't do everything right.

Our family didn't talk much about what had happened, either with each other or our friends. I don't recall being told to keep it a secret, but that's essentially what we did. I retreated into books, reading voraciously, mainly fiction, where I could easily slip into other times, places, and families.

I got another lesson in privacy when I was about thirteen. My parents went through a messy divorce that was fodder for a lot of gossip, in part since divorce was relatively rare in small-town Iowa in the early 1970s. We had a saying in my hometown: You don't need turn signals because everyone knows where you're going. That was comforting on one level. I could choose something at many stores in the town square and just say, "Please charge it to my dad," and they would. Yet once the scandal started, it was stifling. My father began a close relationship with and later married a woman who had been my mother's good friend. In fact, she had been the woman who was in the kitchen making breakfast the morning I woke up and my mother was gone.

Everyone in town seemed to know about my parents' breakup, and my mother was thrown far off-kilter mentally. My brother was away at college across the country, so she ranted to my sister and me about what was going on, and expected us to side with her, which I definitely did. On the day my father told me that he was moving out, I had asked him to take me with him. But he insisted that I stay, saying that he needed me to take care of my sister and mother. So I had my own additional reasons to be angry at him, and feel rejected and abandoned.

Ever the good girl, though, I stepped up even further to support my mother, and she did need it. She had never held a job outside the home other than teaching swimming lessons in the summer. I helped balance her checkbook and navigate situations involving authority, including the bank, along with the phone and gas companies. Our standard of living fell as my mother tried to keep us in the same house, which she really couldn't afford. She started taking in boarders as well as collecting cans and bottles for the deposits in order to supplement the insufficient child support and alimony she received. Ultimately she took one of her first jobs as a department store clerk in the local K-Mart. Operating the cash register was beyond her, so she became the person who gave out and collected the little disks with the number of clothes to be tried on in the dressing room. I walked around town with a real feeling that we were being watched and judged by our neighbors.

There was another isolating factor too. We were one of the only Jewish families in a small Christian town. This added to my sense that we did not fit in. About the time I started high school, an evangelical movement focused on students began growing, led by an organization called the Fellowship of Christian Athletes (FCA). Suddenly kids I had known my whole life started telling me that I was going to hell if I didn't accept Jesus as my personal savior. These were kids who didn't really even know what a Jew was; my impression was that they just looked around for someone to convert and the only person they knew who wasn't already a Christian was me. I wrote a short, satiric essay about this shift for my sophomore writing class and called it, "Hey, Hey, Hey for the FCA." To my horror, my teacher posted it on the wall for everyone to see.

We weren't religious in my family. The Reform synagogue in Des Moines was forty miles away, and we rarely attended. When we did, I felt like an outsider there too, a country bumpkin to the sophisticated Des Moines kids. But we were definitely not Christian. I had friends who felt sorry for me because we didn't have a Christmas tree or visits from the Easter Bunny. In truth, I also felt quite sorry for myself about those things.

But high school was the first time I faced strong efforts to convert me. I started to bristle against them and the ways that everyone in my town seemed to assume that everyone else was also Christian. Our beautiful old courthouse on the central square was always dressed up for Christmas, complete with large lit crosses on the sides and a life-size creche on the lawn.

The last straw came when I was told that our school choir would be singing a set of religious songs for Easter at a local church. We had already performed an entire concert of Christian music for Christmas. Just a few months later we were doing it again, only this time in a church. I hemmed and hawed for a few weeks, but increasingly felt like a fraud singing these songs. Finally I screwed up my courage.

"I don't want to sing in a church for Easter," I said to the director one day after practice.

"You can do what you want, but you are graded on performances so that will impact your grade," he responded, looking back down at the score in front of him and shutting down the conversation. I quickly left the room and ran into the bathroom to compose myself.

Distraught, I went to my father, who had grown up in that little town too. He said I shouldn't make waves; I should just put my head down and do it. He didn't tell me directly, yet I learned later that he had faced much more severe anti-Jewish taunts and attacks when he was a kid. My older brother, eight years my senior and by then living out of state, confirmed that he also had been bullied for being Jewish. I learned that it had long been the case that no Jews or Blacks were hired by the local factory, which explained why there were as few Blacks as there were Jews in my little town. It opened up an ugly page in the town's history that I had not seen before.

Still, I was determined. I went to my good friend Tracy's father, Mr. Lewin, who was a local lawyer. The Lewins were Episcopalian and prominent in our town, with Mrs. Lewin having served a term as the mayor. I originally thought I wanted to be a lawyer because of Mr. Lewin, albeit based on a misinterpretation. Unlike my father, who was a traveling salesman and rarely at home, Mr. Lewin was available to take us to the local reservoir for waterskiing in the summer. In truth, I initially wanted to be a lawyer because I loved waterskiing. It turned out that waterskiing isn't regularly a part of a legal practice, but it would be a few years before I figured that out.

"That's not legal," Mr. Lewin said. "The public school shouldn't force you to sing religious songs at a church." Finally, someone confirmed my concerns. It was like a light turned on. "I'll talk to the principal," he added, cementing my everlasting love.

He did. A few days later, Mr. Lewin told me that I could skip the concert without any impact on my grade. There wasn't any policy change that I could see; I think I just got a pass.

It was a powerful feeling to have someone stand up for me when I was facing an injustice. And even more powerful to see that injustice righted, even if just for me. I felt an energy tingle through my body as I navigated around both the choir teacher and evangelical kids. Whether this little incident was the seed or just another confirmation, it cemented the feeling in my bones that my role in this world was to be the Mr. Lewin for others, to help make things better for those who don't fit in.

TECHNOLOGY AND MUSIC AT IOWA AND MICHIGAN

But finding this role in technology, where I ultimately found it, wasn't an obvious path. I was technology curious, although definitely not magnetically drawn to computers like the hackers I'd meet later. I'd been introduced to computers through the punch card system we programmed in high school; my small hometown in Iowa was far from the cutting edge of technology in the early 1980s.

In college at the University of Iowa, I'd dipped my toes into programming. Yet I noticed that the more advanced classes became more and more male, and less and less friendly. The University of Iowa computer science department, like so many other science, technology, engineering, and mathematics departments in the 1980s, held "weed out" classes designed to have students compete with each other to win seats in advanced courses. While I did well enough to qualify for the advanced classes and really liked programming, I stopped taking computer courses after a male friend who was struggling to make the cut suggested that if I wasn't serious about a career in computer programming, I should not take a spot from someone who was. I'm still not sure that was the right decision.

I ended up as an English major, feeling a bit like I was cheating by getting a degree that involved reading fiction. That decision also involved defying my father, who insisted that I major in business and threatened to withdraw his financial support unless I did. After a few painful conversations, especially after I decided to attend a prelaw semester at the London School of Economics, I decided to pay for my education myself. With the unwavering support of my brother, I secured student loans and a couple of part-time jobs in order to chart my own course.

In college I also found my first community, in part through music. I ended up getting assigned to a dorm room on a floor with an eclectic set of women, most of whom were a year or two ahead of me. They introduced me to the Grateful Dead, along with Elvis Costello, Prince, the Pretenders, Bonnie Raitt, Joan Armatrading, Rickie Lee Jones, Talking Heads, Little Feat, and more. A friend named us the "ees" after our set of mid-1960s' first names: Bonnie, Tammy, Wendee, Kimmy, Laurie, Betsy, Penny, PC, and me. We always had music playing and went to see live music often. Thanks to Wendee, I found a job bartending, first in a dive bar, but later in a blues bar called the Crow's Nest, which was one of the regular college circuit stops for Chicago blues legends like Koko Taylor, Buddy Guy, and Junior Wells. We also hosted punk, postpunk, new wave, and rock bands.

The Grateful Dead scene, though, was where I especially felt at home. It had a way of welcoming me and all the other kids who didn't quite fit into the frequently preppy early 1980s' college town of Iowa City. I appreciated the band's strategy of letting the fans record and spread the music peer to peer too, rather than policing every copy of a song or performance. As a result of this, they had a huge following and sold out shows across the country despite little radio play. I loved the DIY spirit embedded in the scene, dancing to the songs that never seemed to end and the space it made for misfits like me. Little did I realize how important this connection would become.

YOU'RE GOING BACK WHERE YOU STARTED

"Isn't it funny, Cindy? You're going back to where you started out."

My father smiled at me in the rearview mirror as I sat in the back seat of the minivan. We were driving from Iowa to Michigan to drop me off for my first year of law school in Ann Arbor, stopping at Purdue University to drop off my sister on the way. He said it like he was talking about the weather.

"What?" I asked, unsure of what he meant.

"You were conceived in Ann Arbor, remember?" His smile got bigger as I looked more confused. Then it slowly dawned on me. That drive my parents took to get baby me was to Detroit and one of the few things we knew was that my birth mother had been a Michigan student at the time she got pregnant.

I was curious, but I wasn't ready to take any steps forward on this story just yet. I worried it could destabilize my always-fragile mother. It wasn't until my third year at Michigan that I finally screwed up the courage to try to find my birth mother. I used a flimsy story to get the alumni office to give me her address. I pretended to be the daughter of a college friend of hers. I was sternly told that only current students could get alumni addresses, to which I happily provided proof in the form of my student ID number. Privacy? Apparently not.

I decided to write my birth mother a letter and worried over it. What do you say to the person who you have never met but who gave you life? I had always envisioned her floating just above me like a beautiful hidden fairy godmother, taking my side whenever I was upset and generally watching over my life from afar. I wrote at least fifty drafts of the letter, making sure it was in my best longhand and arranging to have a friend take a series of smiling photos of me in the law quad so that I could pick the best one to send.

After a month or so, a typed, formal envelope came in the mail. The letter inside was typed too and signed by my birth mother, Evelyn. The letter gave me some basic medical and background information in a cold, clinical tone, but then instructed me never to contact her again.

That hurt. Deep and hard. I crawled into bed and stayed there for two days.

I suddenly felt unmoored from the world. In an instant that letter shattered my childhood visions of an ethereal second mother who missed me and terribly regretted giving me up. It also represented my deepest fear: that I had actually been rejected and abandoned. After a few days, my brother urged me to get therapy, and after a week or so more, I did.

Intellectually, I understood where Evelyn was coming from. From all I know and have learned, her pregnancy was one of the worst things that ever happened to her. She had apparently ignored or not realized the fact that she was pregnant for a long time, making even an illegal abortion not really possible. This was before *Roe v. Wade*, but an abortion still could have been arranged. Evelyn's parents had hidden her away to ensure that her grandparents wouldn't find out. They first sent her to live with some distant relatives in a fifth-floor walk-up in Paris and then later kept her in a dingy motel outside town until she was ready to give birth. She had to drop out of college.

I had gotten pregnant myself during high school at age seventeen. It had been a stupid mistake; I had not felt powerful enough to insist that my newish, older boyfriend use a condom and had foolishly believed that it couldn't happen to me. I had the good luck that this was during the time after *Roe* and before *Dobbs*, when abortion was legal in Iowa. I also had the strong support from both of my parents. My mother drove me to Des Moines to get an abortion in the privacy of the medical offices of her gynecologist. That turned a mistake that could have dramatically changed the course of my life into just a rotten couple of weeks along with a painful lesson in both using contraception and speaking up for myself. Moreover, the experience made me a lifelong believer in letting people decide when they are ready to have children.

I could understand intellectually why Evelyn might have made the choice to cut off that memory, and me, from her life. I recognized this as her legitimate choice for privacy. Yet it still hurt. It was like someone I didn't even know had grabbed the very root of me and shaken me from the earth. It was like being slapped by a ghost.

I love my adoptive family. My parents were not perfect, and I had always harbored worries about not belonging, but those came from inside me—never from them. They presented my adoption as my special story, and that's how I felt. Still, I had never quite felt fully at home in my family either. Perhaps between being adopted, my mother's illness, and my parents' divorce, or just who I am, I always felt like I needed to present a polished, capable version of myself and not take up any space with my own messiness. I disappeared into books in part to hide out from that feeling. I couldn't help hoping that there was another family somewhere with which I'd feel a better sense of easy belonging. In my fantasy family, I would be seen in a deeper way and wouldn't feel that I had to be perfect all the time.

Evelyn did give me some basic information about my birth father, including his name, but my trick with the alumni office didn't work a second time. To tell the truth, I didn't have the heart to push further. I just couldn't bear having my birth father—who barely knew I existed—reject me too.

GOLDILOCKS

The rest of law school was a time of figuring out where I should be professionally. Despite realizing that my childhood dream of being a lawyer in order to go waterskiing regularly wasn't likely, I was still interested in the law. By then I had solidified the feeling I'd had in high school that I wanted to stand up for the rights of others. Law seemed to be a good way to do that. But I couldn't figure out the right role.

In law school, I tried a child advocacy clinic. One of my clients was a young mother who I helped petition to get her child back from the foster care system. I learned an early lesson in direct legal services when my client showed up to her court hearing in a T-shirt that said "born to be bad." Running with her out to the courthouse parking lot, I scrambled to find her a less problematic shirt to change into. Luckily I had a change of clothes in my car, and we were about the same size.

Direct legal service work is incredibly important, and it taught me a lot about building a narrative in a case. Working with individuals and families that had been most underserved by our legal system was interesting and crucial. But it didn't feel like my calling. Through that work, I realized I wanted to change the world for more than just my individual clients. I wanted to help more than one person at a time.

Figuring out how to do that, though, took time. Thanks to a professor I met at the University of Iowa named Burns Weston, I went as big as I could, focusing on international human rights law. While I wasn't the best law student—definitely somewhere in the middle of my class at best—on law school graduation in 1989, I won a fellowship to the UN Centre for Human Rights in Geneva, Switzerland. I hoped that vantage point would let me work in the law in a way that could help millions of people.

From the gorgeous Palais de Nations, I studied the implementation of international human rights treaties, contributed to research that would inform UN policymakers, and wrote a couple of academic articles.[3] My main project, at the suggestion of the professor who sponsored me, was trying to figure out the effectiveness of the human rights treaty process in improving human rights. I focused on the International Covenant on Civil and Political Rights and the Human Rights Committee that administers it since that was the longest-running human rights treaty process.

Countries that sign the covenant promise to meet a set of standards, submit appropriately named "quadrennial reports," and then come to a hearing at the United Nations to answer questions from the set of experts who made up the Human Rights Committee. I didn't have an easy way to access conditions on the ground, but I did have a set of second (and some third) quadrennial reports from countries, so I reviewed those to see what improvements they reported in their protections of human rights. I found some, but they were not as significant as I had hoped. I ended my research with some suggestions for how the committee could better track changes (and nonchanges), give feedback to the countries that participated, and urge more compliance with the standards set out in the covenant.

Other than a few delegations that came to the United Nations to lobby, however, I never interacted with the people we were trying to help. I felt removed, and the problems we were working on felt academic, bureaucratic, and theoretical. Yet I did meet several people who would become important to me and keep me looped into human rights over the years. One of them was a lawyer from San Francisco named Michael van Walt, who seemed to have the coolest gig in the world as the Dalai Lama's international legal adviser.

When my fellowship ended, I left Geneva and landed in San Francisco—where both my brother and the Grateful Dead were then based. I felt a bit like Goldilocks. Direct legal services didn't give me an avenue to create system-wide change, but the UN advocacy was too far away from the people who needed help. I wanted something in the middle: a way to create systemic change that could help many people while still directly working with clients. But first I had to start paying back my mountain of student loans, which at that point had accumulated to an amount higher than the value of the house I grew up in. I accepted a job with a sixty-person downtown San Francisco law firm while I tried to sort out the right place for myself over the long term.

CINDY'S FRIENDS MEET FRANNIE'S FRIENDS PARTY

Shortly after I landed in San Francisco, I threw a party at my new flat in the Haight Ashbury neighborhood that would change my life. I had just found a terrific roommate, a French woman named Frannie who worked at a café in Palo Alto called Café Verona, where she met a lot of hacker types. She invited them to our housewarming, which we called the "Cindy's Friends Meet Frannie's Friends Party." One of the hackers, who had on bright, tie-dye socks, introduced himself to me as John Gilmore. After a night of dancing in our living room, I ended up dating James, another one of the pack. John, who lived part of the time just on the other side of the Panhandle, became a friend. Frannie fell for one of my law school friends at the same party, so it was a definite success.

To be clear, I am not using the term "hacker" pejoratively here. In this community, "hacking" means plugging away at a problem until you solve it. Quite literally, "hacking at it" means attacking a technical problem somewhat in the same way you would use a small ax on a big tree. I'm also using "hacker" as a shorthand for the quirky, problem-solving community of programmers who prioritize autonomy, knowledge, and personal freedom in developing code as well as building out our digital world. The early internet was thick with them before the business school types showed up.

They weren't perfect. Some of them had serious problems treating women like people. One prominent hacker asked me if I could help him find the right manual to read to get women to date him, using hacker shorthand RTFM for "read the fucking manual." He looked puzzled and sad as I explained that women weren't like computers, and you couldn't just program them to date you. There was also a general lack of recognition that just because you were bullied by others as a kid, didn't mean that you couldn't become a bully to others. Nevertheless, many of those guys were interested in creating something better in the online world than the offline one. There we found a lot of common cause.

Meeting my boyfriend and his hacker friends in San Francisco in 1990 opened a new world for me. The guys from Palo Alto who showed up to dance in my flat in the Haight were doing things far beyond my rudimentary experience with computers. They were living and working online, and typing to each other in ongoing chat-like conversations all day and long into the night, usually with bright green letters on a black background.

They lived largely free from the normal barriers of physical distance for collaboration, friendship, and community. To try to understand them, I read Steven Levy's *Hackers*. We strung Ethernet cable between apartments at a complex on University Avenue where James and several others of them lived. I attended the first Computers, Freedom, and Privacy conference, and saw in person some of this small yet growing community that was living a huge part of their lives online. Most of them weren't in it to become millionaires, much less billionaires. They were there to solve interesting problems. Some, like John, were also thinking about how we could design the coming digital world to be a place that was even better than the physical one—or at the very least, not worse.

THE FOUNDING OF EFF

At the same time as I was discovering the hackers, John, along with Mitch Kapor, the founder of Lotus Development Corp., and John Perry Barlow (whom I'll call Barlow going forward to help keep the two Johns separate) were starting an organization called EFF. These three, who met in an early digital community called the WELL, created EFF to fight for those fledgling online communities.

The WELL, which stood for Whole Earth 'Lectronic Link, was a virtual community that had launched in 1985, but by 1990 was the meeting place for thousands of early internet enthusiasts.[4] It was organized in ways that soon became standard for online communities, and would be familiar to later users of Reddit, Discord, and many social media sites: a set of forums reflecting member interests, with larger forums supervised by conference hosts who helped curate content and gently enforce the rules. In the 1990s, the WELL represented the promise of the internet for many, including EFF's founders. As one early manager, Cliff Figallo, said, "[The] exercise of free speech and assembly in online interaction is among the most significant and important uses of electronic networking." He continued that he hoped the WELL would be a grassroots alternative to "electronic consumer shopping malls," which he feared would otherwise dominate the digital future.[5] While I was never part of the WELL, many early EFF board members and staffers were.

Mitch was already rich and famous at the time he founded EFF. He had designed one of the earliest spreadsheets in Lotus and knew most of the early tech titans personally.[6]

Barlow was famous in a different way. He was a 1960s' counterculture icon and psychedelic pioneer from the East Coast–Timothy Leary faction of hippies. Also, he had been raised in Wyoming and remained fundamentally a cowboy all of his life. He always said he was the official best friend of Grateful Dead guitarist and singer Bob Weir, who he had met when they were wayward youths sent away to the same boarding school.[7] Barlow wrote the lyrics to several of the Dead songs I loved, including "Cassidy" and "Throwing Stones." And that is just the start. At some point I started calling Barlow "the most interesting man in the world," after a character in a popular beer commercial.

Barlow and Mitch had become concerned after each of them were questioned by the FBI about their digital activities. They were both surprised, and shared the view that the law enforcement officers interrogating them had no idea what the internet was or what people were doing there. Barlow wrote an essay about his experience called "Crime and Puzzlement."[8] They also shared the view that the cluelessness of the cops had made them susceptible to wild claims of harm from corporate giants, which turned out to be behind many of those early investigations.

The FBI visits to Barlow and Mitch coincided with a series of raids by the Secret Service on early computer enthusiasts where the feds took everything plugged into the wall, and seemed to have decided that the Fourth Amendment protections against search and seizure did not apply.[9]

The two men connected in person when Mitch diverted his private plane on a flight from Boston to San Francisco to land on Barlow's ranch in Wyoming. Barlow would say, "Mitch literally came down out of the sky to meet me."

At that meeting, they decided to start a fund (thus the "foundation" in the name) that would pay for lawyers for the people impacted by these government raids. John, also a member of the WELL and already a wealthy hacker thanks to being employee number five at Sun Microsystems, joined pretty quickly thereafter as a cofounder.[10] Steve Wozniak gave some of the first significant funding, and while he didn't stay involved, he's credited as a founder as well.

Barlow, true to type as a part-time rancher who was never seen without his cowboy boots, provided the "frontier" metaphor to EFF's name. "Electronic" was likely a nod to the WELL. Pretty quickly, however, Mitch, Barlow, and John realized that there just weren't many lawyers with enough understanding of this new digital world to take the funding from the organization that they had created. So they hired their first in-house lawyer, a newly minted attorney from the University of Texas named Mike Godwin, who already had a reputation for being a fierce online advocate. Godwin is famous for coining Godwin's law, which provides that "as an online discussion grows longer, the probability of a comparison involving Nazis or Hitler approaches 1."[11]

Godwin was definitely right. The small group of people engaged in online discussions in those early days slanted heavily toward the kind of person—generally but not exclusively white and male—who could write long, dense emails full of logical-sounding argument and keep at it until late into the night. After a while, hyperbole frequently took over. The "winner" was often the person who could just keep at it the longest.

Barlow had the strongest pen of the early EFF crew. His essays detailed how clueless government was to the coming digital revolution. He wrote his most inspirational one a few years later, in 1996, called "Declaration of the Independence of Cyberspace." The essay claimed that the online world was a wholly separate space where governments had no jurisdiction. I read it at the time and immediately disagreed with it. I knew that as long as every person whose fingers were on a keyboard also had feet resting on the ground in the jurisdiction of some government somewhere, no one online was really free of governmental control. Nor did I think that a government-free world would ultimately be more just or free. Still, Barlow's writings and vision were powerful.

Barlow much later told me that he didn't mean the declaration literally. He meant that the development of cyberspace was a chance for society to start over and do better, and that the governments of the world needed to allow space for it to do so. He believed that this shift was inevitable too, although he never thought it would occur without a fight. He was focused on the early, bad moves by the US government—the raids that sparked the creation of EFF, the encryption fights, and most immediately when he wrote the essay: the fight over a law that would have prohibited any "indecent" material on the internet.

Barlow said his idea was to bring about a better world by describing it as if it was already here. While we didn't agree on the framing, I wholeheartedly concurred with his belief that if handled right, this new cyberspace could create a "fairer, more just future."

But Mitch, Barlow, and John weren't starry-eyed about what it would take to build this better future and fend off a worse one. You don't start an organization like EFF—and hire fighty lawyers like me—if you think that it will all just happen happily and naturally. Barlow's words to me at one early EFF board meeting remain one of my strongest inspirations: no one gives you your rights; you have to take them.

The people—mostly guys, mostly white—involved in this early internet were an eclectic and interesting bunch of misfits. I've always felt at home among the weird. While I wasn't a coder, neither was Barlow. At some level this attenuated Grateful Dead connection made me feel like I could fit into this strange hacker world. I was especially delighted in about 1994 when John invited me to take a day hike on Mount Tamalpais in Marin County with Barlow. I was completely starstruck; I doubt I said more than a word or two to him the whole time. Eventually Barlow and I would become dear friends as well as collaborators, but that was later.

MIDSIZE LAW FIRM MISFIT

My hacker boyfriend James and I were getting settled into a small flat in the Noe Valley neighborhood of San Francisco. As I was increasingly fascinated and drawn in by the online world inhabited by him and his hacker friends, it became clear that the midsize law firm life was not for me. I had no connection to most of my clients; I even exhausted myself over a bankruptcy memo for a junior partner for weeks only to learn, when I went to turn it in, that the case had settled and the partner had forgotten to tell me. It wasn't really their fault. I didn't connect with the work and wasn't very good at it. I felt like I was just working to move money around between already wealthy people and entities. I knew that in order to be motivated to care about the cases and precedents, I needed to see and feel the real people I was helping. I also needed to know my work was aimed at making the world better.

About that time I heard from Michael van Walt, the lawyer I had met in Geneva who was the Dalai Lama's international legal adviser. Michael was then living in the Bay Area, still working for the Dalai Lama, and had a job available. He needed help starting a new human rights organization. Called the Unrepresented Nations and People's Organization (UNPO), it was a collection of nations and peoples—at the time as varied as people from Tibet, East Timor, and the then Soviet republics of Latvia, Estonia, Georgia, and Armenia. It also included Uyghurs, West Papuans, Aboriginal Australians, Kurds, Sami, Kosovans, and several Native American peoples. One group was the Ogoni, from Nigeria, who were represented by activist and writer Ken Saro-Wiwa, who would turn out to be a critical inspiration.

What all of these groups had in common was that they were "peoples," but lived under the control of another state and so were in effect "stateless nations" under international law. As a result, they did not have a vote at the United Nations but still needed a voice to exercise their self-determination and protect their human rights. The Dalai Lama's foreign minister Lody Gyari, Estonian independence activist Linnart Maell and Michael created an organization—a kind of shadow UN and voice for the voiceless—to help these groups make common cause and share strategies and ideas, especially at the United Nations. Most of the groups were struggling to organize under repression, including surveillance, censorship, and other pressures. By banding together through the UNPO, they found a place for solidarity, skill building, and mutual support.

I left my law firm to help Michael write the UNPO charter and other founding documents from a high-ceiled office in a former convent and girls school located across the street from Mission Dolores in San Francisco. The office was shared with two small organizations working on behalf of Tibet. But after we got the UNPO launched, there really wasn't a place for me. At that point, the organization really needed dedicated fundraiser, and I was a baby lawyer with no fundraising experience.

When the UNPO moved from San Francisco to The Hague in late 1991, I stayed behind. I had a steady boyfriend, a new home we were just making together, and growing set of friends to go see music with. I was deeply in love with San Francisco too. Its mild weather, gorgeous views, architecture, and surrounding ocean pulled me in. But I think the city ultimately won my heart because it was a haven for all sorts of people, like me, who had not fit in where they came from. I started calling San Francisco the "island of misfit toys" after a location in a TV Christmas special that I saw every December when I was a kid.

Instead of moving to Holland, I found a new job as a litigator at a six-attorney law firm called McGlashan and Sarrail in San Mateo, just a bit down the 101 freeway from where I lived in San Francisco. It was here that I finally started to learn the nuts and bolts of how to be someone's lawyer, mainly from my boss, Bill Bauld.

Bill taught me how to listen to someone's story and pick out the legal issues, finding the facts we could use, and the things we needed to guard against. I learned how to bring and maintain litigation without a huge budget, since most of our clients were individuals or small businesses. I also learned how to marshal those facts and tell a story to the court along with how to take depositions, write motions, negotiate, and move a lawsuit from beginning to end.

Bill brought me into his cases from the first client meeting until the end. We'd sit in his sixth-floor office with a view of the incoming airline traffic to the San Francisco airport and talk through how to translate the clients' problems into a legal theory, then how to move that into a lawsuit or brief. Bill showed me how much of lawyering is about building trust between the client and lawyer as well as between the lawyer and judge. He did that by being both absolutely straight about the risks and benefits of each strategy with the client, and absolutely straight with the court about the law and facts. I remember watching him in a courtroom, his power coming not from flash or ego but rather from being trustworthy with every word he said. It was different than most of the other lawyers I saw and a style I would try to emulate.

IT KEEPS THINGS SECRET

In 1993, I was nowhere near a fully baked litigator, much less one ready to take on major constitutional impact litigation when John called me to ask if I would take on the *Bernstein* case. Still, I saw this as a chance to help with this interesting new world, and not incidentally, to impress my boyfriend.

I paced around my living room in our flat in Noe Valley as I talked to John, trying to avoid hitting my shins on our low coffee table.

"What do you need a lawsuit for?" I asked him.

Even then, John spoke in a sort of ponderous, gentle tone that almost belied the seriousness of the issue we were discussing. After a long pause, he said, "There's a grad student at UC Berkeley who wrote a computer program. The government told him that if he publishes it on the internet, he'll go to jail as an arms dealer."

I stopped my pacing. "What? Wait, what does it do? Does it blow things up?"

"No," John explained, and his voice on the phone paused again—a pause I would soon recognize as the mark of how John thought quickly but spoke slowly: "It keeps things secret. It's strong cryptography, and he wants to publish it on the Usenet newsgroup sci.crypt." Newsgroups were discussion groups that functioned kind of like today's Reddit.

I resumed my pacing. This was a lawsuit not about sharing weapons but instead about the right to publish information concerning how to hold a private conversation. I had many questions, but the first was, "How can they tell him he cannot publish something? That sounds like a First Amendment problem to me."

"It sounds like one to us too," John agreed. Then he added, "Will you do it?"

I knew almost nothing about the case and only a little about EFF, but I was sure I wanted to be involved. "Let me talk to my firm," I replied. "But yes, I'm very interested."

I spent a while on the phone with John taking notes on a yellow pad of legal paper, making a list of the first set of things I knew I'd need to research later. I hung up the phone and went to find my hacker boyfriend James in his office in the back bedroom of our Edwardian flat.

"Um, so John just called," I told him, looking down at my notes. "He wants me to take on a lawsuit. What's strong cryptography? And what's sci.crypt?"

I had just agreed to lead the biggest case in my life. I had no real idea about the technologies that were central to it and had never even handled a First Amendment case.

Luckily, my boyfriend knew what John was talking about, and quickly explained enough about the technology and its importance that I could at least start to approach my bosses.

Soon after that, I met John for breakfast at the Pork Store Café on Haight Street in San Francisco. In a booth over eggs and hash browns, with a few drawings on my trusty yellow pad, he diagramed the concepts and technologies that would ultimately set me up for the rest of my career: the science of encryption, public key cryptography, internet security, and Usenet newsgroups.

More broadly, he introduced me to the philosophy behind EFF: that as more of us moved into the coming digital age, civil liberties were going to be subject to new challenges and were going to need protection. Free speech would be challenged when everyone had the ability to speak to potentially millions of others simultaneously through websites and message boards. Privacy would be challenged when people started relying on digital networks to share their most intimate and politically critical conversations, meaning the government would have less control over speech but more ability to invade privacy. Listening, I summarized EFF's mission as making sure that when you go online, your rights go with you.

He told me about the cypherpunks and the broader movement to free up encryption. The lawsuit he proposed was just one piece of an effort to ensure that the coming internet remained free, secure, and private. The first issue of *WIRED* magazine, in May–June 1993, featured John and two other hackers in masks with the headline "Rebels with a Cause (Your Privacy)."[12]

John brought me up to date about how the internet had become a crucial part of how coders write, read, and share code. He also explained how insecure and vulnerable ordinary internet activities were to cops, spies, and criminals alike. We talked about how source code, object code, and machine language work as well as compilers and similar tools. He told me how sharing actual code is the ultimate way to describe and show many ideas about all kinds of science, including cryptography. He noted how the basic ideas of the scientific method I'd first learned in grade school were now being conducted online.

I went to the three partners at my little law firm and asked if I could do the case for free, or what the lawyers call pro bono. I said, "I think this internet thing is going to be big, and it's a chance for us to make a name for ourselves early."

While small, the firm wasn't a bad fit for a project like this. It had been set up by Doug McGlashan, who had also left the midsize firm where I had started out. Doug and the other name partner, Karen Sarrail, along with my direct boss, Bill, had designed the firm to ensure that they could go home on time every night to be with their young kids, coach soccer, and do lots of other things that didn't really work well for those at big, corporate law firms. I didn't have kids, so I proposed that when they went home, I could stay and work on this case. They agreed and were nothing but supportive the whole time, even though I suspect none of us realized how long it would take or how it would suck me in.

Next, I talked to Godwin, who encouraged me and promised that EFF would help me learn any of the technical pieces I needed to know.

I then called EFF director of legal services Shari Steele. Shari would prove an invaluable friend, mentor, and partner in the *Bernstein* case and beyond. She had an optimism that shined through even in her emails, and cheerfully organized weekly calls, found experts, and pulled in interns and other help when we needed it. Shari was smart and strategic too. She helped edit all the briefs as well as handled the press releases and other public-facing work of making sure the case got noticed. Shari was based in DC at the time, and as a result, we didn't meet in person until years later. In a way, she was my first fully online friendship.

CODE ≠ LAW

My client, Dan, was pursuing his doctorate in mathematics at the University of California at Berkeley. Dan had a soft voice and manner, but underneath it I quickly found a will of steel. Like many of the hackers I met in the 1990s, he was very, very smart, especially when it came to logic-based thinking required to manipulate code to make a computer do things. And he was used to being right. From Dan, John, my boyfriend, and many of the other hackers I worked with in the early days, I developed a maxim: "Ninety-nine percent of the time they are right and the other 1 percent can be sheer hell." We didn't conflict often, but when we did, it could take a long time—generally involving many long emails sent and received late into the night—to reach a place where they were willing to change course.

This was especially true in the space between what the words of the law or a court opinion said and what a judge was likely to do. One of the truths about coding is that the computer will do exactly what its instructions say—regardless of whether that is what the coder actually wanted or even if it was a good idea. Computers are hyperliteral that way.

Judges are not computers. Even if you can interpret the words of a law to support a decision you want, a judge—a thoughtful one anyway—is going to resist if that outcome is nonsensical or unreasonable. So when the Constitution says "Congress shall make no law respecting speech," many hackers (and not only hackers) think of that as a computer instruction rather than a constitutional one.

But lawyers quickly learn that while the constitutional language creates a strong and high bar to speech regulation, those words have never meant that there could literally be "no law." Instead, the First Amendment has developed many categories, subcategories, and tests—even within the broad category of "speech"—that determine whether a law can survive constitutional review. That decision depends on things such as context, history, and rationale along with how closely the proposed rule tracks the problem.

SNUFFLE

But Dan wasn't wrong about the overall strategy for his case. Getting the court to rule that publishing computer code was protected speech would maximize our chances of winning.

Dan also knew that the case could take a long time and that the science of cryptography needed to move on while we made our way through the courts. At our first meeting, he confirmed that while the program he wanted to publish was useful, it wasn't the kind of scientific breakthrough that the world needed to have immediately. Rather, signaling how unscary it was, Dan named the program Snuffle.

What Snuffle did was clever. It converted a hash function into an encryptor. A hash function is a widely used technique that allows some data (including, say, the text of a message) to be quickly and efficiently stored as well as retrieved.[13] Hash functions are hugely useful, and were already ubiquitous for various kinds of data storage and authentication in the 1990s. In fact, they were so useful that it would be largely unthinkable that they would be banned or restrictively licensed by the government.

The Snuffle program was meant to demonstrate that the regulation of encryption made no sense technically. Hash functions were not regulated but encryption was. Yet you could turn one into the other with just a few lines of code.

Dan had also written a paper describing the code. He knew that presenting the same information as the code in an academic paper would help demonstrate that the government was actually regulating speech—the sharing of information and ideas—when it regulated what the regulations called "software capable of maintaining secrecy."

I was primarily interested in the case because I saw how encryption would be fundamental to privacy in the digital age. Dan cared about that too, but he was a scientist first. Applying the First Amendment to publishing code online was a core part of his motivation.

BUILDING THE IMPACT CASE

While we were in the case in order to help Dan publish his code, this was a different kind of lawsuit than most—something lawyers call an "impact case." That means we were not just aiming at justice for Dan but to change the law for everyone else too.

The goal of an impact case is to get the decision into the books of published legal decisions that can be cited by lawyers in other cases and thereby create a precedent that is binding on other cases. That only happens to a small subset of cases and only under specific conditions, but we had set the case up to meet them. One factor is to bring a case where the facts are not in dispute, so the only thing the court has to do is to decide how to apply the law to them. Those decisions get published. A jury trial, by contrast, is one where the process is trying to decide which facts are true. Those verdicts are not published in the books that lawyers use to find and cite the law.

In Dan's case, everyone agreed that Snuffle was subject to the export licensing process, so the fight was about whether that requirement was constitutional. A constitutional ruling by the judge would likely be published, and if confirmed on appeal, create a precedent that other judges in that appellate circuit would have to follow. Ultimately, if the Supreme Court agreed, all the courts of the United States would have to follow the precedent. That broader goal made it an impact case.

I started building the case by researching the export regulations. The way the regulations worked meant that a person who wanted to export something had to submit a written request to the State Department. Then if they were allowed to export it, they would be issued a license. This system was set up for companies selling tanks, not graduate students publishing code. The rules were both byzantine and vague. They normally required not only lawyers but export specialist lawyers to navigate them.

Even before we met, Dan had started the licensing process, knowing full well that he would not be granted a license, but also that the law would require him to try before it would allow him to file a lawsuit to challenge the rules. He had actually submitted six different license requests, which the regulations called commodity jurisdiction requests. These requests covered both the code he wanted to publish and the scientific paper that described it. The government combined his six separate requests into one and told him that he needed a license. He appealed that decision, but we knew that with that initial denial, we had clearance to file the lawsuit.

In addition to the complex set of regulations, I researched the First Amendment, especially the law on prior restraint, which governs situations like licensing schemes in which the government requires permission before publication. I was making my way through the doctrines, but somewhat slowly since I was doing my regular work too.

I'LL GIVE YOU SOME OF LEE TO HELP

One day John called to ask how the case was going. I wanted to impress John, but I needed to be honest that I was moving too slow.

"I have a lot to learn," I said, which felt like an enormous understatement.

"I want to give you some of Lee to help," John said.

"What's a lee?" I asked. John explained that he was referring to Lee Tien, his personal attorney.

"I've had him looking into the export regulations for a while now," John told me. "I'm going to pay him to spend some time helping you."

"I'd love the help," I said.

The next thing I knew, I was connected with Lee, who had already mapped out multiple legal arguments that would prove vital to the case. From our first phone call, sitting in my little office and looking out over San Mateo to the Bay, I knew I'd been thrown a lifeline. Lee had a mastery of First Amendment case law and export regulations, and together we figured out which of the many possible arguments were the strongest.

Shari, Lee, and I started having calls, building the pieces we would have to pull together to make this work. Things moved much faster from there. Over time, we pulled in several other lawyers, including two experienced First Amendment attorneys in Jim Wheaton from Oakland and Bob Corn-Revere from Washington, DC. Bob had recently argued a First Amendment case at the Supreme Court, and had a deep well of wisdom and experience. We soon had a merry band plotting together on weekly conference calls.

I turned out to have a knack for big-picture organizing—driving the to-do list forward and figuring out what expertise we needed. Shari invariably found people who could fill any holes we identified, and more critically, convinced them to donate their time to help us. I was good at plugging people into projects too, and stitching together and harmonizing various pieces of legal writing by members of the team, then seeing where we needed to go next. It was great fun, and we all fed each other's enthusiasm.

I also figured out how to bring my English-major love of storytelling into creating a narrative of the case. In any litigation, you need to accomplish two major things: you need to give the judge a legal path to go down and a reason to go down that path instead of the one presented by the other side. Nailing both steps is especially true in impact litigation, where the lawyer is aiming to win not just for their client but in a way that helps everyone else too. We wanted Dan to be able to publish his code, but we really wanted to clear a path for other people, including businesses, to be able to develop as well as deploy the tools to give privacy and security to all of us.

I knew that a recitation of the facts and cold analysis of the case law just wasn't going to cut it here, particularly given the likely strange and new technical environment that we were asking the judge to enter.

This case required a multistep analysis, piling new idea onto new idea, which is never ideal for a court. First, we had to convince the court that code is speech. Then we had to show that publishing code on the internet was a thing that the First Amendment should protect, which meant explaining to the court how the internet was a place where scientists engaged with each other, shared knowledge, and developed ideas. Third, we had to demonstrate that sharing code was critical to this scientific process. Fourth, we had to show that the science of cryptography was like any other science that computers help with, where publication of code is central to its advancement. Fifth, we had to convince the court that the government licensing scheme was a prior restraint on that speech since it required a license before publishing code on the internet. Finally, we had to convince the court that the government licensing scheme contained in the export regulations did not satisfy the law.

FREEDMAN V. MARYLAND AND PROCEDURAL PRIOR RESTRAINT

The central argument was that the export regulations, called the International Traffic in Arms Regulations (ITAR), did not meet the specific procedural requirements set by the Supreme Court for prior restraint. These had been established by the Supreme Court in a 1965 case called *Freedman v. Maryland.* A Baltimore cinema owner named Ronald Freedman had refused to ask for permission from the Maryland State Board of Censors (it was even called that) to show a French film about the 1916 Irish Revolution called *Revenge at Daybreak.* Prior to the creation of the motion picture rating system of G, PG, R, and X that we are all familiar with, many states had such boards, and they were quite active.

While everyone agreed that the film would have been given a license if Freedman had asked, the Supreme Court decided that merely having to submit to the licensing scheme itself violated the First Amendment. That was because the scheme prevented the film's screening until a license was issued, had no timeline for the board to decide, gave wide discretion for the licensing board and required cinema owners to bear the burden and expense of going to court, and the burden of proof once in court, in order to challenge a board decision. Justice William J. Brennan, writing for the Supreme Court, noted that Freedman rightfully charged that under the censorship scheme, "judicial review may be too little and too late."[14]

The procedural requirements articulated in *Freedman* were aimed at making sure speech wasn't held up by government bureaucrats. They specifically required that the bureaucrats make a quick decision based on clear rules and that the decision be immediately reviewable by a court with the government bearing the burden of proof.

Neither *Freedman* nor any of the other cases since 1965 relying on it had anything to do with the internet, code, or cryptography. But all of them addressed situations in which the government required a license or other prior approval for speech—involving things like where to place newsstands or parades, plus censorship boards for books and movies. Getting the court to see that Dan's intended publication was similar to these situations was a huge lift.

Ultimately we ended up with ten claims or causes of action. *Freedman* was our strongest one, but another claimed that the export law and procedures were unconstitutionally vague since they didn't define "software," and also tied themselves to such moving targets as "software capable of maintaining secrecy." Another claim was that the rules were overbroad given that they reached academic and scientific work like Bernstein's, and the term "export" reached any publication online as well. Furthermore, we raised the rights of readers, noting that the prohibition on the publication and discussion of cryptography denied other people the right to learn about his work.

FILING

In February 1995, we were finally ready to file the case. I took the manila packet with the complaint and other papers to the federal district court in San Francisco myself. Full of excitement, I walked into that giant, imposing, rust-colored building on Golden Gate Avenue. My internal butterflies were a big contrast to the gray flatness of the court clerk's office on the sixteenth floor. I also didn't fit in physically. I was a short, dark-haired woman in a suit and flats waiting in line behind bike couriers in helmets and spiked shoes as well as messengers in black leather and Doc Martens.

The clerks behind the glass were efficient but busy, and definitely not interested in hearing about the groundbreaking constitutional litigation I was filing. I felt like someone with a big secret and no one to share it with in that drab little waiting area.

When it was my turn, I watched the clerk stamp the initials M. H. P. on the complaint; the randomized process known as "the wheel" determined that we were assigned Judge Marilyn Hall Patel. I was too green to recognize what good news this was, but it ended up being a terrific stroke of luck. Once we had some initial hearings, I could tell that Judge Patel was willing to dig into this new world of computers and digital networks, even though I suspect she had little personal experience with them when we started. She took us seriously, and as a result, we built the case with an eye toward educating her rather than pummeling her with our arguments. This ended up being a strategy that we would apply to many other cases before many other judges over the years.

I drove down to my office in San Mateo, called Dan and told him we were on file, and sent a message to Lee and the other lawyers.

EFF put out a press release, and I experienced my first rush of media attention. It was great fun, but I had to practice staying on message—saying the same basic thing to each reporter. I found it easy to forget that I was talking to someone new on each call who needed to know everything from scratch. And I learned how horrifying it can be to see a direct transcription of what you actually said, with wandering sentences, oohs and aahs, and painfully vague phrases. The case was covered in the *San Francisco Examiner*, *The Mercury News* (San Jose), local legal newspapers, and still-newish tech press. We even received some national press, coverage in *The Economist*, and a couple of favorable editorials.

We mailed the documents to the government, following the standard process for when you sue the government. That was far less exciting than even the gray clerk's office. A short time later, I got a message from someone named Tony Coppolino at the Department of Justice—a name I would become very familiar with.

LET ME TELL YOU ABOUT YOUR CASE, LITTLE GIRL

At one point early on, I had the kind of call with Tony that I had already become familiar with as a young female attorney. I've dubbed it the "Let me tell you about your case, little girl" call. While the specifics were different each time, this was the gist: in a generally condescending tone, one full of overconfidence or even braggadocio, opposing counsel would go on and on, laying out his theories of the case and defenses, along with all the ways he thought he would win, and I would lose. I guess the idea was to talk me out of my case, but what ended up happening is that I had a road map to his defenses and strategies. The opposing counsel just couldn't seem to help himself.

While Tony was much smoother than some of the other lawyers I tangled with, that first call rang the same bells. It went something like this:

"Ms. Cohn, I'm here with so-and-so at the Department of Justice, and we want to talk to you about this *Bernstein* case. You clearly misunderstand what happened here. Mr. Bernstein's rights have not been violated. He just doesn't understand how the commodity jurisdiction process, US Munitions List, and ITAR work, and he failed to exhaust his administrative remedies. You should reconsider and dismiss the case."

The unspoken part of this is that it's not really about my client, it's about me as the lawyer. Opposing counsel often signal their superior knowledge by use of acronyms and legal jargon. I'm supposed to realize that I'm in over my head in both the law and facts of the situation, and have no idea how poorly this is going to go with the judge. Some lawyers will say all of that out loud.

"Oh, I don't think so," I replied, although later I learned to just say something noncommittal like "Oh really?" Because the good part came next.

"Yes, your argument that the First Amendment applies is obviously wrong because software is functional. These regulations are aimed at protecting national security, so they are not content based and judicial review of specific agency decisions is not permitted under Edler. The ITAR has been fully vindicated."

In the early days, I was a bit cowed by those calls, and would head into my boss's office next to mine to debrief. Bill would point out all the ways opposing counsel was wrong and also all the help they had just given me. A couple of times I fought back in the calls, but I quickly realized that this didn't accomplish anything and only gave my opponents the same kind of information that I was learning from them. As I went on in my career, I would look forward to the call. It often helped clarify where the fights were going to be. I don't know for sure if the same thing happens to young male lawyers, but it didn't seem to be as regular an experience for my male friends. It wasn't for Bill.

Over time, Tony and I became quite cordial, and we built mutual respect—something that tends to start in earnest once you begin winning a big case against the Department of Justice. Yet in the early days, I suspect he must have thought I was some nobody from a tiny law firm in California. Which, come to think of it, I was.

But it didn't stay that way.

MOTION TO DISMISS DENIED: CODE IS SPEECH

The first hearing in the *Bernstein* case happened on October 20, 1995. It was the government's motion to dismiss our case, asserting that our claim was not "colorable" as a First Amendment one. "Colorable" in the law means that our claim did not even come into the general zone of the Constitution—which would be true, for example, if code was not speech or publishing on the internet wasn't an activity protected by the First Amendment. When it comes to export restrictions, which are generally an area where the president and the executive branch have a lot of power, another doctrine, called "nonjusticiability," meant that courts should stay out of the dispute *unless* the Constitution was involved. Overall, the brief was clear and the language understated, yet still portrayed the government as sober advocates and my client as an overwrought crank.

We started our brief with a paragraph laying out what was at stake. It's a practice I would use often. Writing the first paragraph of a brief and sometimes even the entire introduction helps me figure out how to frame the whole case. In the first paragraph of our first brief in the *Bernstein* case, we wrote,

> The US government here claims it can restrain the publication of private ideas about science, specifically ideas that if implemented, can enable others to engage in confidential speech. The restraints come under the guise of export control regulations, but these regulations, if upheld, would not only restrict the rights of scientists and academics to share their ideas with each other but also implicate the future course of the First Amendment in this country as we enter the information age.

As the hearing approached in fall 1995, we drew the first blood. The government suddenly "clarified" that it did not intend to include Dan's academic paper two years earlier when it denied his licensing requests. Dan had submitted six separate requests aimed at smoking out what the government really intended to license, and one of them was an academic paper. He had received a summary response from the government that a license was required for everything. After all the bluster of our telephone conversations and the dismissive tone of its papers, the government was now backing off on one of the things that it had censored.

On the morning of the hearing, I couldn't eat anything. Lee and I, along with another young lawyer whom we had recruited, met in the second-floor cafeteria in the same federal building on Golden Gate Avenue in San Francisco where I had filed the complaint a few months earlier. The dour brown federal building that housed the district court had been built to withstand public protests and attacks. To me it had the countenance of Darth Vader just a block away from the beaux arts cake of a building that is our city hall. The plaza area in front of the federal building had lots of concrete with metal bumps installed to prevent skateboarding or any other sort of fun from lightening its severe demeanor. I was a little intimidated each time I entered.

Judge Patel's majestic wood-paneled courtroom had two long wooden tables with big, high-backed leather chairs lining either side. The tables are in between the public seating area and the dais where the clerks and judge sit. The long table on the left is for defendants, and the one on the right is for the plaintiffs. Those leather chairs were my enemies. In order to be the right height for the table, I had to ratchet them up so high that my feet didn't touch the ground. They also rocked a bit which meant I frequently set the chairs rocking or my feet swinging. At the end of the day, I'd have knee pain. If I set the chair low enough so that my feet touched the ground, I sat too low. Either way, I felt like a little kid sitting at the big kid's table. The table and chairs in that courthouse never let me forget that as a petite woman, I was not in a place that expected me to be there.

Judge Patel was a well-respected, seasoned judge. She was completely prepared on that day, which was normal for her as I'd come to learn. She launched immediately into questions to Tony. It was clear that Judge Patel's idea of the hearing was a smart, interactive discussion with the lawyers. She was in control always, but she let each of us say our piece too.

My interactions with Judge Patel set the tone for all of my later oral arguments: that they go best when they are fundamentally a conversation between you and a smart person in a black robe who wants to do the right thing. Every judge is a bit different, but my experience with Judge Patel taught me a lot about how to be an advocate. I firmly believe the task is not just to argue at a judge but enter into a dialogue with them. As I learned from Bill, part of my power is to be absolutely straightforward and trustworthy about the facts and the law. I always have a clear goal and point of view, but also carefully listen to figure out what the judge needs to know in order to rule for me in a way that meets their goal: a ruling that will survive an appellate review.

In that first hearing, I had to wait a long time. Tony gave lengthy answers to the judge's short questions. The two of them went back and forth for what felt like a few hours—but what was probably only about twenty minutes—before she turned to me.

Sitting there while Tony and Judge Patel talked was frustrating but encouraging. Most of what she was asking about were clarifications related to the government's argument. More important, she didn't seem convinced by his answers. She clearly didn't buy his attempt to explain the government's last-minute change in allowing Dan to publish his academic paper by saying that Dan had simply misunderstood the original commodity jurisdiction determination. She didn't seem convinced when Tony talked about why the source code Dan wanted to publish wasn't speech. About halfway through, she posed this question to Tony: If she agreed that both the First Amendment was triggered and the export restrictions were a prior restraint, did she even have to discuss the rest of our claims?

That was a good question to hear, and while she did not fully show her hand at the hearing, we left with a hopeful feeling.

But then we waited. And waited.

COMPUTER LANGUAGE IS LANGUAGE

Finally, six months later in April 1996, my phone rang, and the front desk told me that the call was from a reporter from the *San Francisco Chronicle* named Bob Egelko. I didn't know him then, but I would in time. This was the first case I handled that was of interest to the press, so I didn't realize that before the courts implemented digital filing and direct internet access to court dockets, a small set of reporters stationed in the federal courts would learn about the court decisions in my case before I did.

It was Bob who told me that we had won: the court had rejected the government's motion to dismiss the case. I stood up and realized I was almost dancing behind my desk as I listened to him. I peppered him with questions about the reasoning before I finally promised him I would call him back first with a comment if he would fax (!) the decision to me. He did, and I read it as quickly as I could, and then refaxed it to Dan, Lee, and Shari at EFF. Then I jotted down a few summary notes and called Bob back.

The decision was strong—stronger even than we had hoped for. It discussed the First Amendment, noting, "Like music and mathematical equations, computer language is just that, language, and it communicates information either to a computer or to those who can read it."[15]

Judge Patel then directly addressed and refuted the government's key argument:

> Defendants argue in their reply that a description of software in English informs the intellect, but source code actually allows someone to encrypt data. Defendants appear to insist that the higher the utility value of speech the less like speech it is. An extension of that argument assumes that once language allows one to actually do something, like play music or make lasagna, the language is no longer speech. The logic of this proposition is dubious at best. Its support in First Amendment law is nonexistent.[16]

First step check: code is speech. We were on our way.

MARSHALING EXPERTISE

The next big step was to seek summary judgment, or a decision that we win, rather than merely fighting off the government's attempt to kill our case. During summary judgment we could submit evidence, but we also needed to be careful to only submit facts that were not in dispute. If there was a factual dispute, then the case would head to trial, and we wouldn't get our written decision for the lawbooks.

We knew our package would have to have several separate pieces. Because so much of the story about the internet and cryptography was likely to be new to the court, we took special care to make sure that we found people with credentials that the judge was likely to recognize. We needed the court to understand two important things that the scientific community already knew: first, that publication of code online was a critical part of developing science and so should be protected as any other kind of scientific, useful speech by the First Amendment, and second, that the science of encryption was going to be crucial for ensuring privacy and security online. Shari, with help from John, found us powerful voices for these points.

In addition, we knew the government would portray Bernstein as either an outlier or crank. That had been its approach from the beginning in our multiple phone calls and the way its motion to dismiss was framed. We needed respected names and a set of stories that demonstrated that what happened to him was intentional, consistent policy, and it had real-world impacts not only on Dan but also for internet users everywhere.

Looking back, I see how these pieces of the case became the basic building blocks of the internet freedom work we would do at EFF for the next thirty years. We continue to show how offline activities translate into the online world and need similar protections. Over and over again, we step in to protect science along with the scientific and innovation processes online. We point out how we all benefit when people can tinker with each other's ideas, codes, and other expressive works. The stories we developed for *Bernstein* recognize how security and privacy are intertwined—you protect one and you also protect the other. These would all become familiar themes as EFF and the internet grew.

First, on the question of whether code is speech, Professor Hal Abelson of MIT was our central voice. A storied professor already when we met in the 1990s, he taught the intro to computer science course Structure and Interpretation of Computer Programs, which initiated so many who would go on to become the world's leading computer scientists. Abelson also coauthored a textbook that was taught in over two hundred colleges and universities worldwide.

Despite having to explain some pretty basic principles to a young non-technical lawyer in California, Abelson was incredibly supportive and gracious with his time as we were putting the case together. A key thing he told me became central to our argument, and we included it directly in his declaration to the court: "Programs must be written for people to read and only incidentally for machines to execute." Abelson explained that as mathematics and logic serve as languages for expressing ideas about truth and falsehood (declarative knowledge), computer programs serve as languages for expressing ideas about how to do things (imperative knowledge). This set the table for the rest of the argument. We used his metaphor of a recipe as an example of speech that teaches people how to do things throughout the case.

The second step was demonstrating that publishing code on the internet is part of the development of science and therefore should be protected as a speech act. For that, Professor Andrew Appel from Princeton University taught me and the court about how even in the mid-1990s, science was increasingly being done over the internet and how publishing code is the way to be as precise as possible about what you are saying about a way to do things with computers.

He placed cryptography firmly in the scientific story too. Appel said,

> Cryptography is an area of applied mathematics, just as many areas of computer science are. It is not, as the government implies, merely a "product" or a "thing" to be used for commercial purposes; it is an academic discipline that is dynamic. This science may also produce useful things for people, as with many sciences, but it changes and grows with new research and insights gained from the academic process. The further development of this discipline requires that cryptographers be able to share their ideas, including the sharing of their computer code.[17]

We didn't stop there. We expanded and buttressed Abelson's and Appel's observations with several other prominent computer scientists to try to demonstrate the breadth of the issues at stake in deciding whether publishing code on the internet should be thought of as part of what the First Amendment protected.

On the role of cryptography itself, we went deeper to show that it is a science like many others, but that export regulations were a real barrier to that science. Cryptographer Bruce Schneier, whose book *Applied Cryptography* is one of the basic texts for anyone seeking to actually build or use encryption systems, took the time to explain to me the applied science of cryptography and helped me develop how to explain it to our judge. Schneier shared how the export restrictions had limited his ability to publish the computer code that would otherwise have been a part of his own book, and how his publisher became scared to distribute floppy disks containing the code along with the book.

Professor Matthew Blaze emphasized the security angle—both how trustworthy cryptography requires widespread publication to allow widespread scrutiny and testing, and how that process makes us all safer. Blaze added examples of how the export restrictions impeded both his research and teaching.

Professor Matthew Bishop of the University of California at Davis described how cryptography works, using the analogy of a locked safe carried between people by a courier. He explained how the export restrictions aided criminals who want to access personal, confidential internet data like credit card and bank information as well as the sensitive computer security information he regularly exchanged with colleagues around the world.

We also gathered more stories of the problems created by the export restrictions. We shared a declaration from Zimmermann, the creator of PGP who was investigated by federal prosecutors for making strong cryptography available to the public. While the case was largely over by the time we filed his formal declaration, his was the most chilling story we presented because he had faced imprisonment for publishing his code.

Coder James Demberger told the court how his publication of a prototype computer program called VOTPCRYP on a computer message board resulted in a threatening letter from the government, and how his attempt to place the code into the public domain, something the regulations nominally allowed, was repeatedly rejected by the agency. Brian Behlendorf, one of the developers of Apache, the most commonly used internet web server, told how it was blocked by the export restrictions merely for having "hooks" that encryption code could be later connected to. We presented a couple more stories too, all involving people thwarted from participating in the development of cryptography.

CRYPTOGRAPHY AND HUMAN RIGHTS

I wanted to talk not just about the science of cryptography but also about how using cryptography was (or was about to be) critically important for protecting human rights. This was one of my main personal reasons for taking the case—along with impressing my boyfriend—and I wanted to present it to the court. Through some digging, I found an email list for international human rights academics, and I sent a note asking if anyone knew someone who was using cryptography in the service of human rights.

I got back multiple emails with one name: Dr. Patrick Ball.

Patrick was working with the American Association for the Advancement of Science, and had been helping activist groups in repressive countries acquire and learn to use strong encryption to keep their data safe.

I reached out to him. In our initial phone call, his voice was intense. Patrick had been working on the ground with democracy activists in Guatemala. These organizers had been targeted by government raids, their offices searched, and their membership lists seized from their computers. People on those lists had been arrested. Many were tortured, and some disappeared and were likely murdered. It was a horrific story and a place where encryption could have literally saved lives.

Patrick was a natural storyteller, and I could hear a ring in his voice as he told me how he'd brought Zimmermann's PGP encryption software to these organizers in Guatemala to help them protect each other and their work. This was exactly the kind of thing I wanted to tell the court, and I knew Patrick could tell it well.

Yet as I talked further with him, it became clear that he was not only rampantly and repeatedly violating the export restrictions but was going to continue to do so. This worried me. If I told his story to the judge in our case, it would become public. Even if we got a protective order hiding his name, his work would definitely become known by the lawyers in the Justice Department and likely the very regulators we were fighting in court. It wouldn't be hard to find him, based on the description of what he was doing. I worried that with those obviously illegal acts being presented to a federal judge, someone on the government side might just think they had to pursue him.

Was it worth risking this work along with the lives it protected in order to increase our chances of getting the regulations thrown out and the work itself protected?

Ultimately, I decided no, it wasn't worth it. We had a robust story we were telling the court already. While the human rights story was important, it wasn't critical. I know for a fact that Patrick has never completely forgiven me for not letting him tell his story to the court.

But Patrick made a strong impression on me. It was the first time I met someone who was focused on the specific conjunction of international human rights and technology that had inspired me. I also recognized an electric connection we seemed to have, even over the phone.

DOES FUNCTIONALITY MATTER IF THIS IS A PRIOR RESTRAINT?

On September 20, 1996, we were back before Judge Patel, having laid out our case in the declarations and law briefs and asking for a summary judgment in our favor. In the first round we had won the fight to get code acknowledged as speech. Now we were asking to win the whole case. The argument started at 9 a.m. and ended about 2 p.m. when the court reporter finally asked for a break. By then I had more confidence. At one point when Tony tried to say I'd conceded something, I broke in to counter, "Let me make my own concessions." Most of the time the argument was about whether or not the regulations were based on the content of the materials or merely targeted the "functional" aspects of the code. If they were based on content, the stringent First Amendment standards for content-based restrictions on speech applied.

About two-thirds of the way through, Judge Patel asked me what would turn out to be the most important question: Does the issue of functionality matter if the export restrictions are a licensing scheme and so are covered by the prior restraint doctrine?

I knew at that moment that we were winning. I quickly answered that the government's claims of interest only in cryptographic codes' potential "functionality" to encrypt communications just didn't matter legally under the prior restraint doctrine. If the government was going to require a license for the publication of the code online—which it clearly did—the protections in the prior restraint doctrine against censorship applied regardless of *why* the government claims it needed a license. Judge Patel understood the argument we were making: that all the government's stated concerns about cryptographic code's potential functionality were not legally relevant to the issue of whether the export licensing scheme was a prior restraint and thus whether it needed to meet the procedural rules of *Freedman v. Maryland.*

The argument continued for quite a while after that, but I knew that the government's main and most important contention—that if it was aimed at the functionality of the code, then it didn't have to meet the First Amendment's requirements—was not going to fly.

Tony must have realized that he was going to lose too. On top of that, I'm sure the steady drumbeat of criticism in the press that Shari and others at EFF kept going also played a role in what happened next.

FROM THE ITAR TO EAR

Just a little over a month later, before the court had ruled, the government radically shifted its regulatory posture, while still attempting to continue what it had been doing. Specifically, it moved the regulation of encryption code from the State Department's ITAR to the Commerce Department's Export Administration Regulations (EAR).

We were floored and flummoxed—all the specific regulatory assertions we had made were going to be moot since a whole new regulatory scheme was going to apply. Yet the actual export of strong cryptography would remain subject to a license—just a different kind.

On December 9, 1996, Judge Patel issued the decision on the summary judgment motions we had argued in September. We won convincingly, but we didn't have time to celebrate. On December 30, the government formally issued its new regulations, and we were back where we started. Dan still couldn't publish his code, and we had to amend our lawsuit to address this change.

BERNSTEIN V. US DEPARTMENT OF STATE BECOMES *BERNSTEIN V. US DEPARTMENT OF COMMERCE*

For me, this shift meant canceling holiday plans so that I could try to master the EAR, an entirely different set of regulations that were just as opaque and complicated as the ITAR had been. But the EAR were not as easy to attack. In challenging the first regulations, we had relied heavily on an analysis from the elite Justice Department's Office of Legal Counsel that in 1978—fifteen years before we launched the case—had advised that the ITAR were unconstitutional under the First Amendment. We had nothing similar for the EAR. While the impact of the regulations was the same for Dan and others, the processes in the EAR were quite different. So we were back to the drawing board.

It took most of spring 1997 for us to shift our arguments over to the EAR and renew our motion for summary judgment. The second motion was argued in June 1997, and on August 27, 1997, I got the now familiar call from Bob at the *San Francisco Chronicle* telling me that we had won. Again. Luckily Judge Patel had not been fooled by the shift. This time the court did chastise us a bit, though, even as it handed us a clear victory:

> Both parties exaggerate the debate needlessly. Plaintiff does so by aggrandizing the First Amendment, by assuming that once one is dealing with speech that it is immaterial what the consequences of that speech may be. Defendants do so by minimizing speech, by constantly referring to "mere speech" or "mere ideas" in their briefs and assuming that the functionality of speech can somehow be divorced from the speech itself. This controversy is before this court precisely because there is no clear line between communication and its consequences. While defendants may have the authority to regulate encryption source code, they must nonetheless do so within the bounds of the First Amendment.

I could take a little criticism for being overly dramatic, especially when we won so completely:

> Where one places a newspaper rack is not an activity associated with expression, but the availability of newspapers generally is. Similarly, while the export of a commercial cryptographic software program may not be undertaken for expressive reasons, that same activity—indisputably regulated under the EAR—is often undertaken by scientists for purely expressive reasons. By the very terms of the encryption regulations, the most common expressive activities of scholars—teaching a class, publishing their ideas, speaking at conferences, or writing to colleagues over the internet—are subject to a prior restraint by the export controls when they involve cryptographic source code or computer programs. . . . This is precisely the kind of law . . . that risks self-censorship on the part of those that must apply for licenses and censorship on the part of the decision maker.[18]

The court issued an injunction against the regulations, which we had asked for. But we knew this was not the end of the case. We expected the government to appeal first to the appellate court—cases from the Northern District of California were appealed to the Ninth Circuit Court of Appeal—and probably to the Supreme Court after that. The national security forces of the United States were not used to losing and certainly wouldn't back down just because one lone federal judge disagreed with them.

We were right. The first thing that the government did was ask the appeals court to delay the injunction and allow it to continue to license encryption code until after the appeal could be heard. We filed a flurry of papers back and forth. When the dust settled in September 1997, the court of appeals had stayed the impact of Judge Patel's ruling pending its own review. We had won, but Dan was still unable to publish. We turned our attention from the ugly brown skyscraper where the district court was housed to the gorgeous Ninth Circuit building a few blocks away.

STARTING FROM SCRATCH AT THE NINTH CIRCUIT

When you win on summary judgment in a constitutional case like we did and an appeal happens, the upper court is really starting from scratch legally. The appellate judges definitely know that the lower court agreed with you and why—that's extremely important—but they don't have to agree at all with the district court's ruling or show any deference to it. You have to make the same arguments again, but you don't want to just cut and paste what you did below. You need to make your old arguments feel new. It's a challenge.

In the *Bernstein* case, we did have a big new thing to talk about on appeal. In June 1997 the Supreme Court had decided *ACLU v. Reno*, the first true internet case.[19] The case challenged a law called the Communications Decency Act that prohibited "indecent" speech online. It grew, in part, out of the hysteria that resulted from a faulty study of porn online conducted by an undergraduate student at Carnegie Melon University. The study was the basis of a cover story (later retracted) by *TIME* magazine.[20] Despite the fact that the study was obviously wrong, it was picked up by members of Congress and used to justify the new law.[21]

It was anger at the passage of this law, and the complete refusal of Congress or the executive branch to even try to understand what was actually happening online, that led Barlow to pen the Declaration of the Independence of Cyberspace.[22]

While I wasn't directly involved, EFF spearheaded lots of public attention around the Communications Decency Act. The subsequent litigation, which was led by the American Civil Liberties Union (ACLU), was a triumph. The Supreme Court unanimously determined that speech on the internet is entitled to full First Amendment protection and rejected the government's various claims to the contrary.

We knew this ruling would set up our question about whether the First Amendment protected publishing code on the internet too. Having a recent unanimous vote of approval of the First Amendment online from the highest court of the land was so important that we put it into the first paragraph of our brief in November 1997.

Once again we created credibility for our side by bringing in lots of prominent voices. I call it "driving the big bus" to court. By this time, the case had a much higher public profile. In a strategy that we would replicate in our other big cases, we welcomed a wide range of voices to file amicus briefs in support of our position from different perspectives and across the political spectrum. For organizations, we had the ACLU, Electronic Privacy Information Center, Center for Democracy and Technology, and Computer Professionals for Social Responsibility. Human Rights Watch filed a brief on the more liberal side, and Free Congress and the Independent Institute filed one on the more conservative or libertarian side.

Furthermore, we welcomed amicus briefs from scientific and technical experts including the US Public Policy Committee of the Association for Computing Machinery. That effort was spearheaded by an indomitable woman named Barbara Simons, who pushed the often staid, historically nonpolitical organization to stand up for science in litigation like ours. We also received support from the National Computer Security Association, and cryptography pioneers Whitfield Diffie, Peter Neumann, and Ron Rivest. We had people who made the internet work like those involved in the Internet Mail Consortium, along with more traditional business groups such as the National Association of Manufacturers.

Supporting briefs were also filed by several prominent law professors and the American Association for the Advancement of Science, where Patrick worked. He was the cryptography spreader focused on human rights whom I'd rejected as an expert, and I suspected he had a voice in convincing the prominent organization to weigh in. That's not even the full list. We may have started as a ragtag legal team, but we now rode with many allies on the big bus.

In December 1997, we were up for an oral argument. The Ninth Circuit Court of Appeals sits in a white stone building stuffed with cornices, statues, mosaics, carved fruit motifs, plaster cupids, and Corinthian columns. That sounds like a mess, but it is actually one of the most beautiful courthouses in the country. It has a Grecian countenance that is both calming and creates respect.

The court staff seemed to know that the *Bernstein* case was important. We were assigned to the most ornate courtroom, which had multiple diamond-shaped mosaics behind the dais. Our usual crew of hackers all came, with cypherpunk dress-up day in full swing. But that crew was outnumbered by people in suits who clearly wore them every day. As I walked up to the building, I saw a scrum of press and TV cameras.

While some of this attention was due to EFF's outreach and the ongoing attention brought by the cypherpunks, much of it was because people beyond that geeky world were starting to understand why this was an important fight. As public use of the internet grew, the need for security and privacy as well as the recognition of encryption's potential role grew along with it.

When we started the case in 1993, the basic codebase that would become the World Wide Web we all now rely on had recently been released free to the public. The organization that would steward it, the W3C foundation, had just been founded by World Wide Web creator Sir Tim Berners-Lee. There were about two hundred web servers total in the world, and the internet had just been opened for commercial use. "Information superhighway" was the predominant descriptor of this new online world.

Four years later when we were at the Ninth Circuit in 1997, over seventy million people were online. A couple of graduate students at Stanford University registered the domain Google.com, but searchers online had several choices, including search engines called Yahoo, Lycos, AltaVista, and WebCrawler.

In the courtroom, I was once again dressed in a new suit sent by my mother from the Denver department store where she worked. I was once again hoping to look a little less nervous than I was.

The government went first because it lost below in the district court. What felt like hours of conversation between the three judges and government attorney, Scott McIntosh, was probably less than ten minutes. I was itching to stand up and tell our story. Our three-judge panel included Judges Betty Fletcher and Thomas Nelson, and a very senior one named Melvin Bright. Judge Bright had been appointed by President Richard Nixon and definitely had never used the internet. I wondered whether he had ever used computers at all. Most older judges had secretaries who handled word processing, calendaring, and other tasks that are done by computer. Even many younger judges still had their emails printed out for them and then dictated their replies.

Within the first few minutes, Scott invoked national security and the need to protect signals intelligence, clearly trying to set this up as a case of wild-eyed activists trying to second-guess the government on a matter of serious national importance. This opening gambit would become familiar. By the time of the NSA spying cases, we would make internal bets on our team about how many minutes a government lawyer would take in oral argument before mentioning national security. It was rarely more than one or two minutes; usually it was in the first sentence.

It quickly became clear that Judge Fletcher was not buying the government's contentions. As Scott tried to explain that the government regulations were not trying to suppress information from people, she responded, "They're just keeping them from using it."

Scott replied, "Not using the information, your honor, using the software, because . . ."

"That's just words, counsel," she interrupted, getting a laugh from the packed gallery.

I knew she, like Judge Patel before her, was not accepting the idea that you could somehow parse the functionality of software out from its publication, and then suppress publication and learning.

We had practiced my presentation several times during mock oral arguments—what are called "moots"—with outside lawyers and law professors who volunteered to prepare me. Some played hostile judges and asked questions that ended up being much more tricky than the ones that the panel ultimately asked.

When my turn came, I walked the three judges through the four cases that we thought controlled the decision-making and answered a few questions, all of which we had anticipated in our prep sessions. I then had the good sense to sit down.

Once again we waited.

CONGRESSIONAL TESTIMONY

In the meantime, my law practice was developing, and the firm was starting to talk about making me a partner. The *Bernstein* case sparked some clients, including some advising about cryptography regulations, but not that much. It was still a labor of love for me and the firm.

Public momentum against the export regulations was growing, though, as were governmental attempts to salvage its authority. Republicans like Senator John Ashcroft were actively on our side, using the issue of encryption and privacy to attack then president Bill Clinton and his vice president, Al Gore, who was preparing his run for the presidency.

In March 1998, I was invited to testify before the Senate Judiciary Committee's Subcommittee on Constitution, Federalism, and Property Rights, alongside two prominent law professors, Richard Epstein from the University of Chicago and Kathleen Sullivan, then of Harvard. I was nervous, but with Lee alongside me, and the district court decision and Ninth Circuit arguments under my belt, I felt that I was in the right place and on the right side of history.

My goal was to explain the case to the members of the subcommittee. But even more urgently, it was to dissuade them from passing a new law that could make our job harder in the courts, or at least make us have to start all over yet again. The proposed law, called the SAFE Act, was largely well-intentioned, but it represented a compromise that would be a step back from our clean win in the courts. Additionally, the Clinton administration was pushing several even worse "compromises" that would have largely continued the licensing scheme. The administration was hoping to use the legislative process to insert those into the law under cover of "reform."

One thing I've learned is that while "reforming" an old law in the legislature can often be a good idea, you have to look closely at the entire context to figure out whether a proposed fix is a good one. Frequently what comes dressed up as a sheep of reform is really a wolf. Of course, sometimes, especially in the digital age, updating laws and regulations to reflect the more modern context is important. I have a list of those, including lots of our privacy laws that were written before modern networks made pervasive surveillance so easy that a prominent law professor named Peter Swire called this the "Golden Age for Surveillance."[23]

But here the proposed legislative reforms were relatively small improvements, and we were winning much bigger ones in the courts under the Constitution. A judicial win would be much better, cleaner, and longer lasting than a legislative compromise fix, particularly since constitutional decisions are not as easy to dislodge as legislative ones. My job was to convince Congress to let that process play out instead of stepping in now to "reform" the law.

Sitting in the wood-paneled hearing room nestled among the statues and stately buildings of the National Mall, I emphasized how the US founders relied on encryption:

> Even the Constitution and the Bill of Rights themselves were often encoded, as Thomas Jefferson and James Madison exchanged drafts of those seminal documents. Cryptography was used by a virtual Who's Who of American Founding Fathers—not only Jefferson and Madison, but Benjamin Franklin, Alexander Hamilton, John and Abigail Adams, Aaron Burr, and many others. In sharp contrast to the Administration's arguments today, they viewed cryptography as an essential instrument for protecting information, both political and personal. Our research indicates that when the First and Fourth Amendments were enacted in the late 1700s, any suggestion that the Government should have the ability to prevent individuals from encrypting their messages, or that the Government should have a back-door key to all encrypted messages, would have struck the Constitution's framers as ridiculous.

FINDING COMMUNITY

About this same time, my personal life was shifting. My hacker boyfriend and I were moving in different directions, in part because he didn't want children and I was thinking that maybe I did. Ultimately we reached a breaking point, and I knew I had to move on. The breakup was not easy. James and I had pretty much turned into adults together and we had shared a lot, including two cats that I ultimately had to leave with him.

But by that time I had a few solid friends who rushed to my side. Two of them helped me find a roommate and even got me a kitten as a housewarming gift for my new apartment, which had a view of the Bay in the Potrero Hill neighborhood.

Newly single, these friends brought me deeper into their community. One of them had started an annual music-centered festival in the early 1990s that James and I had attended a few times. By 1998, when my breakup was happening, this community was holding the annual festival plus a few regular events throughout the year. I was invited—cajoled really—by the kitten givers to join about thirty-five folks from the community on a trip to Death Valley in a converted bus called the Green Tortoise.

That four-day weekend brought me something that has sustained me for nearly thirty years and counting. A rattling green bus full of people somehow bonded in the alchemy between seeing the spring flowers and flailing in the sand dunes. We cooked shared meals and sang during the long drives in between stops. We flopped into hot springs and got stuck on the bus for hours while a wicked dust storm raged outside. We partied, but we also talked and shared about our lives. I ended the weekend with an invitation to join a book club, plan to start a women's singing circle, and standing invitation to a monthly jam session where real musicians frequently showed up. But more important, I now had a community.

Other than the couple who invited me, most of these folks knew nothing about what I did for a living, much less about the minutiae of encryption, lawsuits, or national security. I later learned that most of my bus mates were tremendously accomplished in their professional lives too: including a dentist, a journalist, and several teachers. But honestly, it didn't matter. What did matter was that I now belonged someplace, with some people. I also had a solid personal balance for my professional life that I've never let go of.

Having this place of solace coupled with an identity outside law and technology has been critical to my ability to keep doing the work, even when it's hard and we don't win, or have our wins snatched away. I can put down the weight of being a woman in a male-dominated world as well as someone who needs to constantly be on top of all the facts, laws, and strategies. Community is my refueling place, and turning off my brain and just joining in to the song, even if a bit off-key, is one of the ways that I've been able to stay in these fights for the long run.

LAW WHERE THERE IS NO LAND

"We're doing a piece about lawyers doing work on the internet. I want to interview you and have a photographer come take your picture," said *New York Times* reporter Amy Harmon on a phone call while I was waiting for the Ninth Circuit's decision in March 1998. My heart started racing. A picture in *The New York Times*! My family would be so proud. I started humming and vowed to buy five copies for my mother.

The next day, a disheveled photographer out of central casting showed up at my San Mateo law firm. I took him into the tiny book-filled law library that we shared with several other offices on our floor. I'd had a few photos taken of me for the news at this point. The photographers had generally tried to give a technical flavor. I'd been in grainy shots with numbers, mathematical symbols or some vague approximation of computer code superimposed on top. They made me look like some sort of technical-focused specter, a future ghost from the land of technology.

The photo that *The New York Times* ran has me in my then favorite deep-blue blouse, posed behind my gray, blocky Toshiba laptop, and surrounded by law books.[24] It was an improvement from the "I'm from the land of the computers" weird photos, but I look about twelve years old. The mid-1990s' blouse looks ridiculous to me today, just a tiny step away from the frowsy bows that women lawyers wore instead of ties.

The photo ran on the front page of the Business section in *The New York Times* under the headline, "Law Where There Is No Land." It had a big photo of me, with smaller inserts of three Harvard law professors: Larry Lessig, Charles Nesson, and Jonathan Zittrain.

My father was delighted. He didn't subscribe to *The New York Times* and didn't really even know what the case was about, but it didn't matter. His daughter-the-lawyer was in the paper. My mother was happy too, although she understood even less about what I was doing and was largely afraid of computers her whole life. Yet she showed her love in her own way, including as my dedicated personal clothes shopper.

But that was only the beginning.

FINDING FAMILY

A month or so after I got back from testifying in Congress, I heard a voicemail message at work. A woman said, "I saw your photo in *The New York Times*. If you're the Cindy Cohn who was born in Detroit in November 1963 and adopted, I'm a good friend of your birth mother. Here is my number. Please call me."

I froze. The cryptography world is full of ex-spies along with people who have fabulous tales of espionage and secret dealings. Several people had asked me if I felt I was targeted by the government for the case, but I definitely did not. The government attorneys had been condescending at times yet never threatening. I had never even talked directly with the NSA folks who were their clients; they were generally silent the few times they were introduced on our calls or in court. But still. Was this some sort of trick? How could someone know this little bit of my history?

I worried about it. I kept staring at my phone all day, as if willing it to ring again. Finally, at the end of the day, sitting safe in my office, but with my stomach clenching, I called the number she left.

"Hello, this is Cindy Cohn. You called me after my photo was in . . ."

"*The New York Times*, yes!" she interrupted with a warm, high-pitched voice. "I'm so glad you called back! I'm Charlotte. I was best friends with your birth mother in high school and college. I'm so happy that we found you."

Still unsure what was going on, I stammered a bit, "I, I, I'm curious . . ."

"Yes, we wondered so much about you over the years," she interrupted again. "I told Evelyn she was wrong to not talk to you when you wrote before and I'm not going to let it happen again."

"You knew about the letter?"

"Yes, when you were in law school. She showed it to me, along with your photo. I told Evelyn at the time that she should really talk to you, but she wouldn't. I wasn't sure that it was the same person in *The New York Times* photo, but I just had to find out. I'd like to try again."

I had trouble catching my breath and felt myself start to shake a bit, remembering back to my days in Ann Arbor and that cold, typewritten letter I'd receive telling me never to contact her again. This emotional history flooded my head and my heart. Should I take up Charlotte's offer to try again to connect me? Maybe Evelyn felt differently now. But if not, could I handle that kind of deep rejection a second time?

After a long pause, I stuttered, "Um, sure. I would like that." I wasn't actually sure. Yet she seemed so enthusiastic and confident that things would be different this time, and I really wanted to believe her.

I didn't hear from her for at least a month. When she called back, she said that Evelyn had refused once again.

"But I just couldn't let it go," she continued immediately. Before I could really process what she was saying, she added, "I called your grandfather, who now lives in Florida with your aunt. I asked them if they wanted to meet the baby. They both immediately said yes. They are overjoyed."

I don't remember much else from the call, and when I got off the phone, I just looked into the distance for a long time, goose bumps covering my arms.

A FAMILY AFFAIR

My first call was to my brother, then to my mother, father, and sister. I still couldn't really believe it. Neither could they.

The next day, February 2, 1999, I received an email from my birth mother's sister, my aunt Deidre, and my birth mother's father, my grandfather, Harold. They included photos of themselves. It was the first time I ever saw someone who was genetically related to me. I searched the photos for similarities, and found some with my brown eyes, some with my mouth, and some with the shape of my head. I kept feeling shivers. I ended up wrapped in several blankets on the couch as I drank in those photos—some old black-and-white ones that they had scanned, and others more recent. The ones of my birth mother looked very little like me, but the ones of my birth aunt were uncanny.

My birth mother herself was another story, though. She apparently threatened my grandfather that she would never talk to him again if he had contact with me. She wrote an angry letter to Charlotte accusing her of interfering and cutting off all contact with her too—and she cc'd me. She later wrote a similarly scathing letter to me, and I wrote an angry one right back. It was not my best moment.

I was scared but also overjoyed that Harold decided to meet me anyway. As happy as I was to be connected, it was painful and unnerving to see how much of a conflict my emergence was causing. Harold and Deidre assured me that this was just the last straw in what had become a stressed relationship long before I showed up. Still, I couldn't help but feel conflicted. My birth mother made good on her threat, however, and never talked to her father again.

But Harold and Deidre were warm and excited. Harold said he had thought about what had become of me nearly every single day since I was born. They both immediately invited me to come to Florida to meet them.

I wanted to visit my birth family, but it was a scary prospect. I already had experienced my birth mother rejecting me twice, and as warm as they seemed on the phone, I had no idea how these people were going to be in person. I called my brother to tell him about the offer, and he immediately said he was going to come with me. I nearly burst into tears.

Less than an hour after I got off the phone with him, I got a call from my sister.

"You two cannot do this without me!" she cried. "This is a family affair, and I want in." At that I did cry.

A few weeks later my brother flew down from Portland, and we flew together from San Francisco to Orlando, where my sister met us at our gate, having flown in separately from Virginia. Then the three of us walked past security and met my birth grandfather and aunt.

All of my fears were dissolved in the few days we spent with them poring over family photos, hearing stories, and trying to find the ways in which we were connected. It turned out that my birth family was quite political as well as engaged with literature and music—things I had always been more interested in than my adopted family. Harold loved books, musical comedy, classical music, and jazz. He had owned a record store in Detroit before becoming a humanities professor at a community college. His wife, my grandmother, had already passed away. She had been a tennis teacher and sporty—something I definitely was not. But I saw my eyes in hers, clear and plain. And the whole family was academically oriented, like me. My grandmother had a master's degree in public health, and her sister, my great aunt, had been one of the first female graduates of Wayne

State Law School. It was a revelation. I felt a kind of tether to the world, to these people, that was unlike anything I had ever felt.

Yet at the same time, this family moved and talked fast. Too fast for me, really. They were quick to anger and just as quick to come back from it. As much as I felt newly connected, I also didn't. I felt my Midwest, small-town slowness and calm in contrast to the anxious, interrupting nature of this family originally from Detroit. I was startled by their emotional reactions. Nature and nurture seemed to have divided me neatly in two.

So in addition to the connection with my birth family, the trip showed me how deeply connected I was to my adopted family. My brother and sister coming to meet my birth family with me kind of fixed something inside me: it calmed me about being a part of the family I was raised in. What I thought was my adoption story was really our story together. Definitely a family affair.

ENCRYPTIONS BOUNTY

Not too long after I returned from Florida, on May 5, 1999, the Ninth Circuit decision in the *Bernstein* case came out. We won. The decision was a strong validation. Judge Fletcher wrote the opinion, and she agreed with us that the export licensing scheme burdens scientific expression, vested "boundless discretion" in government officials, and had inadequate procedural safeguards. In other words, we were right that it was a prior restraint and one that didn't have the proper processes to protect against censorship.

There are few better feelings than seeing your language and argument adopted, and even sharpened and made better, by a court ruling in your favor. And when that happens in the context of making the world a better and safer place—well, the glow is off the charts. I couldn't stop smiling for a week at least. Forgive me if I quote extensively here, but the decision spoke to all of us who had believed that our little band of lawyers and computer scientists could explain this new, complicated world to the courts. We not only explained it, we got them to understand what was at stake, see why we were right, and why the national security powers of the United States were wrong.

First and most important, the court agreed with us that code is speech, and adopted a clear and straightforward description:

> We conclude that encryption software, in its source code form and as employed by those in the field of cryptography, must be viewed as expressive for First Amendment purposes, and thus is entitled to the protections of the prior restraint doctrine. If the government required that mathematicians obtain a pre-publication license prior to publishing material that included mathematical equations, we have no doubt that such a regime would be subject to scrutiny as a prior restraint. The availability of alternate means of expression, moreover, does not diminish the censorial power of such a restraint—that Adam Smith wrote *Wealth of Nations* without resorting to equations or graphs surely would not justify governmental prepublication review of economics literature that contain these modes of expression.

Next, the court addressed and rejected the government's "functionality" arguments:

> The government's argument, distilled to its essence, suggests that even one drop of "direct functionality" overwhelms any constitutional protections that expression might otherwise enjoy. This cannot be so. . . . The distinction urged on us by the government would prove too much in this era of rapidly evolving computer capabilities. The fact that computers will soon be able to respond directly to spoken commands, for example, should not confer on the government the unfettered power to impose prior restraints on speech in an effort to control its "functional" aspects. The First Amendment is concerned with expression, and we reject the notion that the admixture of functionality necessarily puts expression beyond the protections of the Constitution.

Finally, as we had expected, the court focused on the prior restraint argument as the easiest way to see how the export regulations failed the First Amendment. The court was careful to limit its opinion to just that doctrine, but in closing it recognized the broader context of the dispute, in words that continue to resonate even today:

> The availability and use of secure encryption may offer an opportunity to reclaim some portion of the privacy we have lost. Government efforts to control encryption thus may well implicate not only the First Amendment rights of cryptographers intent on pushing the boundaries of their science, but also the constitutional rights of each of us as potential recipients of encryption's bounty.[25]

That was the good news. The bad news was that the decision was two to one. Judge Nelson wrote a strong dissent, siding with the government on functionality. Judge Bright wrote that while he joined with the majority, he thought the issue was difficult and believed that the US Supreme Court should weigh in. We knew the fight was not over.

The next step after the Ninth Circuit decision might have been the Supreme Court, but the government had another option first—something called en banc review. Because the Ninth Circuit is so large, with so many judges who often have very different opinions, the practice is frequently to ask for a larger group of eleven judges, called an en banc panel, to reconsider the ruling of a three-judge panel. Over summer 1999, the government sought this additional review. When this happens, the full court takes a vote, and if enough judges believe that the initial decision should be reconsidered, it grants the petition for en banc review, and the opinion is suspended until the eleven-judge review is over.

After filing briefs back and forth, the Ninth Circuit court granted the en banc review on September 30, 1999. This meant that after six long years of litigation, winning every significant step of the way, our beautiful Ninth Circuit precedential decision was suspended.

We filed additional briefs to the en banc court, once again trying to make our arguments strong and fresh even as we made the same basic claims about code as speech and the prior restraint analysis as we had made from the beginning. Then we waited.

JUNGER V. DALEY IN CLEVELAND

We kept ourselves busy by helping our friends Gino Scarselli and Ray Vasvari in Ohio prepare for their case, *Junger v. Daley*, on the same issue. That case, brought by a law professor at Case Western University, had lost in a district court. Lee and I flew to Cleveland to help Gino and Ray prepare in December 1999. The lower court decision was heavily relied on by Judge Nelson in his dissent in our case.

IS SHE STRAIGHT? IS SHE SINGLE?

Also in fall 1999, I got a call from a relative who I had always called my cousin, Max. Max and I shared an aunt and uncle in common—his mother's sister was married to my father's brother. Max had come to Michigan as a first-year law student during my third year and we became quite close. He had clerked for Judge Fletcher, albeit long before the *Bernstein* case came before her. Max was one of the people I called for advice when I learned Judge Fletcher would be on our Ninth Circuit panel.

"I'm coming to visit San Francisco, and I'd love to see you," he said. "And while I'm there, do you want to meet the clerk who worked on your case when he clerked for Judge Fletcher? He finished his clerkship and now works at a law firm in San Francisco."

"I absolutely want to see you," I responded. "But wait, what? How do you know the clerk in my case? I'd love to meet the person who helped Judge Fletcher write that beautiful opinion."

That's how I showed up at a small Italian restaurant near my home in Potrero Hill and met the next man who I would fall in love with. The spark we had at that dinner was palpable, and poor Max ended up sitting there while we bantered back and forth about the internet, law, and music.

The next day Max called to tell me that the clerk had called Max with two questions: Is she straight? Is she single? Told that both of those were yeses, the clerk had asked for my number. I told Max to give it. With that, I was off on my next personal adventure.

WANT MY OLD JOB?

A little later, but still in fall 1999, I was driving over the coastal hills from San Mateo to Half Moon Bay with my mind flip-flopping. Shari, who had been my solid partner at EFF during the *Bernstein* case, had just moved to California and wanted to have dinner. As the sun set over the Pacific, at one of those classic seafood places perched over the water, Shari confirmed what I had guessed: she was taking over as executive director of EFF. Then in her always direct way, she said,

"You want my old job? Join me and we'll turn EFF into the kick-ass civil liberties organization that you and I know it can be."

I jumped to my first thought.

"I couldn't do it without Lee," referring to my lifeline.

Shari laughed out loud. "Well, that's perfect. I already talked to Lee, and he said he couldn't do it without you! Of course I want you both."

Shari wasn't just taking over as executive director. She was putting the organization on a different path. Before Shari, in the late 1990s, the leadership of the organization was focused more on becoming a think tank, or advisers and consultants to the new tech companies, helping them to center privacy and free speech. As the director of legal services, most of what Shari did was to wrangle administrative comments to regulators thinking about the early internet, and find and support outside lawyers like me to carry a few court cases. What Shari was proposing in 1999 was moving the organization toward a much more aggressive role of defending and defining civil liberties. And with me as legal director, we would start building an internal legal team that could directly handle litigation.

It was tempting. But I hesitated and told her I needed a little time to think about it. That's because I was also considering taking a big step in a nondigital direction.

BOWOTO V. CHEVRON

When Shari asked me to join EFF, I had just been offered a chance to jump into more direct human rights lawyering. I was asked to serve pro bono as local counsel for a big international human rights case against the multinational energy corporation Chevron, arising out of Chevron's orchestration of a military-style attack on environmental protesters in the Niger Delta. The case was important to me because I felt it was a way to honor the legacy of Ken Saro-Wiwa, one of the activists I had connected strongly with during my time at the Unrepresented Nations and Peoples Organization. Ken had been illegally arrested in Nigeria for organizing protests against Shell Oil's activities in his Ogoni homeland. I watched, feeling helpless, as he was subjected to an obviously rigged trial based on phony murder charges. In 1995, he was hanged along with eight others. They were called the Ogoni Nine.

In 1991, Ken had come to a training in UN advocacy that the UNPO had sponsored and I had helped teach in Geneva. We became fast friends. He was a powerful polymath. In addition to sparking the Nigerian environmental movement by fighting the pollution caused by oil drilling, he was an acclaimed fiction author. Ken had written a book called *Sozaboy: A Novel in Rotten English* that I'd read in a course on African fiction as an undergrad in Iowa. He had also written the screenplays for one of the most popular sitcoms in Nigeria, called *Basi and Company*. Ken was charming, hilarious, and a bit of a flirt, although we were always just friends. He loved that I had read some of his writings for a class. We talked about books and writing along with their connection to human rights and activism.

I spoke at several memorials held for Ken after his horrific murder, including one sponsored by the Los Angeles chapter of PEN America, where the organization showed one of the most famous episodes of his sitcom. But I wanted to do more. In 1999 at an environmental awards ceremony called the Goldman Awards, a friend told me about a case that had just been filed in federal court in California called *Bowoto v. Chevron*, and that the lawyers were looking for local counsel. The case also arose from environmental protests against oil drilling in Nigeria, the heart of Ken's work, but focused on Chevron rather than Shell. The protesters were from different tribal groups and a different location in Niger Delta than Ogoniland, where Ken was from. But they, like me, had been inspired by Ken.

Bowoto v. Chevron was about as far away from internet law as was possible. It arose from the damage caused by Chevron's oil drilling activities on the offshore Parabe platform. In order to facilitate moving oil from the platform to its onshore facilities, Chevron had breached the berm that separated the swampy freshwater from the seawater. The influx of saltwater had killed the freshwater fish that the community depended on, hurt its drinking water supplies, and caused a tremendous amount of erosion. It resulted in the loss of whole villages, and many people, especially young people, had been forced to move away.

The local community—led by four or five men who were called "youths" but were actually my age, in their late thirties—had tried to support their frontline community and get Chevron to address the damage. Chevron refused. After being ignored for a long time, about a hundred unarmed members of the community mounted a protest by taking their canoes out to Chevron's giant offshore Parabe platform and refusing to leave until their concerns were heard. They stayed for three days, repeating their demands that Chevron work with them to mitigate the damage it had done to this community, both through environmental repair, and by employing the people who could not now fish to support their families.

On the morning of the third day, Chevron's pilots in Chevron's helicopters flew some Nigerian forces known locally as the "Kill and Go" to the platform. These soldiers were routinely stationed and provisioned at Chevron's facilities, and Chevron paid them. So quite literally, Chevron bought the bullets and guns that these forces used. True to their name, the Kill and Go opened fire on the protesters, killing two and injuring several more, including our lead client, a man named Larry Bowoto, who was shot in the arm.

The goal of *Bowoto v. Chevron* was to bring Chevron to justice for the attack in federal court in San Francisco, near its San Ramon headquarters. It was one of a number of cases trying to hold US multinational corporations liable in the United States for the human rights violations that they were responsible for abroad. The case had already been filed when I heard about it, but the legal team needed a lawyer in San Francisco who was familiar with the local court processes.

Joining EFF to work on digital rights seemed so cushy and niche in comparison to the *Bowoto* case. Yet even then I knew that human rights work like that done by and in support of protesters such as those on the Parabe platform could be hurt or helped depending on how the internet developed.

I had other questions too. Would I like nonprofit life? Would the funding be stable? Would I have to raise my own money? I had just made partner at my tiny law firm a couple of years earlier. I was lucky enough to work with people I adored and who had taught me how to practice law. They had also let me do the *Bernstein* case and now the *Bowoto* one pro bono, which was a huge kindness. I didn't want to seem ungrateful.

The flip-flopping I'd felt on the drive over highway 92 continued as I drove home and for the next couple weeks. My newish boyfriend, the former clerk in the *Bernstein* case, strongly encouraged me to take Shari's old job. I asked a lot of people, both inside and outside EFF. At a music festival, I polled all of my friends. I walked around my office feeling like I was a bit of a traitor for even considering leaving.

But I finally got clear on the path forward and decided to make the leap. What made it possible was that when I screwed up my courage to ask, Shari immediately agreed to let me continue to work on the *Bowoto* case from EFF. I told my law firm partners individually, and while they were sad, they were all supportive. I started packing up boxes from a decade of legal practice to move into the nonprofit world.

The *Bowoto* case took me to Nigeria several times to meet with our clients from 1999 until the case finally ended in 2010. We also brought Larry to California, where he stayed with me in my Noe Valley flat as we found a way to get his arm treated for the damage done as a result of the shooting. After several days visiting local emergency rooms and otherwise trying to arrange for care for a Nigerian with no insurance, some kind doctors at Stanford agreed to examine him and ultimately perform surgery for free.

The Chevron case experience gave me a powerful perspective on the privacy needed to stand up for human rights violations. We knew that we were being closely monitored by Chevron and agents working with Chevron throughout the case, particularly when we were in Nigeria but also likely when Larry was in California for his surgery and recovery.

THE PRINCESS OF LIGHT

In January 2000, between when I said yes to EFF and actually made the move in September 2000, Tony from the Department of Justice called. He told me that the government was going to change the export regulations again. For a quick moment my heart sank. Were they going to make us start all over again like we had to when moving from the State Department's ITAR to the Commerce Department's EAR?

But it wasn't that. This time it felt different, even on that first call. Tony invited me to a meeting in DC to discuss the proposed changes. I eagerly hopped on a plane, and arranged for Shari, Dan, and Bob to join me. I even reached out to Patrick, who I'd stayed in touch with despite rejecting him as a declarant in the case. We discovered that in addition to a shared view of human rights and the internet, we shared a love for the Grateful Dead. I ended up staying with him and his wife in Washington, DC.

The meeting was in one of those majestic DC buildings. I could smell the wood polish on the wainscoting. I always tense up when I'm stepping into the halls of power, and this one felt especially powerful. Portraits of generals and other senior military officials—mostly men—looked judgingly down at me from the walls on either side of the room. As always, the chairs were too big for me, just like the ones in the courthouse in San Francisco where this all began.

In those big chairs along both sides of the table were people in various uniforms. I saw lots of shiny medals and even a couple of epaulets. It was more brass than I'd ever seen in person. I knew that the military was deeply interested in encryption, and that the export regulations—both under the Department of State and Department of Commerce—were largely aimed at ensuring that the US military kept an edge in its tools and information. Yet this was the first time I saw the power that we had gone up against in the same room.

There were at least twenty people there, and it was obvious they'd gathered for another meeting ahead of our arrival.

This kind of physical formality is often used strategically during negotiations. Big law firms have their own version, but this was the national security flavor, with lots of stars and bars. The primary goal is to reinforce the government's position as powerful and inevitable—no matter how outlandish or unreasonable it actually was. The unspoken implication is that any disagreement with the government is the wrong place to be. Of course another goal is not-so-subtle intimidation so that I (or whomever the government was negotiating with) would feel nervous about pushing back.

At the far end of the long table, backlit because of the windows behind him, was Tony. He said hello and told us to find seats near the other end of the table, near the door. I sat at the end, Bob and Shari flanked me on either side.

While the setup was intimidating, the underlying truth was quite different. We'd come to negotiate the terms of the government's surrender. Part of me was elated at our victory. Another part of me was disbelieving. But it was true. Likely due to some combination of the court rulings, the mounting congressional action, and Silicon Valley corporate pressure, the government had decided to give in.

I've come to believe that a big factor behind the scenes was the fact that Al Gore was running for president in 2000 and needed strong Silicon Valley support. Gore had a pioneering role from the 1970s to the 1990s in passing several laws as well as leading other initiatives that supported and funded the fledgling internet. Gore was a true geek; he and others were called the "Atari Democrats" in Congress.[26] But he had been widely mocked for allegedly saying that he had "invented the internet," even though he hadn't actually said it. Regardless, it seemed that dropping the export restrictions on encryption was part of an overall strategy for his candidacy to win support from the increasingly powerful folks in Silicon Valley.

There were other factors as well. Congress was moving closer to passing a law to loosen the controls, and the rumor was that the NSA was getting a bunch of funds to focus on network exploitation in return for backing off on encryption.

I wondered at that moment what Tony was feeling. Was he angry that he'd been bested in court by a handful of attorneys with few resources and little experience? Upset that the politics of the moment had swung in our favor? I also wondered how he thought about me, a small woman who took on the national security infrastructure and helped to make it bend.

Once we had settled in and pulled out our notes and files, Tony, still in the shadows, started the meeting.

He took a breath and we braced ourselves, but he didn't sound angry. "I want to thank you for flying in from California to meet with us," he said to me, his voice bemused and perhaps a little resigned. "I guess for our purposes today, I am the Prince of Darkness."

I felt a smile kick at the corner of my mouth. Without really thinking, I quipped, "I guess that makes me the Princess of Light."

I caught Shari's eyes as they widened, somewhere between surprised and impressed. On my other side, I heard Bob's quiet chuckle. I was lucky to have them both there, not only as trusted colleagues, but as friends. I was too unnerved by my own quip to see how it landed with the bars, medals, and suits. I don't recall hearing any laughter from them.

Then we began. Tony had sent me a proposed set of revised export regulations for review. They dropped the onerous and uncertain requirement of prepublication review for open-source and other publicly available encryption software. That had been the basis for our procedural prior restraint claims.

The new regulations replaced that process with a simple requirement that someone "exporting" (that is, publishing) such encryption software merely send a link to or copy of the code to the government at the time of publication. It was 95 percent of what we wanted. We had a few suggestions and objections.

The meeting lasted for about an hour. In the end, we didn't get much of our additional wish list, but we didn't really need to. The draft regulations were going to allow Dan to publish his code, plus much, much more. The government was relinquishing nearly all of its grip on strong encryption and the science of cryptography. The benefits would reach Dan and other academics, of course, but would also reach deep into the public side of the internet, allowing companies and individuals to implement strong encryption into the tools and systems that the rest of us rely on. We had ensured that the tools that protect privacy and security online were legal, and that the science that they came from could continue.

The biggest downside was really more about my ego than anything else. Because the government gave up while the decision of the Ninth Circuit was legally suspended due to the grant of en banc review, that decision stayed suspended. Our beautiful Ninth Circuit opinion was never reinstated. In the words of the law, our decision is not a citable precedent. Although it can still be found and informally relied on, it doesn't bind other courts. This is something I'll never get over. Our legal team felt cheated, yet there was nothing we could do about it.

The truth is that for all practical purposes, we had won, and won for everyone. A few months later, the *Junger* decision came out and its analysis followed the one in *Bernstein*, although without as much soaring language. While we didn't get our own citable decision, we were happy for our friends, Gino, Ray, and their client Peter Junger. We were also happy for everyone else who now had case law to rely on for the prospect that code is speech and the previous export licensing scheme had been unconstitutional.

Of course, it wasn't a total victory. As is so often the case in life and especially digital rights cases, each triumph is tempered with some loss. Dan made it clear that he wasn't satisfied. He bristled at the requirement to email the government on publication. He wanted complete vindication and no regulatory hoops to jump through. Dan continued the case, albeit with new counsel, and later, even represented himself for a bit. Ultimately, several years later, Judge Patel dismissed his challenge, accepting the government's representations that its new regulations simply didn't reach Dan and so he had no standing.

Thanks in part to the work we did in the *Bernstein* case, however, strong cryptography exists throughout the internet—letting you safely use services ranging from PayPal and Venmo to Signal, WhatsApp, and more. If you lose your phone or laptop, you don't lose everything that it can connect to. Thanks to encryption, you can have confidence that when you visit your bank's website, it's the real thing and not an imposter site. Without strong cryptography, it wouldn't even be possible to envision, much less create, a reasonably secure, trustworthy internet.

Most important, we secured the right to develop and share the tools of privacy in the digital world.

OPEN-SOURCE LAW

In September 2000, I started my first day at EFF. Thanks to the *Bernstein* case, I discovered I had a natural affinity for putting together a team along with building and managing that team through a case. I liked learning and explaining technical matters, serving as a translator as much as an advocate. I realized that the coming internet was going to need a posse of people to help ensure that it fulfilled its promise of being something that contributed to human rights rather than undermining them.

I also discovered how much fun it could be to do impact litigation, and it gave me hope. The thing about litigation, unlike legislative, policy, or even public activism work, is that if you bring a lawsuit, the judge has to read your briefs to decide your case. It gives you a voice and vehicle even if you have little or no political power or money. I saw that we could use the courts to help fend off the worst encroachments on our rights that would otherwise occur with the coming new technologies. The *Bernstein* case proved that we could successfully explain this new digital world to a judge and could win even when we were basically nobodies.

I learned some practical lessons that have become the EFF way to do impact litigation. From Shari, I learned how to pull in pro bono lawyers and outside resources when you have only a tiny budget. I saw how to marshal the power of your cause and ideas in the public debate as well as the pleadings. I learned how to drive the big bus, bringing in experts and other amici to provide ballast as well as trustworthiness to the legal points.

Lee and I established patterns of writing and thinking together too—what a friend later called "open-source law." We gave everyone on the team a shot at editing the main brief and passing around redlined versions. A single person, whom we call the keeper of the brief, integrates and makes the call when there are multiple competing ideas or strategies. We kept everything moving through weekly conference calls and an email list.

In addition, I met a range of women who were playing critical roles in this movement, starting with Shari, and including ACLU lawyers Ann Beeson and Ann Brick, along with EFF's early leaders Pam Samuelson, Esther Dyson, Lori Fena, and Tara Lemmey. In the 2000s, we were joined by Gigi Sohn, who started Public Knowledge, and Leslie Harris of the Center for Democracy and Technology, such that three of the first national digital rights organizations were led by women. I met Barbara Simons, a computer scientist who pushed the respected Association of Computer Machinery into taking a stand in critical public policy conversations. The *Bernstein* case featured Judge Patel in the district court and Judge Fletcher in the Ninth Circuit—two female judges who were fearless in listening to our arguments about this strange new world and siding with us when we were right even in the face of the not-so-subtle national security claims of the government.

Each of these women were not only present in the early days of the digital revolution but also led the way in ensuring that the internet had a fighting chance of becoming a place with more freedom and privacy than what came before.

2

NATIONAL SECURITY AGENCY SPYING: *HEPTING* AND *JEWEL*

DO YOU PEOPLE CARE ABOUT PRIVACY?

On January 20, 2006, the front doorbell rang at EFF's offices in a red-brick building on Shotwell Street in the Mission District in San Francisco. At the time, Shotwell Street wasn't the glamorous part of the Mission. Our offices sat between two auto repair shops, across the street from a utility substation. The sidewalk was often dotted with tents of homeless people. At one point San Francisco did a survey and our block of Shotwell Street had the highest reported amount of human feces in the whole city.

We had many people down on their luck ring that doorbell. Some were just lost. Others sought us out because they believed, quite sincerely, that the government or aliens had put a chip or magnet in their brains. We tried to be sympathetic and point them to other resources, but generally we had to turn them away.

Because of this, it was with friendliness but some caution that our executive director, Shari, answered the bell.

"Do you folks care about privacy?" the guy asked. He was in a tan trench coat, looked to be in his early sixties, with gray hair, intense eyes, and a raspy voice.

"Why yes, we do," Shari answered.

"Then I have some information for you. I am a retired AT&T technician. I know how the NSA is tapping into the internet at an AT&T facility downtown."

"Well come on in."

Shari found EFF attorney Kevin Bankston in his tiny office. We'd specifically hired Kevin in 2003 to focus on combatting the Patriot Act and the rest of the post-9/11 spying, so he was the right choice for a first person to talk to. Kevin quickly brought Lee into the meeting too. They talked for a long time.

After the man left, Kevin and Lee burst into my office.

"This guy named Mark Klein who just came to the door has something," Kevin said, with more excitement than I had seen from him in a long time. I was immediately intrigued, but what they told me blew past my highest expectations.

Mark had presented us with unequivocal evidence that the NSA was engaged in mass, untargeted spying in the United States by tapping into the internet backbone. And it was doing this from an AT&T building just a short distance from our offices. It would change everything.

OPEN AT THE NEXT CRISIS: USA PATRIOT ACT

The backstory to Klein knocking on EFF's door starts in 2001 with the government's responses to the horrific 9/11 attacks. The first of these was the USA Patriot Act.

In the seven weeks between its introduction and passage in 2001, Lee and I stayed up nights trying to parse through the three-inch-thick printout of the proposed legislation for the pieces that impacted the internet. We were part of a coalition of civil liberties, immigrant rights, and civil rights nongovernmental organizations that had split up the giant bill to attempt to figure out what it contained. We needed to understand what laws the government wanted to change, spot overreach and unconstitutionality, and marshal appropriate support or resistance where necessary.

The draft legislation had been rolled out so fast that we had the impression it was just sitting in an envelope on someone's desk with a note on it that read, "Open at the next crisis." Our theory was confirmed when we saw that a good chunk of the proposed law was nearly the same package of legal changes that the FBI had tried to push after the Oklahoma City bombing in 1995.[1] As we had come to learn, the FBI can bide its time. President Clinton had threatened to veto the FBI's suggestions in 1995 because the changes cut back too sharply on civil liberties. President George W. Bush raised no such concerns to those same changes six years later.

One big change impacting surveillance was clear: prior to September 11, the United States had what was reasonably called a "wall" separating foreign surveillance for national security purposes done by the NSA from domestic surveillance for law enforcement purposes done by the FBI. The "wall," which was created by both law and policies, was the fundamental trade-off that allowed the NSA to develop deeply invasive spying capabilities. The theory was that those powers would never be turned on in the United States and used against its own people. We knew that the NSA was frustrated with the wall and that the FBI coveted the power to spy domestically in the same way the NSA did internationally. The Patriot Act tore down major parts of that wall, subjecting people in the United States, at least in some instances, to US foreign surveillance capabilities.

We had a few important victories in the short fight around the Patriot Act. One was that we were able to push back on congressional staff and get them to reject any restriction on encryption. But the overall outcome was dismal. We were steamrolled. Congressmembers had an urgent desire to "do something" in response to the attacks, and the governmental forces in favor of a panopticon approach to surveillance were all too ready to hand them things to do. The administration pushed Congress to act quickly, even before the 9/11 Commission had started its investigation about what failures of US law might have contributed to the attacks. Many who should have known better adopted an either-or mentality, arguing that sacrificing our privacy was necessary to make us more secure. The assertion assumed that these two values are on a scale, and a reduction in one was going to automatically result in an increase in the other.

The Patriot Act passed Congress within two months of the attacks, and President Bush quickly signed it into law.[2]

The thing that was overlooked then, and is still often overlooked, is that none of the changes to surveillance law in the Patriot Act actually addressed the problems that led to the attack on the United States. When the 9/11 Commission later looked closely at how the NSA, Central Intelligence Agency (CIA), and FBI had failed to uncover as well as stop the plot, it did not conclude that the wall separating the NSA from the FBI was the problem.[3] The commission did not conclude that our civil liberties were the problem either.

In fact, the NSA and CIA officials who had picked up many signs of the coming attack were not only *able* but also *tried* to tell the FBI about these threats. Throughout spring and summer 2001, FBI officials were briefed about the "blinking red" systems that the NSA and CIA were seeing about attacks inside the United States, but that information was not shared with field offices. Even as late as July 2001, FBI acting director Thomas Pickford, while telling all special agents in charge to "be ready to move" if an attack happened, did not ask the FBI field offices to try to locate or disrupt any plots. The FBI did issue several threat advisories that mentioned the possibility of an attack inside the United States, yet the domestic agencies "did not have a game plan" to respond to the threats they were hearing about. The 9/11 Commission found little evidence that concerns about a heightened terrorist threat inside the United States had reached any FBI personnel beyond the New York field office.[4]

Inside the FBI, some officials tried to alert their superiors and failed. One of them, an FBI agent in Phoenix, raised concerns about al-Qaeda founder Osama bin Laden sending students to the United States to attend civil aviation schools. Another, Colleen Rowley in Minneapolis, had tried to tell her FBI superiors about the specific flight school trainings of later convicted terrorist Zacarias Moussaoui. Both were brushed aside.[5] A US Department of Justice report did find that some key FBI agents were confused about the rules on sharing information, and as a result, some leads were lost or not followed up on, but those failures were based on a misunderstanding of the rules, not the rules themselves.

One of the actual problems was that the leaders of these agencies, who were in a position to authorize larger investigations, ignored multiple attempts to get them to take this risk seriously.[6] The FBI along with the entire defense infrastructure were caught up in what is called groupthink. They were so convinced of their own internal stories of what to expect and what our opponents were planning that they just couldn't take in information inconsistent with it, even though there was a lot of it. They had plenty of broad, general intelligence about possible terrorist attacks inside the United States from the CIA and NSA, but they failed to connect that with the information coming in from FBI agents and others on the ground in the United States who were seeing how those broad threats were actually being developed.

Groupthink is a problem that has been documented over and over again—and it is especially noxious when the "group" has access to secret information, and so believes it has superior knowledge and insight. This is a lesson that Daniel Ellsberg, the famous leaker of the Pentagon Papers who helped stop the war in Vietnam, taught me later when we worked together at the Freedom of the Press Foundation. Based on his own experience working with classified information, Ellsberg said that people with access to secret information often come to believe that they are smarter than the rest of us. That arrogance, combined with rampant and unchecked secrecy, can be deadly. President Bush also famously fell prey to it. He had, after all, dismissed a briefing that specifically warned that bin Laden was aiming to strike inside the United States.[7]

Rather than a mistaken protection of civil liberties, the primary factors that left us so vulnerable included a mix of groupthink, long-standing turf issues between the FBI, CIA, and NSA, the unwillingness of leaders to listen to NSA and CIA analysts who were tracking the situation, and the FBI's internal failure to have working escalation paths for its own agents.[8]

But this didn't stop either the NSA or FBI from blaming their own failures on the wall as well as the protections it provided for privacy and civil liberties. I even had a former NSA general counsel publicly accuse me, personally, of causing the 9/11 attacks because of criticisms that EFF had made in the 1990s. Of course that was ridiculous, yet it showed the lengths that members in the law enforcement and intelligence communities would go to in order to avoid taking responsibility for the deadliest intelligence failure in US history.

SECRETLY SITTING ON THE WIRE

The Patriot Act was bad enough, but it wasn't actually the worst attack on our privacy after 9/11. Even before 9/11, it was well-known in national security circles that the NSA was hoping to find a way to sit "on the wire" in the United States, giving it dragnet-level access to our domestic telecommunications infrastructure.[9] They had a model: the NSA already had similar access to foreign telecommunications channels through a program called Echelon.[10] The NSA argued that because so much foreign internet traffic was routed through the United States, its inability to actually spy from the United States hurt its ability to be comprehensive. Of course, the power it sought also conveniently let the NSA more easily spy domestically on people in the United States.

We know now that the 9/11 attack was secretly taken up as the reason for the NSA to get what it had long wanted: the ability to sit on the wire in the United States. Ultimately, the FBI did too, gaining access to the NSA's vast new collection of communications from US telecommunication companies. But even in the immediate aftermath of the attack, the agencies did not seek these powers publicly—I suspect recognizing that it would be a bridge too far. Neither the text nor the debate around the Patriot Act mentioned anything like the mass surveillance programs that were later uncovered.

There was a public attempt to create tools for analysis of the information the government already had. It was called Total Information Awareness, and it was championed by Admiral John Poindexter.[11] When it was publicly announced as part of the government's response to 9/11, however, the program was still a research project, albeit a giant and expensive one. Even so, the public loudly rejected the idea of mass analysis of government surveillance of people in the United States. Poindexter was ridiculed for it, and after two years, Congress publicly defunded the program in 2003.

Yet despite this clear public rejection of "total information," at EFF we almost immediately started to hear whispers of mass domestic surveillance programs secretly run by the NSA. We were told, confidentially, that the NSA was gathering up all the telephone records from the United States' leading telecommunications carriers. We separately heard that the NSA was now sitting on the wire in the United States. We even heard that the NSA was collecting the metadata of our activities online from both the telecommunication and some internet companies. Friends in the industry would say things like, "You wouldn't believe what the NSA is doing in the United States now," and "I can't tell you anything without getting in trouble, but it's massive."

We heard something like this many times, and it all sounded wildly illegal under the Foreign Intelligence Surveillance Act (FISA) and the Patriot Act, and inconsistent with the rejection and defunding of the Total Information Awareness project. But we couldn't get any hard evidence. Several people reached out to us, and each time we sat down with them to see if we had enough provable facts to bring a case. No one who reached out to talk to us was willing to go on the record, much less give us documentary proof we could use in court. For most of them, the information was either classified, which meant going to jail if they were caught leaking it, or confidential, protected by nondisclosure agreements they had signed—or both. People, including well-meaning patriotic ones, are reasonably cowed by towering civil and criminal penalties. Even when they were uneasy with what they knew or were being asked to do, they were scared to put their necks on the line by giving us actual evidence we could present in court.

So while we had heard from multiple sources that the NSA was conducting mass surveillance of people in the United States, and even had some information about the specific programs, we didn't have the hard evidence we needed to bring a case to the courts.

FINDING PRECEDENT

Despite this lack of evidence, from 2001 onward, we plotted out possible legal challenges based on what we were hearing. This work was led by Kevin, working with Lee, my longtime friend and colleague who started at EFF on the same day I did.

We were thinking about how to explain to a court why this new mass surveillance was illegal and unconstitutional. Judges are generally looking backward as they decide cases. The US legal system is based on the idea of precedent: that once a court has decided something, the next time that issue comes up it should do the same thing. This makes sense most of the time. Case law should provide a stable understanding of what the rules are so that people can be sure they are acting legally. This system also helps ensure that everyone who does the same thing receives the same justice, even from different courts or across time.

Since the world is complex, however, it's not always the case that a situation comes up that is exactly like what happened before. That means in practice that lawyers will try to find an analogous situation in the past and say, "This current situation is just like that past one," as a way to convince the court to rule for them. The other side will find a different case that supplies a different analogy and point to that one as why they should win. This battle of analogies happens a lot, especially when the situation is new factually, as it often is in digital cases.

GENERAL WARRANTS AND *KATZ*

We did have some good analogies on our side for attacking the ongoing surveillance we were hearing about, starting with one of the key founding stories of the United States. One of the problems that spurred the American Revolution was called "writs of assistance," or general warrants. These documents gave the king's people, here usually customs officials, the authority to search anywhere, anytime, for as long as the king lived. In 1760, a group of Boston merchants objected to general warrants in court and were represented by an attorney named James Otis. Otis argued against giving the government the ability to search without the specificity of who, where, or limits on how long. He said these warrants would "totally annihilate" the "freedom of one's house."[12] A young lawyer named John Adams was in the courtroom watching Otis and later wrote of Otis's argument, "There and then the child Independence was born."[13]

Otis lost, but that case, plus another where the British officials raided the offices of a journalist who had criticized the king and other high officials in a newspaper, directly sparked the creation of the Fourth Amendment to the Constitution. The modern Supreme Court has confirmed that "indiscriminate searches and seizures conducted under the authority of 'general warrants' were the immediate evils that motivated the framing and adoption of the Fourth Amendment."[14] And of course this all happened in the midst of a national security crisis. I suspect this explains why there is no national security exception written into the text of the Constitution.

We had a second analogy too. In 1967, in a case called *Katz v. United States*, the Supreme Court had affirmed that the Fourth Amendment's protection against searches and seizures extended beyond physical places, like homes and offices, to include telephone conversations captured on wiretaps.[15] The court confirmed that the Fourth Amendment protects "people not places," meaning that the mere fact that our private conversations were carried on a wire outside our homes didn't eliminate the Fourth Amendment protections they should receive. That protection was expressly extended in 2007 to include the content of an email in a case called *U.S. v. Warshak*, where Kevin had represented EFF as amicus.[16]

FIGHTING A METAPHOR

One area that we knew would be legally sticky was the difference between the content of telephone and email conversations and the records of those conversations. While we believed the government was collecting and using both, and it turned out that was true, we also knew that the government would try to focus on the metadata collection in order to minimize public and judicial concern about what they were doing. That required us to fight a metaphor.

The predigital metaphor for metadata comes, unsurprisingly, from postal mail. "Metadata" is what is written on the outside of an envelope, while "content" is what is on the inside. While it's true that the outside of an envelope is metadata in the technical sense, using this distinction as a general metaphor to determine the level of legal protection is misleading.

First, it assumes that the information on the outside of an envelope is not very revealing about people. As I note below, if it was ever true in a predigital era, that is certainly not true now.

Second, the metaphor feeds the wrong idea that privacy is just a synonym for secrecy. But privacy isn't just about secrecy. Privacy is not, and shouldn't be, a one-way door that as soon as you open it for any purpose, evaporates. There are legal doctrines based on secrecy in the United States; the most prominent is called trade secrecy. If you post your trade secrets—one famous one is the spices used in Kentucky Fried Chicken—on the outside of an envelope, they will lose legal protection. In contrast, privacy rightfully includes much more, such as control over who can have access to information about you and limiting what they can do with it. For instance, both the US Tax Code and the Privacy Act protect information we reveal to the government for one purpose from being used for another. Regardless, we knew that to secure real privacy online, we needed to break the court's reliance on the envelope metaphor.

ILLNESS, CANNABIS, RIFLES, AND PREGNANCY

In fact, there is a ton of evidence about the power of metadata. A 2016 Stanford study, conducted in part by former EFF intern Jonathan Mayer, now a Princeton professor, looked at what researchers could glean from reviewing the telephone records of around eight hundred volunteers for a thirty-week period. As one news report summarized,

> They found they could draw even more highly sensitive inferences from metadata—connecting the dots from a series of phone calls to infer that one participant might have multiple sclerosis, for example, and that another might have a specific heart condition, and that a third may be involved with growing cannabis, and that a fourth might own a semi-automatic rifle, and that a fifth might be pregnant.[17]

And that's just from the metadata for calls and texts on telephones.

It means that someone with access to the logs of your local internet service provider (ISP) could tell not only that you and I had communicated but also how many times we did so. It can tell if we are casual acquaintances or intimates. By analyzing various logs, that same person—whether they were inside a company hosting our email or an FBI agent with a subpoena—could build a detailed picture of us and our communities, including our religious, political, or social groups. Metadata, especially collectively and over time, gives many insights that would be unavailable in a nondigital world, and many more that would not occur without tremendous effort.

This is an area where the surveillance business model is the perfect henchperson for the surveillance state. Companies also want to collect and analyze metadata because it reveals so much about you and the people you communicate with. They use it to do tings like place ads or help predict what you want to see next in your social media feed. Both the government and the corporate world know the power of metadata. Neither one of them wants you to have control over it.

"WE KILL PEOPLE BASED ON METADATA"

The national security establishment knows the power of metadata too. The national security folks call this kind of mapping of communities and relationships "contact chaining." The NSA's own newsletters, released by Snowden, confirm that targeted metadata collection helped it track down terror suspects Khalid Sheikh Mohammed and Abu Zubaida.[18] Most famously, in the wake of the Snowden revelations, former NSA and CIA chief Michael Hayden said, "We kill people based on metadata."[19]

Former NSA general counsel Stewart Baker agreed, stating, "Metadata absolutely tells you everything about somebody's life. If you have enough metadata, you don't really need content."[20] Baker and I have known each other since the 1990s, and we rarely agree on anything, but here he's right.

That's why it was especially frustrating to hear President Barack Obama dismiss reasonable privacy concerns about the NSA collecting metadata as mere hype. "Nobody is listening to your telephone calls," the president told reporters in his first public comments after the programs were disclosed. "They are not looking at people's names, and they're not looking at content."[21]

THIRD-PARTY DOCTRINE

This envelope metaphor has led to legal problems too. While the Fourth Amendment to the Constitution has soaring words about not violating "the right of the people to be secure in their persons, houses, papers, and effects, against unreasonable searches and seizures," the case law has developed to shrink that right down to something narrow and full of exceptions, including placing "envelope" information generally outside the Fourth Amendment entirely. As a result, while Congress has created some low-level protections in statutes, government requests for metadata traditionally require less process and less court oversight than warrants that seek the content of communications.

Worse, in the 1970s, a legal interpretation of the Constitution, called the "third-party doctrine," eliminated Fourth Amendment protections for your "papers and effects" when you don't hold them yourself. This doctrine holds that when a third party—like your ISP, phone company, or even bank—has private metadata about you in the form of your telephone calling or bank records, that information loses its Fourth Amendment protection.[22] So much for protecting "people not places" when it comes to metadata.

There's a strong argument to be made that these distinctions between content and noncontent, and between "papers" stored at your home and those stored with a provider like your ISP or bank, never made any sense. Metadata should have always been inside the Fourth Amendment given it ability to reveal your associations, thoughts, and beliefs. Regardless, these distinctions make absolutely no sense now, when collecting metadata is easy and cheap, and its power is so strong.

We knew as we put together our legal arguments that we were going to have to take on this metaphor.

SOLID EFF AND SOLID INTERNET

Between 2001 and 2006 when Mark showed up at our door, we were building our reputation at EFF. We had moved to Shotwell Street in 2001, not long after Lee and I joined, and by 2004, had filled up our initial office space. To expand, we broke through a brick wall on the north side, doubling our size. We filled both sides with tiny offices, generally just large enough for a desk and chair. Our conference room sported a long wooden table that a staffer found on the street and beautifully refinished. We also had a kitchen and some open space with dorm-room-style couches and chairs. Near my office sat a battered old pool table that someone had given us. The pool table sometimes sported a ping-pong table topper. In the afternoons, I could often hear the pop of a ping-pong ball or click of pool balls.

The north-side building had been a sweatshop at some point in the past, so at the back it had a narrow staircase with a large office at the top, spanning the width of the building, with windows looking down over the rest of the space. The upstairs office had clearly been used by an overseer. Our two staff technologists, Peter Eckersley and Seth Schoen, took it over. As the ones who made sure we correctly described the technologies we were discussing in court or Congress, or to the press, the overseer's location seemed fitting.

EFF grew from a staff of thirteen people when I joined in September 2000 to twenty-four people by 2005.[23] We grew along with the internet, and the issues we took on reflected the leading concerns of the day. Our program work was done mainly by lawyers, but we also had a small international team, the two technologists, and a couple of activists who led our public-facing blogging and actions like asking our community to write to Congress.

The internet was solid too; people not involved in technology now used email regularly. Google had largely won out over its search engine competitors. Gmail was launched on April Fools' Day 2004.[24] We greeted its original business model of contextual ads which is ad placement based on the text of what you were writing in the email, as "creepy but legal." We didn't know that soon we'd be fighting much more invasive and creepy ads, called behavioral ads, which are based on tracking everything you do and say across various websites. Later this would be called "surveillance capitalism" by professor emerita at Harvard Business School Shoshana Zuboff.[25] Contextual ads are not fully privacy protective, but they turned out to be much better for privacy than what came later.

We were also in the early days of social media. The upstart named Facebook, which actually featured user privacy in its early marketing, was still limited to university students as of late 2005.[26] But it was already challenging older services like Friendster.

Privacy wasn't the only issue that we worked on at that time. EFF has long focused on three core issues: privacy, free speech, and innovation. We were the first, and for a while, the only organization that recognized the importance of getting the balance right for copyright, trademark, and patent claims online. Our work spanned all three of those, plus trade secrets, contract, and various other legal claims that were being used to censor speech or harm innovation.

We represented many users who faced various kinds of claims arising out of their art, critical or satiric commentary, or even the simple act of making a video of their toddler dancing in the kitchen to the Prince song "Let's Go Crazy." Our clients included an American Sign Language instructor who reshot popular music videos using American Sign Language to make them more accessible to the hearing impaired, as well as parodists who made fun of Kermit the Frog and Barney the Dinosaur. Barney's lawyers became extremely aggressive online for a while, issuing cease and desist letters.

The cases were colorful and we tried to have fun with them with our small but mighty community. We took over a bar in San Francisco to re-create a virtual "cage match" that had resulted in a litigation threat to our clients.[27] The match was between Barney the Dinosaur (one of our lawyers in a purple costume) and Wil Wheaton, the actor who had played Wesley Crusher on *Star Trek: The Next Generation*.[28] Staffers dressed up as lawyers for Barney threw out fake cease and desist orders into the crowd. Ultimately, as is right and proper, Wil vanquished the dinosaur in the ring.

EFF had developed a reputation for standing up for users facing copyright claims, including when the music industry started suing college students for file sharing in 2003. When I met Mark Zuckerberg in person, he told me that EFF first caught his attention when we defended his fellow Harvard students who had been caught up in those music industry mass copyright lawsuits. Sadly, Zuckerberg's appreciation for us in the copyright cases wasn't enough to convince him to listen to us about protecting the privacy of Facebook users. Instead, Facebook marched relentlessly toward surveillance capitalism.

We were often one of the first larger organizations to see and articulate new digital issues, as we did in 2004 after several prominent computer scientists, including Barbara Simons, who I'd met through the cryptography case years before, came for a visit to our Shotwell offices. They told us about how the early electronic voting machines were extremely insecure and vulnerable to attack, and that they had no way to perform audits or recounts.[29] We partnered with their fledgling organization, called the Verified Voter Foundation. Ultimately, together we marshaled hundreds of groups from across the country to ensure that most voters had access to voter-verified paper ballots that created a separate audit and recount trail for risk limiting audits.

As important as these cases and issues were, I was still most focused on how we could protect privacy online.

COSMO AND COMMUNITY

My personal life was progressing nicely too. The former judicial clerk and I had moved in together and were talking about marriage, both as in love with each other as with his 115 lb. brown Newfoundland dog named Cosmo. Cosmo came to EFF every day, and was much adored by the EFF staff and visitors. He was sweet, gentle, and extremely lazy. He set me up for a life of loving giant, slow-moving, fluffy dogs. He also helped set

EFF's offices up as a place where dogs, kittens, ducks, and rabbits are welcomed and celebrated.

By then I had built several circles of friends. My music community was still going strong and growing. Many of them had started to have children and build families. My boyfriend and I were still uncertain about whether we should take that step together, but I gladly served as the "cool aunt" to a growing flock of kids.

In addition, we were building a real community of digital rights activists, technologists, and lawyers in the Bay Area. We were a tight-knit crew in those days, seeing movies and going to concerts fairly regularly; we loved the Mountain Goats and a few of us were dedicated Wilco fans, but there were also punk, metal, pop, electronic dance music, and emo fans in the mix. We created an email "fun list" open to staffers, interns, and the broader group where we organized activities. We fielded teams to compete in the Chinese New Year's treasure hunt that happens every year in San Francisco. My boyfriend and I hosted regular wine tasting events at our Noe Valley flat—even though I actually hate wine.

GRANDFATHER

I also continued to keep in touch with my birth grandfather, Harold. We were both determined to try to make up for the time we had lost. I visited several times over those years, and we spoke on the phone every month or so. We created an ad hoc book and politics discussion club. On one trip, he let my boyfriend bring home a bunch of his classical music albums and we reported back what we liked and disliked. We talked about fiction along with current affairs. We tended to agree on the politics, but disagreed quite a bit about books. One ongoing theme was that he thought writer Haruki Murakami was much funnier than I did. But we enjoyed gently ribbing each other.

I attended his ninetieth birthday party in July 2005, where I met many far-flung birth family members, who were, I suspect, a bit shocked to find out that I existed. Everyone acted on the surface as if nothing unusual had happened, though—which was a strange yet welcome bit of denial. My birth mother, true to her threat, did not participate. That still stung, but Harold and I leaned into our relationship even more as a result.

Just a month after the big party, in August 2005, I packed two bags. One had my best suit—again picked out by my mother—so that I could attend the oral arguments in *MGM v. Grokster*, EFF's first case at the Supreme Court. It was a copyright case arising from peer-to-peer filesharing, and I'd organized a record number of amicus briefs in support of our side. After the Supreme Court hearing, I'd leave that bag in DC to be sent back to San Francisco by a friend. The second bag was filled with long skirts and modest blouses, since the next day I was flying to Nigeria to prepare our clients and witnesses for depositions in the *Bowoto v. Chevron* human rights case.

I was in Nigeria when I learned, on a scratchy phone call from my boyfriend, that Harold had passed away. I was both heartbroken over his death and thankful for our time together. I wasn't able to get back in time for the funeral, which in the Jewish tradition happens quickly, so I missed a formal final goodbye.

In June 2005, we learned we lost the *Grokster* case.

"BUSH LETS U.S. SPY ON CALLERS WITHOUT COURTS"

In December 2005, the dam finally broke on the secret surveillance actions the government had taken after 9/11. Or at least it sprang a major leak. After sitting on the story for over a year, past the presidential reelection of Bush, *The New York Times* published the fact that the NSA was secretly spying on people in the United States. The headline was, "Bush Lets U.S. Spy on Callers Without Courts."[30]

It was huge news, and galvanized not only the civil liberties community but the nation and world too. The story confirmed that the wall that had assured many people that the NSA was prohibited from using its spy powers at home had been torn down. While it wasn't a huge surprise to us at this point, many people, including the media, were shocked to learn that the government could use its national security powers domestically without any court approval.

Mass surveillance on people not suspected of any crimes amounts to a huge encroachment on rights, whether those people are in the United State or not. Privacy isn't just a US value; it is a universal human right. While EFF's courtroom work on this issue has been based in constitutional and statutory protections that only reach people in the United States, the overall fight is much bigger. Everyone deserves to be protected against dragnet surveillance, not just those deemed to be "US persons" by virtue of our passports, visa statuses, or locations. Our work in the United States was matched by litigation and advocacy in the European Union and around the world. By this time, EFF was part of a growing global digital privacy community.

TAXI FULL OF HELP

The first press calls for comment about NSA spying came to me while I was in a taxi in New York City heading to the airport with some class action specialists. We were headed home after a federal court hearing in a case against Sony for the privacy and security violations that it caused for users by installing a piece of software called a rootkit on music CDs. It was EFF's first class action case. Class actions are a kind of case that has some separate procedural rules to handle when a lot of people are harmed by the same illegal acts.

I knew that if we launched a case out of *The New York Times* story on behalf of all the people harmed by the spying, it would likely also be a class action. They knew it too. Even before the taxi crossed the East River, they offered to join us, and I had the first piece of what would soon become a dream team to fight NSA Spying.

I read *The New York Times* story closely, hoping we finally had enough evidence to bring a lawsuit, but it was still a close call. We needed admissible evidence, which has much stricter requirements than newspapers generally observe. News stories, especially those about national security, are often filled with unverified hearsay and unnamed sources, neither of which would fly in a court of law.

We were considering all the angles as the year came to a close.

"I WANT TO SUE AT&T"

"I want to sue AT&T," Kevin said on New Year's Eve 2005 when I opened the door at the base of the stairs in my second-floor Noe Valley flat. He was holding a bottle of champagne.

"Happy New Year to you too," I answered. "Come in and tell me more."

Kevin and I walked up the stairs, and he was so excited that I could barely get him to give me his coat. A few of the other lawyers from EFF were at the party, and we took over the living room as Kevin laid out his idea.

"We know that the government is going to have sovereign immunity, qualified immunity, and all sorts of legal protections if we sue them directly," he began. I nodded. Those were some of the biggest challenges we needed to overcome—a set of doctrines prohibiting many direct lawsuits against the government. Qualified immunity was a judge-made rule that basically gave government officials a first free pass to violate people's rights—allowing liability only if an official clearly knew that what they were doing was illegal. Given that what the NSA was doing had never been revealed, much less litigated, this and the other immunities loomed large.

"The Fourth Amendment law is not great around national security. We could win, but it's a hard hill to climb," Kevin noted. "But there are clear statutory prohibitions on telephone companies doing anything with your calls and records beyond what they need to do to provide you with service or protect their own networks. We can win against the telcos for users without having to fight the big constitutional issues with the government. It's an easier path, and we should do it."

We all thought it was a brilliant idea, and like so many EFF cases, a hell of a long shot. After a little while, my boyfriend, now my fiancé, poked his head into the room and demanded that we come celebrate before the clock struck midnight. So we did.

HOW TO SPY ON THE WHOLE INTERNET

Because of Kevin's New Year's Eve idea, we were already hard at work on a case against AT&T when Mark knocked on our door just a few weeks later. We had recruited the lawyer who I would come to think of as EFF's secret weapon: Rick Wiebe. Rick was an experienced lawyer with a solo practice who had contacted me in my first year of EFF. Over lunch at a Vietnamese restaurant near our Shotwell Street offices, I immediately recognized Rick as a fellow traveler—a smart, committed, and experienced litigator with a soft voice and twinkle in his eye. Rick had offered to help with one of our early copyright and trade secrecy cases, and since then, had jumped into our open-source law approach with both feet. He is also one of the most dogged and persistent lawyers I have ever worked with, and that is a high bar indeed among us civil liberties types.

The information Mark gave us made the whispers we had heard over the years from our friends at telecommunication companies make more sense. The way the mass spying worked had to do with the way the internet is set up at the deepest layer, called the internet backbone.[31] The internet is a series of networked computers that talk to each other in a set of shared languages, usually called protocols, in order to route messages and information from a sender to a recipient. It is not centrally controlled, but not all of these computers are equal. A set of large providers—big companies, academic institutions, and governments—operate a series of powerful computers that provide the main data routes for these messages, and these are called the internet backbone.

AT&T operated a part of the internet backbone out of the Folsom Street facility. Part of Mark's job was to maintain the section of the AT&T system that passed traffic from AT&T's internal networks to the internet backbone, which happened through a set of connections called peering links. What Mark was telling us, and what his documents were showing, was that the NSA was now tapping in at these junctures.

Mark's revelation was not completely unexpected; what was unexpected was having someone knock on our front door and hand the actual schematics to us.

When I met Mark in person a short time later, he told the story to me too. I tried hard to keep my jaw from dropping as he explained both the banality of the technical infrastructure—so clear that I could easily understand how it worked—and the audacity of what the NSA and AT&T had built together to undermine the privacy of likely hundreds of millions of innocent people, including millions of AT&T's own customers.

HOOKING UP THE BIG BROTHER MACHINE

Mark had been a technician at AT&T for many years. In mid-2003, he was transferred to the Folsom Street building and charged with maintaining the room where AT&T's own fiber-optic network connected to the rest of the internet.

Figure 2.1 Room 641A in the Folsom Street AT&T building. Photo by Mark Klein / licensed under CC BY-SA 3.0 (https://creativecommons.org/licenses/by-sa/3.0/).

Mark told us that the fiber-optic cables carrying traffic headed to or from the internet backbone hosted by AT&T came together on the seventh floor of the Folsom Street building. This was reasonable.

But he showed us that those cables also connected down to the sixth floor of the building. The sixth floor was where the weirdness happened. Sometime in 2002, a "secret room" had been built on the sixth floor of that building where only workers with NSA clearances could go. Mark didn't have a clearance himself, but he knew and worked with the person with the clearance who had access to that room. The secret room was called 641A (fig. 2.1).

Next to the secret room was a "splitter cabinet." On one side, the internet-connecting fiber-optic cables that came down from the seventh floor fed into it. On the other side, two sets of fiber-optic cables came out. One set snaked back up to the seventh floor to carry traffic onto the wider internet. But a second set of cables went into the secret room.

The way the surveillance program worked was clever. Fiber-optic cables carry our digital data and communications on beams of light. The cool thing about these light beams is that if you split them, which happens in the fiber-optic splitter cabinet, you don't split the data. Instead you end up with two copies of the information carried on them. Outside room 641A, the splitter cabinet and newly installed wiring meant that when the communications came down from the seventh floor, they were "split" in the cabinet. One copy of the communications went into the secret room, while the other copy continued to the intended recipient. In this way, the NSA could be sitting "on the wire" inside the United States of the fiber-optic cables that carry everyone's communications since it made and captured a copy of all the traffic going through the juncture. The NSA could then review the traffic separately, without slowing down the traffic or leaving any trace of what it was actually doing on the public network (fig. 2.2).

Mark called it the "Big Brother machine," which seemed appropriate. Mark had taken a photo of the door to room 641A, which we later turned into a poster-size image that we hung on the wall at EFF. More important, Mark had copies of some of the internal plans and specifications for the room. The specifications included the setup in San Francisco, but also appeared to be directions for technicians installing such rooms up and down the West Coast. The documents referenced similar setups for what they called "cutting into" peering links to install splitters at sixteen other major internet carriers and internet exchange points too. They revealed that the work was completed by the end of February 2003.

While this location on Folsom Street handled a lot of internet traffic, both for AT&T customers and others, it was not the location closest to the US border. There are physical places where the undersea cables and satellite waves that carry our communications from people abroad to people inside the United States first hit US soil. If the NSA was only aiming to have access to foreign or international communications, the place to put the spying apparatus was at those first connection spots. None of them are in downtown San Francisco. The closest undersea cables, for instance, are over two hundred miles, either north in Eureka or south in Morro Bay, California. The Folsom Street facility is several hops from any "first stops" for traffic coming in or out of the United States.

THIS ISN'T A WIRETAP, IT'S A COUNTRY TAP

We talked with several telecommunications experts, and they confirmed that this setup was a reasonable method for the NSA to "sit on the wire" in a way that would let it operate surreptitiously but still be effective.

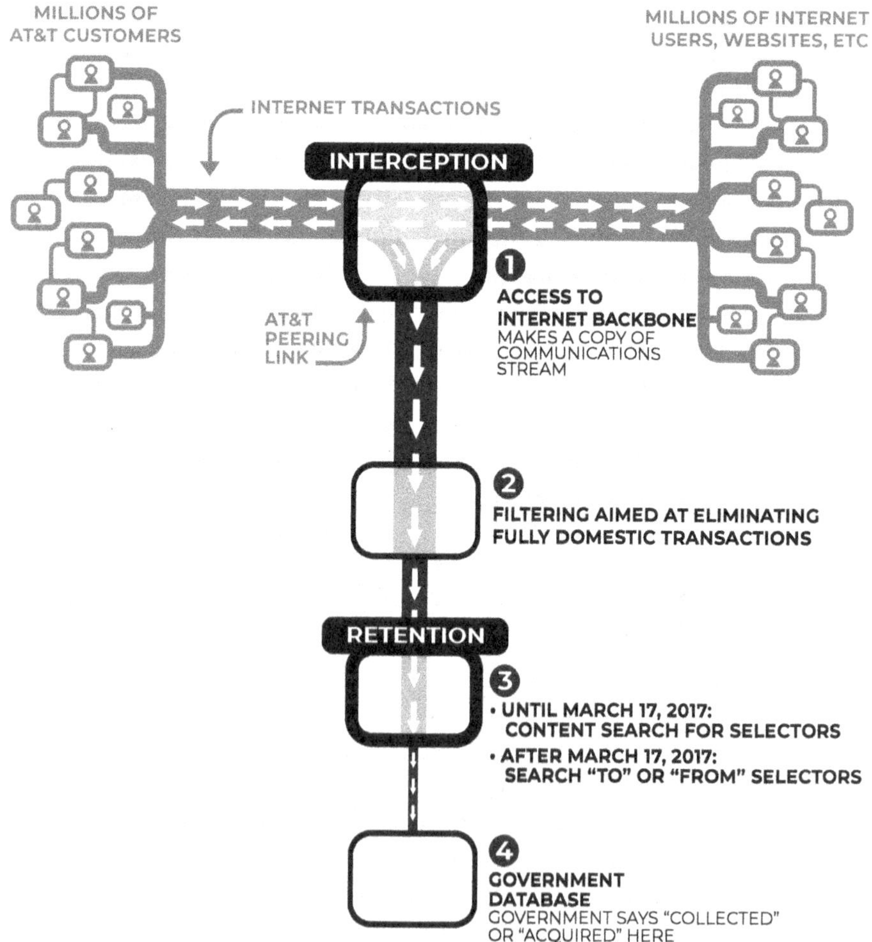

Figure 2.2 NSA spying Upstream graphic by Hugh D'Andrade / EFF licensed under CC BY 4.0 (https://creativecommons.org/licenses/by/4.0/).

They also confirmed that the documents and information Mark had all seemed legitimate—that this is what the implementation would look like at a large telecommunications company like AT&T. One expert we talked to, Brian Reid, who had been involved in the development of several critical internet technologies, including email, web, and document representation and transmission, said, "This isn't a wiretap, it's a country tap."

We had our evidence. This was that crucial confirmation, in a form admissible in court, that we had been hoping for. We knew and could now prove that AT&T had facilitated illegal surveillance of internet communications domestically. Added to the legal strategy we had been crafting, this evidence would help us bring a lawsuit against mass surveillance.

It was nearing the end of January. With Mark Klein's direct evidence about AT&T in hand, the next thing to do was to get him his own lawyers. We needed him as a star witness, so we couldn't have him be our client. The risk of conflicts of interest between Mark and AT&T customers wasn't great, but it was real, especially if Mark faced prosecution or a civil claim from AT&T. We all knew—as did Mark—that he had serious legal risk.

We made some calls and were overjoyed when an all-star team readily signed on. Thanks to the persuasive skills of our cocounsel Rick, two prominent attorneys, Jim Brosnahan and Tony West, agreed to represent Mark on the civil side. Then they recruited two of the Bay Area's leading criminal defense attorneys, Miles Erlich and Izzy Ramsey. It was a dream team.

Jim is a legendary litigator based in San Francisco. When I was a new lawyer, a presentation by Jim taught me (and likely thousands of other young lawyers) the technique I still used to chart out the legal arguments in a case that I call "finding where the fight is." I'll give an example later. Tony was also a well-respected lawyer who would go on to work at the Obama Justice Department. We knew Mark was in good legal hands.

FIRST TO FILE

Since we had already thought through most of the case before Mark showed up at our front door on January 20, we were ready to file almost immediately after we had digested the evidence and found him counsel.

With the leadership of my colleague Corynne McSherry, we quickly gathered three California AT&T customers as our clients, all of whom wanted to see the spying stopped. Based on their physical locations, each of them had a reasonable belief that at least some of their communications had gone through the specific fiber-optic splitters that Mark had seen in San Francisco, meaning that their communications had also been copied and sent to the NSA-controlled room 641A. The case was called *Hepting v. AT&T*, after our lead plaintiff, a Bay Area computer programmer and EFF supporter named Tash Hepting, who stepped forward after we published a blog post asking for volunteers.

We were moving fast because we were concerned that others might get ahead of us. We suspected, rightly, that we weren't the only folks thinking about suing over the revelations in *The New York Times*. We had much more evidence than the newspaper story, of course, but we wanted to get a case going quickly. We needed to be sure Mark and his counsel were ready as well as have our experts all lined up for what we knew would be a big fight.

So while the claims and plaintiffs were all set up to support it, we kept the new and potentially classified information Mark gave us out of the initial complaint. We filed the lawsuit just eleven days after Mark showed up, on January 31, 2006, and were assigned to Judge Vaughn Walker.

We were happy that we had our case on file by the end of January because the news kept breaking. On February 5, 2006, *USA Today* released a blockbuster story that the NSA was sweeping up people's telephone records in a mass US spying program. This confirmed another rumor we had heard. *USA Today* was able to discover that nearly all the major telecommunications companies were participating, including our target AT&T. More coverage followed, with reporters racing each other to find scoops, and flesh out the stories and coverage in *Bloomberg*, *Slate*, *The Washington Post*, *National Journal*, *The New Yorker*, and others.

With all of that attention and all of those well-funded corporations implicated, we knew that many other lawsuits would be filed.

WAITING ON THE PRESS

One of the most important reasons we kept Mark's evidence out of the initial lawsuit was because we wanted the press to publish it first. After they did, we could move forward seeking a quick ruling, called a preliminary injunction, to put a temporary stop to the spying.

The reason we chose this strategy was because we weren't sure the information wasn't classified. Mere possession of classified information without a proper clearance is a criminal violation with severe penalties. But historically, at least as of 2006, if the same information was already broadly publicly available, the risk of criminal prosecution for us presenting it to a federal court was pretty low. The risk to the press for initially publishing it was low too. We also thought that the chances that the judge would actually consider Mark's evidence, and not just require us to give it back to the government, increased if the information had already been front-page news.

Mark had already talked to *The New York Times* and *Los Angeles Times* on his own. At the *Los Angeles Times*, the reporter was Joe Menn, one of the best tech reporters in the country. Joe was doggedly following up and building out the story from Mark's evidence. We kept in touch with Joe, but just as we were told the story was ready to go, everything went quiet. We tried to reach *The New York Times* too, but weren't able to get a callback from the reporters Mark had talked to.

We scoured the news every day for the next few weeks waiting for a story to come out. But nothing did. Every few days we called Joe trying to get clarity about when the story would run. At first he gave apologetic responses, but then he stopped responding altogether.

Much later we would learn that after Joe had reached out to the NSA for a comment, the executive editor of the *Los Angeles Times*, Dean Baquet, had talked to Michael Hayden, who was then the principal deputy director of national intelligence. While the details are unclear, Hayden convinced Baquet to spike the story. This was the first of many, many times during the NSA cases that we would find out that the government was pulling strings behind the scenes to try to stymie us.

Waiting was extremely frustrating. Every day at some point we'd all gather in the office, where we'd fret about the time going by without any press on Mark's information. In the shared space on the legal team side of the office, we had a burgundy, velvet, Victorian-style couch that had been donated by my fiancé. Our new apartment didn't have room for it when we moved in together in early 2001, not long after I joined EFF. That couch became our central scheming and worrying spot. We'd call a "red couch" meeting whenever some news broke that we needed to process together.

In between worrying on the red couch, we worked on our preliminary injunction package to the court. Mark's testimony and evidence was so solid and clear that in any ordinary case, it would be more than sufficient for the court to order at least a temporary halt to illegal behavior. But we knew this wasn't an ordinary case.

We worked with Mark and his lawyers to draft a declaration laying out what he had, giving context, and adding what he knew from personal experience. In addition, we presented written expert testimony and were lucky that a person with deep experience in telecommunications infrastructure, J. Scott Marcus, volunteered to provide a declaration that put Mark's information about the Folsom Street setup into perspective as a piece of a larger story about NSA internet backbone tapping.[32]

I'M BAAACK

Finally we didn't feel we could wait any longer. On March 31, we filed our preliminary injunction motion, including Mark's declaration and the AT&T documents he had provided. Because we were still hoping to follow, not lead, the press story, we filed under seal, meaning that none of the information would be publicly available from the court records. Also, as a courtesy, I called the Department of Justice, and left a message letting it know about Mark's declaration and evidence.

The person who returned my call was Tony Coppolino, the attorney who had been my opposing counsel in the *Bernstein* case. Tony and I had actually become friendly over the years. He was a nice guy, and a smart and fair-minded opponent. I'll never forget the first voicemail I got from him after we filed Mark's evidence.

"Hi Cindy, it's Tony Coppolino calling about your *Hepting* case. I'm baaaack. Call me."

I did, on a Friday afternoon. "Hi Tony, are you handling this case? This will be fun."

"Yes, it looks like it. But this is serious, we need to see the documents you filed right away to see if they are classified. If so, it is illegal for you to even have them."

"I don't think they are classified, Tony. The aren't marked as 'classified' or anything like that. I'm happy to show them to you. Can't you get them directly from the court?"

"With all due respect, Cindy, you don't know if they are classified since they don't have to have markings and can still be classified. Only we can tell. We also can't get them from the court if they are classified. Can you have someone bring another copy down to the SCIF [sensitive compartmentalized information facility] in the federal building so that they can be sent to us in DC?" A SCIF is a protected part of the federal building where classified information can be stored and accessed.

"Sure. We'll do that right away. How will you get them?"

"Well, there is a very slow but very secure fax machine in the San Francisco SCIF that will get them to us in DC, page by page."

"Well, OK, but I could FedEx them, or fax or even email them . . ."

"No. None of those ways are secure enough. This is the only way. And if they are classified, you are likely in trouble."

After I got off the phone, we quickly arranged for another set of the documents to be delivered to the federal building, just on a different floor from where we'd filed the motion papers. I think Kevin took them down there personally, borrowing my car to do so. Several years later, my friend Jon Eisenberg would write an entire brief from the San Francisco SCIF in one of the NSA spying cases called *Al-Haramain*. He gleefully reported that when he left, they shredded everything he had brought in with him, even his banana peel.

After we sent off the documents, we all started to get a little nervous. We looked up, again, the potential prison sentence for illegal possession of classified information. Unlike most other kinds of contraband, where you have to know something is illegal or have to have acquired it illegally, merely possessing classified information without the proper governmental clearances is a serious offense.

We reminded ourselves that we didn't think the documents were classified, and even if they were, they revealed a flatly illegal and unconstitutional program. The classification system is not supposed to be used to hide illegal government actions.[33] After all, we were only showing them to a federal court, under seal, to try to get the law applied to have the program stopped. That couldn't get us in trouble, right?

The truth is we were all a little worried.

That weekend we had one of our monthly wine tastings at my home, and many of the lawyers who worked on the case showed up. We gave a little toast, clinking our glasses with the hope that we wouldn't all be carted off to jail that next week.

Monday came and no word from Tony. Then Tuesday dragged by. Finally, at about 4 p.m. on Tuesday afternoon, my phone rang and it was Tony.

"It's a little late for you, isn't it?" I noted, since it was 7 p.m. in Washington, DC.

"Justice never sleeps, Cindy," he deadpanned.

"What's the story? You have us all a little nervous here."

"You're in luck. The documents are not classified, and neither is the other information your witness has presented. So you're not in trouble with the government. But you are in trouble with AT&T and so is Mr. Klein. Those documents are theirs. They are claiming trade secrecy and confidentiality over them. Your guy stole them, and they want them back."

My shoulders relaxed. This I could handle. Indeed, this was excellent news.

BIG FIRM BLUSTER

"I'm glad to hear I won't be going to jail," I responded, "Please tell AT&T's counsel to call me."

A few minutes later I got an angry call from one of AT&T's lawyers, who had me on speakerphone in what seemed to be a roomful of male voices. Fierce and full of big, legal phrases, the lead lawyer said something like, "Ms. Cohn, those documents you just filed are the internal, confidential property of AT&T. They contain trade secrets and confidential business information. Mr. Klein stole them, and violated his nondisclosure agreement and other contractual obligations to AT&T in doing so." He continued for a while, threatening Mark with a lawsuit and maybe even prison. He also told me I was facing sanctions. He demanded immediate return of the documents and all copies that we had, that we immediately retract the filing and make sure all copies were removed from the court files. It was full litigator bluster combined with a somewhat more intense version of the "Let me tell you about your case, little girl," speeches I had been hearing ever since I started my legal practice.

Having just been reprieved from a possible federal prosecution for illegally possessing classified information, and over a decade more experienced than I'd been when the *Bernstein* case started, there was no way I was going to be scared by a bullying corporate lawyer.

"I don't represent Mr. Klein," I responded. "You'll have to talk to his lawyers about any issues you have with him." I gave them contact information for Miles, Izzy, Tony, and Jim. I thought I heard them swallow hard when I mentioned who Mark's lawyers were, but that could have just been my imagination.

"As for EFF, we will not retract the filing and we do not believe that we have done anything improper." I knew better than to argue with him; I wasn't going to convince him any more than he was going to convince me at this point.

He blustered a bit more, and I just listened. Finally he said that since I had refused AT&T's demands, the corporation was going to go to court immediately. I responded with a phrase I rarely get to use but that always gives me a smile: "I'll see you in court."

I hung up the phone and immediately picked it back up to notify Mark's attorneys so that they were ready for the angry call now headed their way.

But I couldn't stop smiling. By calling the documents trade secrets and confidential AT&T business documents, AT&T had just resolved one of our big worries going into the case. While we believed Mark, we had not been able to find any other employee to publicly corroborate his story. They were all unwilling to talk to us, just as so many other people had been before Mark showed up at our door. We worried that AT&T would just claim that Mark made it up and the documents were false. You cannot both claim trade secrets and say that the documents are fake, though.

AT&T had just confirmed that Mark was telling the truth and authenticated the documents as legitimate.

Finally, on April 7, 2006, *The New York Times* covered the story of Mark's evidence in a small piece basically noting that it had been presented by us in the lawsuit.[34] The *Los Angeles Times* finally printed something in May.[35] Apparently just as we had wanted to follow them, they wanted to follow us. This was disappointing, and I think led to a general failure of the media and public to recognize what Mark had confirmed: the NSA was sitting on the wire in the United States, monitoring a huge amount of domestic communications traffic as people went about their business online. It was as big, if not bigger, than the December 2005 *New York Times* story. While we worked mightily to get it the attention and outrage it deserved in order to get Congress or the courts to stop the spying, it never has.

EMERGENCY MOTION

AT&T lawyers did immediately file an emergency motion demanding that Klein's information be returned. As for their threats to sue him personally or unleash the police on him, those didn't materialize. After a flurry of briefs filed by both sides, including the government, the case was set for its first hearing in May 2006. By that time, the question of NSA spying had been front-page news for several months.

When I arrived at the federal courthouse that morning, I saw quite a few TV vans pulled up and people setting up cameras. I knew they were there for us. Once I got to the nineteenth floor where Judge Walker's courtroom was, I could barely thread my way from the elevator to the courtroom. I had to show my name on a page of our pleadings to the federal marshal at the door of the courtroom because it was already full and they were turning away spectators. There were whole rows of reporters. Our normal EFF "dress-up day" crew of hackers were there too, joined by many others. We weren't just talking about an obscure technological future anymore.

As I walked up to the long tables where the lawyers sat, the contrast between the sides was remarkable. The defense side table was crowded with lawyers from AT&T and the Department of Justice, plus some representatives from the NSA and the other government agencies we had implicated. They all seemed to be white men in sleek dark suits with ties that were either American flag red or American flag blue. Those suits looked expensive. You could feel the power and prestige wafting off them. As I walked over to greet them, they basically ignored me until Tony looked up and said hello. Only then did I matter.

Our side was different. We had fewer lawyers, at least four of us were women, and we didn't all look cut from the same cloth. But we were strong. In fact, in our own way we had an all-star team, and it was the largest litigation team I'd ever managed. We had the class action lawyers, our EFF crew, and several longtime pro bono outside collaborators.

One was Jim Tyre. Jim was one of the small cadre of lawyers who first embraced the internet in the 1990s. In true 1990s' fashion, we had met through a mailing list, called Cyberia-L, where lawyers and law professors interested in the internet hung out. Since I'd joined EFF, Jim had regularly helped out on our cases, especially on First Amendment issues, even as he resisted the many times I tried to get him to move to the Bay from his beloved Los Angeles to formally join us. During one of our first cases together, Jim had suffered the first of several serious eye issues starting with a detached retina. He was functionally blind by 2006, but that didn't stop him from jumping into our cases and carrying heavy legal loads.

Once the news broke about the NSA spying in *The New York Times*, a prominent Bay Area litigator named Rob Fram reached out and brought along his team. To me, it seemed like we had our own fancy suits now, but I think Rob and his crew thought of themselves as more of the rumpled professorial types.

By the time we put the *Hepting* case together, I also had the confidence to pull together a team that could handle seriously complex litigation challenges, which this case definitely was. At one point, as mentioned earlier, Rob called our process open-source law. We had weekly team calls to discuss strategy, and in between, we would email around a brief or other important document among the eight or more people on the team. For each major issue, we named a lead who would drive the issue and have the final say. Jim was our lead on jurisdiction, for instance.

In the meantime I served as ringmaster, keeping all of us on task. I also handled the endless number of smaller issues that came up—from negotiating briefing schedules and protective orders to making sure that all the pieces continued to move forward. I was the lead on all the calls with AT&T's lawyers and kept my eye on the overall story too; I tended to write the introductory paragraphs for every brief that would summarize the story we were telling. I pulled in and recruited help as we needed it, and kept our clients updated on our progress.

JUDGE WALKER

Back in the courtroom (fig. 2.3), we all rose as Judge Walker walked in and we were called to order. Judge Walker was a venerable, somewhat gruff judge who had been in the Northern District of California federal court for a long time. We were not sure he was a good draw for us. He had a well-earned reputation for being a judicial conservative. Judge Walker had even sentenced a defendant to march in front of the federal building wearing a sign that said, "I stole mail and this is my punishment." While I'm not a fan of stealing mail, I'm also not a fan of public humiliation. On the other hand, he was an equal opportunity gruff, and not likely to be scared off by government or corporate bluster.

AT&T's attorney came out strong; his first words to Judge Walker asked that everything stop until the courtroom could be cleared of spectators. We heard a murmur through the audience as the observers and journalists wondered if they were all going to have to leave.

Figure 2.3 Courtroom drawing of Cindy Cohn at *Hepting v. AT&T* hearing by Vicki Behringer, www.courtroomartist.com.

But it quickly became clear who was in charge. Judge Walker breezed right past him, noting that he'd handled many cases involving trade secrets and rarely had to limit public access. The judge then asked the AT&T's lawyer for the precise legal authority backing their demands to return the documents.

Not only did Judge Walker understand what the case was about and how important it was, he saw that beyond the bluster, AT&T really didn't have a leg to stand on in demanding that we return the documents, much less to clear the courtroom. We knew we were in the right, but we still breathed a sigh of relief, catching each other's eyes across the conference table while trying to maintain our poker faces.

Maria Morris, one of the class action attorneys who had signed on from the New York taxi ride, argued for us. Maria ably knocked down AT&T's arguments demanding return of the documents, while assuring the court that we were being careful with them, and had limited who had access to them to only the lawyers and experts we needed to pursue the case.

After a few more back and forths, Judge Walker announced his ruling: he let us keep the documents and ordered AT&T to negotiate a reasonable protective order with us to allow the non-trade-secret parts of the documents to be made public. First round: EFF and Mark.

The hearing wasn't over, though. Tony and the other government lawyers were there because the Department of Justice had filed a brief demanding to join the case. It had even filed the first of what would become many secret briefs. Justice Department lawyer Carl Nichols stood up to argue and I was on tap to respond to him. We heard, for the first time, the claim that we would be fighting over for the next thirteen years: that the state secrets privilege required the case to be dismissed.

The state secrets privilege is a judge-made doctrine, meaning that Congress never passed a law to create it. Instead, the Supreme Court created it in 1953 in a case called *U.S. v. Reynolds*, brought by the widows of three men who had worked for an Air Force military contractor and were killed in a military plane crash.[36] The Air Force claimed that the release of the crash reports would harm national security. The court created a new "evidentiary privilege" to allow the government to withhold the crash reports, but not to dismiss the whole case. The case then settled.

Much later it came out that the crash reports had no national security value whatsoever; they just demonstrated that the Air Force had been negligent.[37] Regardless, the state secrets privilege was created and continues to be a powerful tool for the government to block national security information from being used in the courts. Over time the doctrine grew, allowing full dismissal of the case at least in a few instances where the person suing had promised to keep government secrets.[38]

But in our case, the information revealed arguably illegal and unconstitutional behavior by the government. Our clients were just normal people who had been spied on and were suing AT&T, not the government. They were not members of the military, military contractors, or otherwise bound to government secrecy in any way. Dismissal of the case at the outset should not have even been on the table. Yet the government argued that the state secrets privilege meant that the case should be immediately dismissed.

Judge Walker was respectful but skeptical at the breadth of the governments' argument, which was essentially that the courts had to step aside immediately and dismiss a case if the government merely invoked national security.

I laid out our response to the state secrets claim for the first time, "We'd like the opportunity to demonstrate to you that the state secrets information is not important for us to win this case, it's not necessary for us to win this case, and that there is a path, I think a fairly clear path, that you can follow to decide this without implicating state secrets."

To my delight, Judge Walker asked exactly what I had hoped, "Can you strike that path for me?"

"I sure can," I responded, and laid out our central contention. Under the law applicable to all telephone companies, AT&T was forbidden from disclosing customer information to the government without proper authorization. AT&T's liability was triggered by that moment of disclosure. What the government did with the information after it received it, whether from the internet backbone, or collecting everyone's telephone records or internet metadata, was not necessary for AT&T to be liable for handing it over in the first place.

This was one of the insights that Kevin presented back on New Year's Eve. Privacy law in the United States prohibited telecommunications companies from handing over customer data except in limited circumstances, and none of those circumstances fit the kind of mass collection that we were suing over. The government did have an argument that secrecy should protect it from having to reveal its actual targets—the people it was tracking along with the details of how and why it selected them—and it could even largely protect what the government did with the data after it got information. But the fact that AT&T was handing over the user data of millions of people in rampant violation of both state and federal law should not be a secret, much less one that risked national security. National security is not supposed to be a cover for violating the laws that Congress specifically passed to protect our privacy.

Judge Walker heard me out and then moved to questions like whether he could review the classified briefing that the government had just filed. He next focused on scheduling, saying he wanted to move quickly. He wanted to move so quickly that I, embarrassed, had to ask him for a little more time to accommodate my upcoming wedding, which was scheduled in Hawaii in late May. That tickled him. The government and AT&T attorneys also made a great show of congratulating me even as I turned bright red standing at the dais in front of the packed courtroom.

ROCK, PAPER, SCISSORS AND THE STATE SECRETS PRIVILEGE

So after a wedding on a Maui beach and a flurry of briefing, we were back in front of Judge Walker on June 23, 2006.

The government had by then formally intervened in the case and asserted that the state secrets privilege required immediate dismissal. AT&T had filed motions to dismiss too, first arguing that it was simply an innocent company caught in the middle, and then trying to claim that the part of AT&T we had sued couldn't be sued in California—a jurisdictional issue that Jim took on.

In our response to the government, we laid out our interpretation of the state secrets doctrine. In addition to the government's secrets not being necessary for us to win on the law, we argued that the state secrets privilege just didn't apply because of FISA.

FISA, passed in 1978, was Congress's response to a previous time that the national security parts of the government had been caught spying on innocent people in the United States. In an investigation led by Senator Church, called the Church Committee, the public discovered that the government had been spying on people that the FBI and NSA deemed "subversive," including peace activists like singer John Lennon and civil rights icon Reverend Martin Luther King Jr. Another portion of the spying, code-named Project SHAMROCK, involved the NSA collecting all the cables and telegrams passing through key transit points like New York City, Washington, DC, and San Francisco, all without any judicial involvement or congressional oversight. This was the pre-internet version of the NSA sitting on the wire. As a result of this scandal, Congress specifically created rules in FISA about how and why the government could spy domestically in the name of national security. It created a special court made up of judges selected by the chief justice of the Supreme Court to review such requests individually. It was called the Foreign Intelligence Surveillance Court or FISC.

I like to think of the question of whether a judge-made doctrine like the state secrets privilege should prevail over a law that Congress passes like FISA as similar to the game of rock, paper, scissors. If the judge creates a doctrine, that is important. It's the rock. But if Congress writes legislation on the same topic, that's the paper. And as every second grader knows, paper covers rock, and the statute should win.[39]

That was our basic argument about the state secrets privilege being applied to national security surveillance. FISA was created, in part, to stop mass spying, so overall, it should prevail, or what lawyers call "preempt," the state secrets privilege. There was even a part of the FISA paper, called section 1806(f), that covered the rock of the state secrets privilege for our specific kind of case.[40] This provides a process by which a regular court can determine if and how to use evidence that the government claims has national security implications to determine whether challenged surveillance was "lawfully authorized and conducted." That's exactly what we were doing.

My colleague Kurt Opsahl found this specific part in the larger FISA law when we were researching the case and trying to figure out what to do if the government made a state secrets privilege claim. 1806(f) didn't allow evidence to become public just because it was being used in a lawsuit, but it also didn't allow the government to simply remove it entirely from a case. Instead, 1806(f) created a process for the secret presentation of national security evidence to the court—called *ex parte, en camera*—to allow a judge to determine whether the spying was legal. It was a way forward, and for our immediate purposes, it meant that the state secrets privilege just didn't apply.

We presented all of this in the June hearing. Judge Walker listened closely and asked a few questions, but didn't show his hand. We were nervous, yet tried to remain hopeful. He did tell us that he wanted to rule quickly, and for that we were grateful.

KATRINA RELIEF AND MULTIDISTRICT LITIGATION

Attacking the state secrets privilege wasn't the only thing we were doing that spring and summer. As we had anticipated, starting shortly after the *USA Today* article came out about the mass telephone records collection, a flood of new lawsuits against the NSA's spying were filed all across the country. We were right to have rushed to get our case on file first. In all, there were nearly sixty cases, and that triggered a federal process known as multidistrict litigation, which sought to coordinate them.

Most of the cases were brought by traditional plaintiffs' class action attorneys who saw an opportunity to hold the telecommunications companies accountable to their millions of customers. Several state public utility commissions sued since in addition to the federal statutes we were relying on, state regulators had the power to hold companies accountable for failing to protect the privacy of their customers' communications and records. A few other civil liberties groups filed suits too. The ACLU of Illinois filed a case on behalf of radio legend Studs Terkel. The ACLU of Northern California also brought a case, led by my friend Ann Brick, based in part on California state law as well as federal law.

There were a couple of cases directly against the government too. A smart lawyer named Ilann Maazel who worked at a large progressive law firm in New York City brought one called *Shubert*. Ilann would become a stalwart partner throughout the long run of the NSA spying cases.

The Center for Constitutional Rights, which was also my cocounsel in the *Bowoto v. Chevron* case, brought a lawsuit directly against the government based on the presumption that its lawyers, who were representing prisoners being held as terrorism suspects in Guantanamo Bay, Cuba, were likely targets.

In the mix as well was a case called *Al-Haramain*, which was directly against the government but had different facts. Rather than arising from people who had little reason to be caught up in the NSA dragnet or those who had a good reason to believe they were under surveillance like the Center for Constitutional Rights plaintiffs, the plaintiffs in *Al-Haramain* actually knew they were the targets of the phone surveillance. The government had accidentally provided them with a document proving it. Because of this, the *Al-Haramain* lawsuit did not have the same threshold standing obstacle that all the other cases had. That case was led by one of California's best appellate attorneys, a man named Jon Eisenberg.

With all of these cases flooding into the courts, it was time for the class action specialists, who had been riding with me in the taxi when the first *New York Times* story broke, to kick into gear. That's because the first question raised whenever a bunch of lawsuits are all filed on the same basic facts is whether they should be combined under one umbrella case before one federal judge in what's called multidistrict litigation. The second is which of the lawyers should lead them.

We wanted the judge to be Walker because he had shown an openness to our argument as well as skepticism about the broad claims of the companies and government. We wanted EFF to help lead the multidistrict litigation because we wanted to keep the focus of the cases on stopping the spying and ensuring it couldn't happen again. We had several giant conference calls with all the plaintiffs' lawyers to try to get everyone on the same page. The lawyers were a cantankerous bunch, and several of them wanted to lead. Most of the plaintiffs' class action lawyers also had very different ideas about how the case should go; several focused on racing to a settlement with the telecommunication companies and a large payday. The class action specialists we had on our team, led by Reed Kathrein, Jeff Friedman, Maria Morris, and Shana Scarlett, were invaluable in helping us navigate this new terrain for EFF.

A panel of three judges handles the multidistrict litigation cases, deciding whether to combine multiple cases with the same laws and facts as well as choosing which district court judge would hear the combined cases at the trial court level.

We lobbied hard for Judge Walker within the big group of plaintiffs as well as with the government and telecommunications lawyers. Other counsel wanted a range of options, including one lawyer who kept interrupting the calls to say, "We need the cases assigned to New Orleans for Katrina relief," referring to the hurricane that had devastated New Orleans in 2005. That one puzzled us.

Our decision to file our case right after Mark showed up at our door paid off. *Hepting v. AT&T* was the first filed case of all of them. That gave us an edge in the multidistrict litigation process, especially since we had already briefed and argued both the trade secrets question and the initial motions to dismiss by the time the case came before the multidistrict litigation panel. Ultimately, we won exactly what we wanted: EFF and the ACLU of Illinois, with lead lawyer Harvey Grossman, were named colead counsel. Judge Walker retained control of all the cases.

Suddenly I was at the helm of a huge, unwieldy set of cases known as *In Re National Security Agency Telecommunications Records Litigation*.

EVEN THE STATE SECRETS PRIVILEGE HAS ITS LIMITS

On July 20, 2006, as we were knee-deep in trying to negotiate for the leadership of the multidistrict litigation, Judge Walker issued his decision on the motions to dismiss. As with the *Bernstein* case, we had no warning, but by then we didn't have a reporter call to give us the news either. Instead, we received an email notification with a link to the court's docket on its website. The decision was seventy pages long, and we had won.[41]

The government's and AT&T's motions to dismiss were denied, and while the court did not rely on Mark's evidence as we had hoped, it firmly rejected the government's state secrets arguments. The opinion noted the obvious: that the mass spying was not a secret. It had been front-page news. By then it had even been confirmed by the attorney General, Alberto Gonzales. That conclusion wasn't undone by the fact that some of the telecommunications companies flatly denied participating in it. Verizon's denial of participating in mass surveillance was particularly unequivocal—which made it a flat-out lie when five years later in 2013, Edward Snowden revealed one of the specific documents ordering the company to provide all of its customers' phone records to the NSA.[42]

The decision said that

> the very subject matter of this action is hardly a secret. As described above, public disclosures by the government and AT&T indicate that AT&T is assisting the government to implement some kind of surveillance program.[43]

The court went on to say that while some evidence may be excluded by the state secrets privilege or otherwise, it was premature to decide what that should be and that the case should be allowed to take its course.

Judge Walker continued, in words that warmed my heart,

> But it is important to note that even the state secrets privilege has its limits. While the court recognizes and respects the executive's constitutional duty to protect the nation from threats, the court also takes seriously its constitutional duty to adjudicate the disputes that come before it. To defer to a blanket assertion of secrecy here would be to abdicate that duty, particularly because the very subject matter of this litigation has been so publicly aired. The compromise between liberty and security remains a difficult one. But dismissing this case at the outset would sacrifice liberty for no apparent enhancement of security.[44]

The judge then noted that based on what the government had admitted, if it was telling the truth, merely requiring it to turn over any document by which it accomplished this (a "certification" in the language of the statute) shouldn't reveal any state secrets.

It wasn't a total victory. While the judge allowed us to move forward with the internet backbone claims, he prevented us from pursuing additional information—a process lawyers call discovery—about phone records and internet metadata. He based his decision on his view that despite the *USA Today* story and follow-on reporting, the amount of information that was already public about those two programs was not enough. He did say that we could come back and seek further information if more facts did become public. We were not happy about being stopped for two of the three programs we had challenged, but remained hopeful that if public attention continued on this issue, more would be revealed and we would be able to come back to ask for more.

In the part of the opinion focused on AT&T, the court rejected all of AT&T's initial defenses and jurisdictional arguments. It ordered both parties to brief whether he should appoint an expert with an appropriate security clearance to assist the court in reviewing and handling any secret evidence. As an experienced trial court judge, Walker had carefully thought through the practical issues in handling the case.

We were overjoyed. All other work stopped on Shotwell Street as we read the decision. We fielded a ton of initial press calls while we quickly put together a press release. At least one TV news station sent out a camera team to our red-brick building that day.

In between, we couldn't stop smiling at each other, hugging, high-fiving, and laughing. We had taken on both the national security infrastructure of the United States and one of the country's largest companies. We had beaten them both.

I was walking on air for weeks. I even publicly thanked Judge Walker at our San Francisco post-wedding celebration, held at a basement speakeasy music venue called Cafe du Nord in San Francisco the weekend after the decision came out. All of our communities were in attendance. Some of my camping and music friends played in the band, and others lifted my new husband and me up on chairs during a "Hava Nagila" that seemed to go on forever. John came, as did most of the EFF staff and even a couple of our volunteer lawyers. Patrick even attended. He had since gotten a divorce and moved to Palo Alto, and we had the occasional dinner together. I don't think Judge Walker meant his decision as a wedding gift, but I accepted it anyway.

Another quick round of briefing followed, but unsurprisingly, as the government and AT&T had requested, Judge Walker sent his initial decision to the Ninth Circuit for what is called "interlocutory review."

ALL THE MONEY IN THE WORLD VERSUS US

Walking up to the Ninth Circuit building in August 2007, I saw an absolute circus. TV crews, a huge number of people, and a long line already forming to enter the court. It was all for our case. The overflow room filled, and then a second one was set up. I was wearing another suit sent by my mother from Denver. We passed through security and walked up the marble stairs, entering the gorgeous ceremonial courtroom, the same one where I had argued the *Bernstein* case. I was ready to stand up to the intelligence community in favor of privacy once again.

This time I wasn't the one arguing. Our cocounsel Rob, who had reached out to me outraged about the mass spying and brought his downtown legal team into the case, was the one standing up this time. We may have been a nonprofit team, but now we looked a little less raggedy with Rob arguing for us.

On the other side, though, was what my father would have called "all the money in the world." At this point, all the major telecommunications companies were defendants in the various multidistrict litigation cases that had been consolidated before Judge Walker. While our case was just against AT&T, all the companies had skin in the game in this appeal since if either AT&T or the government defeated us, they would likely be off the hook too. Each of them brought a team in fancy suits and shiny shoes. It seemed every large, corporate defense law firm in the country was represented, and once again they all seemed overwhelmingly white and male. The phalanx of defense lawyers filled the first rows of the audience.

But those weren't the only lawyers on the other side. In addition to the Department of Justice lawyers who represented the government, I saw many lawyers from the various agencies involved in the NSA spying, including the FBI and NSA along with several other agencies involved in national security. The government lawyers weren't quite as posh a crew as the telecommunications lawyers, yet like them, they were almost all white men. I made sure to introduce myself to each of them.

The clerk called the case. Our three-judge panel was Michael Hawkins, Margaret McKeon, and Harry Pregerson, a legendary liberal. They were all solid, experienced judges, and we hoped they would stand firm for privacy against what we knew would be an attempt to scare them with national security. Indeed, the first sentence out of the government attorney's mouth after introducing himself was,

> Your honors, the nation's top officials, whose job it is to assess and protect foreign intelligence, have determined that litigating this action could result in exceptionally grave harm to the national security of the United States.

The second question from Judge Hawkins warmed my heart, though: "Why shouldn't we view the FISA law as having supplanted the common law doctrine?" He meant the common law doctrine of the state secrets privilege.

"Yes!" I said, despite myself, then looked up and hoped I hadn't said it too loudly. Luckily, no one seemed to notice. All eyes were on the judges, not me at the counsel table.

The judge's question meant that he understood the central fight: whether the government could use the judge-made state secrets privilege to get our case dismissed, or if, as we had argued, in passing the FISA law, Congress had created a statutory structure to let these cases be considered while still protecting national security. Judge Hawkins had basically asked if paper covered rock.

The rest of the hearing wasn't as fun as those first moments, but it wasn't bad either. The judges asked hard questions of everyone, and seemed both unsatisfied with the idea that the courts should just function as a rubber stamp on government claims of national security secrecy and concerned about what we would need to have access to in order to prove our case. Rob ably pointed out what I had also explained to Judge Walker in that first hearing: that once internet communications were copied and those copies were put into NSA control, we had won our claim for illegal interception regardless of what happened afterward. We didn't need any state secrets information to prove that; we already had Mark's evidence showing the splitters on the sixth floor copying everything that passed over the fiber-optic cables at AT&T's peering links on the seventh floor.

We left the courthouse in high spirits. We weren't sure we would win, but we knew we had a chance and that the judges took our arguments seriously, even if we were outnumbered and outdressed in the courtroom.

WTF IS RETROACTIVE IMMUNITY?

It soon became clear that we weren't the only ones who thought that the Ninth Circuit argument had gone well for us. Shortly after the hearing, we learned that the government and telecommunications companies were making a big push for Congress to end our case. We saw the proposed legislation they were pushing that would grant them something called "retroactive immunity." On our weekly conference call with the litigation team, we puzzled over the new term.

"What is retroactive immunity?" I asked. Lee was now EFF's legislative lead. He explained what he had been told by our allies in DC. "They are going to let the telcos off the hook for everything they've done since 2001 on mass spying regardless of whether it was illegal, and do so without ever formally confirming whether they actually did it or not."

"What? I don't get it. Has this ever been done before? How do they get out of breaking the law like that? And how do you get immunity for a thing you won't even admit you did?"

"We don't think it has ever been done. We think they just made it up and gave it a formal-sounding name."

There was no mistaking it. The government and these powerful companies didn't like their chances in the courts, and had jumped to the legislature to bail them out.

When we heard that Congress was being pressed to kill our lawsuit and let the companies evade responsibility, it put us at a crossroads. We had to decide whether to take a big step on a path that EFF had largely abandoned over ten years before: engaging directly in DC.

TO DC OR NOT TO DC

While I wasn't directly involved, EFF's aversion to engaging deeply in DC came out of a hard early episode that happened in 1994. EFF had been based in DC in those days, having moved to better focus on lobbying from where it was founded in Mitch's offices in Cambridge, Massachusetts.

The organization was immersed in a legislative fight over the proposed Communications Access for Law Enforcement Act. As originally drafted, the act would have required both telecommunications carriers and ISPs to build their communications systems to be massively tappable. EFF had first opposed the bill, but then was able to get Congress to take ISPs out of it. Based on that change, EFF's leadership had flipped to supporting the law. To the EFF lobbyists involved, this seemed like a good deal: protecting the baby internet from massive wiretapping capability requirements in exchange for not opposing them for legacy telecommunications carriers.

But that wasn't how it landed for many EFF members and several of EFF's key board members. John, as cofounder, led others who felt strongly that EFF needed to stand up for the principle of privacy for all users in all technologies. They noted that the telecommunications and internet infrastructures weren't really separate. They also thought it was wrong for EFF to be involved in backroom DC negotiations where it traded off telecommunication privacy rights for internet ones. Both online and offline, they protested loudly. There was a big, ugly split inside the organization, and it caused some shouting as well as deep existential agonizing.

As a result of this split over DC compromising, EFF itself split. The lobbying arm—and the corporate money that EFF had been receiving—stayed in DC along with executive director Jerry Berman. Jerry formed a new organization called the Center for Democracy and Technology.

The rest of EFF moved to San Francisco with little money and no leaders other than the remaining board members. For a while both the system administrators and servers lived in John's attic. It wasn't clear if EFF would survive. But slowly the organization regained its footing and hired new leadership.

Today EFF and Center for Democracy and Technology are strong allies, and while we differ in some areas and approaches, we tend to be broadly aligned and stand together most of the time. Yet the hangover from the Communications Access for Law Enforcement Act fight remained at EFF for many years. While we did lots of lobbying on various bills, we have never hired anyone based in DC to focus on it. The board was deeply afraid of getting caught up in the daily scrum of DC lobbyists and falling prey to the temptation to make compromises like that one.

Ultimately, despite this history, we decided to engage directly in DC for this fight with the NSA. We had reason to think we could succeed. The outrage about NSA spying domestically still had huge political and public attention even over a year and a half after the first *New York Times* article. I had been on *FRONTLINE*, Fox, NBC, ABC, and MSNBC, and in nearly every major newspaper in the country. The overall public sentiment was definitely against the NSA. The issue was covered by Jon Stewart's *Daily Show*, which was almost required watching for political wonks at that time. Senator Chris Dodd was a strong champion on our side, as was Senator Ron Wyden, who has never wavered in seeking to rein in the NSA to protect people's privacy. The libertarian wing of the Republican Party was also firmly with us—led by Senators Mike Lee and Rand Paul. We had bipartisan support and bipartisan favorable coverage in the press.

We had other support too. A dozen prominent former government attorneys and law professors published an open letter in *The New York Review of Books* taking down the various arguments for mass spying, agreeing with us on our paper-covers-rock theory of FISA preempting the state secrets privilege. There was also strong resistance to some administration claims of unilateral presidential authority to engage in domestic wiretapping on the grounds of national security. Senators Obama and Joe Biden, who were separately running for president before they later joined forces, made restraining the NSA's spying part of their standard stump speeches. Obama even promised to filibuster any bill that did not protect people's privacy in the United States. We knew a Congressional fight wouldn't be easy, but we were confident that we were right and believed that we had some high-profile wind in our sails.

We went as big as we thought we could given EFF's small size. We got a small financial boost from some folks who ran big political advocacy mailing lists. I knew them because I had helped them in the early 2000s to convince the major ISPs not to mark their emails as spam. At the time, I had reached out to my contacts at the major ISPs and basically said, "You really don't want the press and public to hear that you are blocking people from getting political messages that they signed up for, do you?" Suddenly their emails were white-listed, and my clients thought I was magic.

We used the grant to hire a public relations firm and some lobbyists, including Adam Eisgrau, a mensch and former staffer to Senator Dianne Feinstein. Feinstein sat on the Senate Intelligence Committee and was the former mayor of San Francisco. We knew that if we got Feinstein's support, we would have a good chance of winning, and without her we'd have almost no chance. We also hoped she would especially care since Mark's evidence showed that the internet backbone tapping was occurring in San Francisco, and of course that's where our case was pending too. We also hired a former congressperson named Tom Downey.

Our goal was big: we didn't want to just protect our case and the other multidistrict litigation cases; we wanted to stop the NSA mass spying in its tracks. The retroactive immunity was only one portion of the bill, called the FISA Amendments Act, that we lobbied against. The rest of the bill was problematic as well since it essentially legalized most of what the president had been doing illegally for many years.

Figure 2.4 EFF parody of the NSA eagle by Hugh D'Andrade / EFF licensed under CC BY 4.0 (https://creativecommons.org/licenses/by/4.0/).

We did all the things that we thought we could do. We wrote one-pagers, took out ads in local and national newspapers, and issued press releases. The public relations firm tried to get press to cover the story, and they did get Mark onto the Keith Olbermann show. Our staff artist, Hugh D'Andrade, created some terrific visuals, including parodying the NSA logo, with a scary red-eyed eagle holding fiber-optic cables in its claws (fig. 2.4).[45] We put it on a hoodie that later became famous after Snowden showed up wearing one.

We engaged directly with key congressional offices, especially those on the judiciary and intelligence oversight committees. Since we had asked Mark to come with us to DC, Hugh created a cartoon version of Mark called "Mr. Klein Goes to Washington" (fig. 2.5). We also brought Brian, the internet expert who had told me that this wasn't just a wiretap, it was a country tap. We held a press conference inside the Capitol building, and ran all over Capitol Hill letting Mark and Brian present the evidence directly to any members of Congress or their staff who would meet with us.

The one thing we couldn't do was the most powerful thing in DC. While the presidential and many congressional campaigns were in full

Figure 2.5 "Mr. Klein goes to Washington" by Hugh D'Andrade / EFF licensed under CC BY 4.0 (https://creativecommons.org/licenses/by/4.0/).

swing, and while leading candidates were campaigning on our issue, we could not get involved. As a kind of nonprofit called a 501(c)(3) in the tax code, we could not participate in the election by giving any support to or opposing any candidates, including endorsing candidates or telling voters to vote for candidates who would end mass surveillance, even though several candidates were campaigning on surveillance reform. We knew that unlike us, AT&T, Verizon, and the other telecommunications companies could engage in electioneering, including directly giving campaign contributions. I cannot overemphasize how frustrating this was, and how this prohibition gives an unfair advantage to corporate voices over nonprofit ones. It also hamstrings organizations from speaking frankly about issues that voters deserve to know about.

Soon the cold reality of Washington, DC, the limits of what a nonprofit can do, and the power of national security arguments in Congress came into focus. Neither EFF nor Mark were asked to testify as the FISA Amendments Act was considered. No actual member of Congress would even meet with us; the closest we got was when Nancy Pelosi walked in early for another meeting in the room where we had just met with some of her staff. Even the staff who did meet with us were clearly not interested in engaging seriously with Mark's evidence. I saw one staffer's eyes glaze over as Mark showed him the photos and schematics of the actual equipment tapping into the internet backbone. One bright spot was Senator Dodd, who had his staff make a video of Mark and discussed Mark's evidence during the hearing on the bill. Still, it was obvious that the lobbying game was over even before we showed up.

We learned another thing too about the political people we thought were on our side. While we were trying to regain the right to a private conversation in the digital age, the powerful voices who seemed like they were on our side in public were not actually trying to stop the spying, or hold anyone accountable for what had been a bald-faced end run around the law and Constitution. The draft FISA Amendments Act did contain a bit more congressional oversight and provided for the secret, unaccountable FISA court to generally approve the program as a whole—basically a modern form of a general warrant. But neither of these were intended to, nor did they, stop any of the mass spying programs. Instead they legalized what had been done illegally.

This was a far cry from what we knew the Constitution demanded: a full stop to mass data collections and consequences for those who had authorized the illegal spying. We also wanted the requirement of a warrant or at least some sort of individualized approvals of any demands for information from telecommunications companies or other providers about a specific person or group of people. And of course the proposed law contained the retroactive immunity that would kill our *Hepting* lawsuit and all the other lawsuits against telecommunications companies, blocking that avenue of accountability.

These fissures became obvious as the fight wore on, culminating in Senator Obama reneging on his vow to filibuster and instead voting for the FISA Amendments Act. Ultimately, the folks we had hoped would be powerful champions of the public interest were willing to accept the most mealymouthed versions of reform. While a few of the transparency provisions for the FISA court were good, they were still miniscule compared to the need.

It was a horrible outcome.

The retroactive immunity passed too. Those seemingly sympathetic congressional staffers who actually did meet with us told us, over and over, that our cause was just, but that we'd just named the wrong defendant. We should have sued the NSA, they said, not the poor telecommunications companies. It was almost funny, listening to staffers paint the giant telecommunications companies as weaklings who were simply powerless to abide by the laws that required them to protect their customers' privacy. We knew that sob story had come to them from the extremely well-paid, full-time telecom lobbyists who line K Street in DC, who had already met with them several times before we showed up.

Meanwhile, we struggled to scrape together enough money to spend a week in DC and buy a couple of months of lobbyist time to even get to talk to them. At one point I remarked that if this fight was like David and Goliath, we didn't even have the slingshot David had, much less the five stones.

Nonetheless, once the law passed, we decided to take those congressional apologists at their word. We launched a new case against the same spying programs, only this time we left off the telecommunications companies and sued the NSA directly. The case was called *Jewel v. NSA*.

JEWEL V. NSA

When we saw *Hepting* was likely going to be dismissed due to the retroactive immunity, we reached out to the patient and stalwart folks who had signed up as plaintiffs in the first case to ask if they were up for a second one. They all agreed, and we even added one more. We intentionally picked clients who could stand in for millions of others who had AT&T as their provider. The point was that ordinary people were being swept up in the mass surveillance, and our plaintiffs were our reference points.

The *Hepting v. AT&T* case had been named after Tash Hepting, one of the first to sign up, but also the first name alphabetically of the plaintiffs. Carolyn Jewel, who had joined a little later, was next alphabetically. We picked hers to be the name of the new case. I admit that we also liked saying "the Jewel case," even as CDs (and their cases) were fading into history. Carolyn was an AT&T internet customer based in Northern California. She is a database administrator and developer as well as the author of several romance novels. Carolyn often did research for her novels that involved talking to and emailing with people all over the world and throughout the United States, including people who were not AT&T customers. This underscored that her communications, like so many others, likely went over the peering links and fiber-optic splitters, with copies going to the NSA secret room Mark had revealed.

We knew that suing the NSA rather than AT&T would make the case harder. Kevin had been right at that New Year's Eve party long ago at my house. Sadly, the US government enjoys a thicket of immunities that protect it even when it flagrantly violates people's rights. The doctrines have names like sovereign immunity, qualified immunity, special needs, and the good faith exception. The result of each is that the courthouse doors are effectively shut for those impacted by the government violating the law. So while state secrets was definitely center stage, we knew there were other obstacles as well. The truth is, outside a few areas—generally where Congress has specifically and unequivocally created statutory processes for victims—it can be difficult to hold the US government itself accountable for violating the law or Constitution.

I've frequently thought of trying to design a video game where the person who is harmed by illegal governmental action has to try to get a remedy. Kind of like a frustrating *Frogger* or *Super Mario Brothers*, I'd show the poor, hurt plaintiffs dodging immunities, leaping over judicially created doctrines even as the courts dreamed up new ones to toss at them, and all while holding up a fragile copy of the US Constitution. I'm not sure who would play it; it's definitely an infuriating game to play in real life.

But even with the new obstacles, we knew we had to try. The story kept leaking out, piece by piece. By the time we filed *Jewel v. NSA* in 2008, we had learned the NSA's internal name for that part of the mass interception taking place on the fiber-optic cables of the internet backbone that Mark had revealed. It was called, appropriately, Upstream.

The initial filing in *Jewel v. NSA* included all the written evidence we had by 2008. The evidence also now included declarations from three brave NSA whistleblowers: Thomas Drake, William Binney, and J. Kirk Wiebe.[46]

Jewel v. NSA was assigned to Judge Walker, who still had all the multidistrict litigation cases in front of him. He also had the original case, *Hepting*, because the Ninth Circuit had sent it back for reconsideration in light of the new FISA Amendments Act. Judge Walker moved quickly to dismiss all the thirty-odd other cases against various telecommunications carriers based on the new retroactive immunity law.

I'm used to political actors jumping in to support civil liberties when it suits their needs and then abandoning the cause when the political winds shift. Republicans like Senator Ashcroft joined us in the encryption fight and talked about the need for privacy online when it let him attack President Clinton. Ashcroft flipped into broad support for government access to everyone's communications when he became attorney general under President Bush.

But the first motion by the government in *Jewel v. NSA* still flabbergasted me. As I noted above, both President Obama and Vice President Biden campaigned against the mass spying, and not just a little. It was part of both of their stump speeches. While they later voted for the FISA Amendments Act and its retroactive immunity, their staffers had been some of the ones trying to reassure us that they only did so to let the poor telecoms out of the middle and that they weren't trying to block a case against the NSA directly. Yet despite this broad public awareness, including President Obama going on national TV to discuss the changes in the FISA Amendments Act, the Department of Justice lawyers continued to officially deny the existence of these programs. It increasingly felt like we were living in one world in the federal district court building in San Francisco and a different one outside it.

Especially upsetting to me was the fact that one of Klein's former attorneys, Tony West, had been named by President Obama as assistant attorney general in charge of the civil division of the Justice Department. That meant he was in the direct chain of command over the lawyers who were handling our case. Tony hadn't represented Mark for a while when that happened; AT&T had backed down on its threats against Mark pretty quickly when Judge Walker didn't agree. And since Mark was only a witness in our lawsuit, there was no formal legal conflict with Tony in the Justice Department.

Yet still, despite having someone high up in the Justice Department chain of command who knew the truth and knew that it was already public, the Obama Justice Department moved to dismiss *Jewel* in early 2009 on the exact same grounds as the Bush administration had done in *Hepting* in 2006: that the state secrets privilege required immediate dismissal of the case without a ruling on whether the spying was illegal. The pleadings were so similar that it almost seemed like a cut-and-paste job.

I felt confident Judge Walker would quickly reject this argument since he had rejected it before in *Hepting*. I thought he might even be angry that the government was acting as though his earlier consideration had never happened.

GENERALIZED GRIEVANCE

But when we got back before Judge Walker, we got an unpleasant surprise. Walker held that our clients didn't present a "concrete injury" sufficient for standing because they were complaining about only an "abstract, generalized grievance." Basically he ruled that our clients didn't have any individual claim, despite being spied on, and instead were just suing over a general policy decision that didn't directly impact them.

We knew that Judge Walker's analysis was wrong. Obviously the fact that lots of people are being subjected to surveillance doesn't mean that each person swept up in it isn't individually harmed. Our clients each had their own individual communications subject to government surveillance. We were confused about what had happened to switch Walker's position so dramatically.

We'll never know for sure, but his change of heart came just as he took a courageous step and threw out a California proposition that banned gay marriage. For a conservative judge, who had earlier made his name by being the lead counsel attacking the "gay Olympics" on behalf of the US Olympic Committee, that decision meant something. I think one could argue that it eventually helped contribute to the Supreme Court approving gay marriage a few years later. Maybe he felt he could only do one brave case at a time.

For whatever reason, Judge Walker's "generalized grievance" decision meant that we had to take another trip to the Ninth Circuit to even get our case off the ground. The trip burned up nearly two more years.

CRYING AND COLBERT

At about the same time that Judge Walker abandoned our case, my marriage fell apart, also with little notice and as a complete surprise to me. After a vacation together in Thailand, my husband told me that he had fallen in love with someone else, revealing an affair that I had known nothing about. I felt disoriented and uncertain, as if the world had become a fun house with shifting floors and trapdoors. I alternated between being hurt, angry, confused, and sad. I got a glimpse of what my mother must have felt when something similar happened to her years before.

By summer 2010, I was in the midst of a strange moment, with my career soaring while my personal life was a wreck. Due to some smart work by our press director, Rebecca Jeschke, I ended up being invited to be a guest on the original Stephen Colbert show, called the *Colbert Report*, on Comedy Central. After a day spent crying on the cross-country flight, the makeup artists did wonders. I got to go "onto the internet" with Stephen via a green screen. Everyone there was nice, even though they could have made a laughingstock of me and EFF. I held it together for the hours of taping and then lost my composure in the limousine that the show had arranged to take me to the airport. I sobbed the whole six-hour flight home. When I finally got to our Noe Valley flat, I told my husband he needed to move out.

Yet with my personal life in tatters, my friends showed up again. That same group that took me to Death Valley in a bus after my hacker boyfriend and I broke up in the late 1990s had stayed close, even as they had themselves started settling down and having children. Our annual event, which started as a bit of a bacchanalia for bluegrass, rock, folk, and jam band fans, had grown into a family-filled community weekend.

It wasn't just the one party. We held regular events large and small, generally centered on music. A core set of my friends were in a band called Hot Buttered Rum. Others were in a band called ALO, and still others in bands called New Monsoon and JP Orbit. We saw them, plus other music, regularly. Once the news got out that my marriage was falling apart, these friends circled around me tightly. I was showered with offers of dinners, shows, hikes around the Bay, dog walks, trips to Jazz Fest in New Orleans, and more. One friend, Emma, even moved into my now-empty house. She made sure the fridge stayed full and watched endless hours of bad TV with me.

In December 2010, I was just slowly starting to feel alive again when an old connection showed up to the EFF holiday party with John. Patrick, who I had met long ago during the *Bernstein* case, was just back from a year spent in the Congo. Still involved in human rights and technology, Patrick had built a database of central African human rights abusers for the United Nations to help make sure that one hand of the giant bureaucracy didn't inadvertently support people who the other hand knew were bad actors. At the after-party in the bar of a fancy hotel, Patrick sat down and started telling stories, captivating all of us with what he called "there I was" tales from his adventures around the world. He was still just as compelling as he had been in the 1990s, but he had softened a bit around the edges too.

On a whim, a couple of weeks later, I asked him to dinner. Sitting in a little window in a restaurant looking out on Guerrero Street, we talked and talked. He was now single, and I told him the sad story of the breakup of my marriage, which was still fresh in my bones. In the car on the way home, he turned and asked me out.

I refused.

"I'm a mess, I'm afraid," I said. "I'm just not ready to date."

"We can go as slow as you need," he responded. "But I'm not taking no for an answer. I've had a thing for you since we met in the 1990s, and I suspect you feel the same. First I wasn't free, then you weren't free. If we're both finally available, I'm not going to let you slip away."

I was skeptical. I still literally had heartaches nearly every day. I was in mourning not just for my husband but also for the life I thought we were going to have. Giving up that vision of my own future was, in many ways, more difficult than losing my husband as a person.

Patrick was persistent, but not pushy. He was true to his word about going slow. And he was right that I had been intrigued by him as much as he by me when we first connected over cryptography all of those years ago. We started dating, first going on dog walks around San Francisco with the 150-pound black Newfoundland named Kodiak Bear that my now ex-husband and I had adopted after Cosmo passed away. Patrick had evolved into a war crimes investigator using data science as a tool. For us, this meant he was frequently away on trips that included meeting with local communities, testifying in trials, and helping to analyze evidence of human rights violations all over the world. I began introducing him to my big Bay Area community of friends, and taking him to music shows and festivals. Ever the geek, he used a piece of software called Mindmap to try to keep track of everyone. It was a challenge for an introvert, but he kept at it, and his devotion to me, to us, never wavered.

HEPTING AND *JEWEL* IN THE NINTH CIRCUIT

The Ninth Circuit hearings for both *Jewel* and *Hepting* occurred in late August 2011 in Seattle. That courthouse is art deco, built in the 1940s, so it was rectangular and far less ornate than the beaux arts San Francisco Ninth Circuit courthouse. By comparison, it felt more stale and staid. Kevin was arguing the appeal in *Jewel*, seeking to overturn Judge Walker's rotten decision dismissing our case as a "generalized grievance." That hearing was combined with our final stab at saving *Hepting*, which I argued in an attempt to attack Congress's creation of retroactive immunity for the telecommunications carriers.

A documentary filmmaker who I would later get to know well, Laura Poitras, attended the hearing. With the court's permission, she filmed pieces of the argument—including a shot of the back of my head. That shot, along with several minutes of Kevin's argument, ended up in her Academy award-winning documentary, *Citizen Four*.

I stood up to argue against the retroactive immunity that Congress had created to shelter the telecommunications companies. I gave it my best shot. As with most appellate arguments, I had prepared a short initial statement and an even shorter ending one, but otherwise had a set of recipe cards that carried citations and answers to the expected questions from the judges. I finished my initial presentation and then—silence. I waited a beat or two, but still nothing from the judges, who all seemed to be looking down or away from me. After a few more minutes, which felt like hours, Judge McKeon said to me, "Don't you have any more, Ms. Cohn?"

I stammered and almost muttered, "I thought you were going to ask me questions."

"Well, if that's all, you may sit down," Judge McKeon responded.

That was it. My face was burning, and the government attorney didn't really even bother to respond to the points I tried to make. It was obvious that the court wasn't going to revive the *Hepting* case, regardless of how unfair it was for the millions of AT&T customers who should have had the protection of settled law for their privacy. Apparently the companies could just run to Congress and avoid accountability after flagrantly ignoring the law and then lying about it for over seven years.

Kevin went next, and his argument went well. The judges were lively, including Judge Pregerson, who was still in Los Angeles and so appeared on a large screen above the other judges' heads. The contrast with my argument made it clear. The judges had chosen which case they wanted to succeed. I was happy for us—we only needed to win one of the cases that day—but also a bit wrecked by my own experience.

THREE BAGS FULL

I had three bags with me in Seattle that day: one full of the briefs and other documents I used to prepare for the nonexistent argument, and one with my suit—this one I purchased myself, but still had my mother approve. Those two bags would be carried back to San Francisco by my colleagues. The third was a smaller case that held large goggles, a bandana, some used cowboy boots, and a steampunk outfit.

The reason for the third case was my heart. Immediately after the Ninth Circuit hearing, I caught a plane to Reno, Nevada. After about five hours of sleep at a surreal casino hotel, and before daybreak the next morning, I climbed into a tiny puddle jumper to fly over the Black Rock Desert and into Burning Man to meet up with Patrick.

It's not really possible to capture the dislocation I felt shifting from a formal, staid courtroom (and baffling oral argument), through a loud, plinking casino, and into a tiny plane in the darkness just before dawn. But all of that cracked open as the sunrise brought yellows and pinks over the brown mountains, revealing the half-circle outline of Black Rock City with a large figure in the middle. I didn't really know what I was seeing yet, but as my plane approached the tiny landing strip, I saw little specs that turned into Patrick and John standing on the dusty ground, holding a third bike for me.

I was still in a daze, trying to process the day before, but this new reality sucked me in pretty quickly. Patrick and I were still moving slowly; I camped with some other folks rather than with him. Yet I knew that it was important for him to show me this world. Tons of my friends had been to Burning Man over the years. It was an event based in the Bay Area, and I even knew some of the founders and its main lawyer, Terry Gross, who had worked on an early EFF case. But the event had never interested me. It seemed a lot of expense and work to go all the way to a hostile environment just to party, especially when my friends and I already threw some epic parties each year. I also knew, though, that when you wanted to love someone who had a religion, every now and then you had to go to church. And for Patrick, like so many others, Burning Man was as close to church as it got.

Following him on a bike into the deep playa, we spotted amazing art, and heading toward it, then, often as not, climbed up on it. We hunkered down in dust storms, and stumbled into little bars and chill spots together. I started to see how we could navigate all of life together. He was even smarter than I had thought, but more than that, he was fun, silly, and open. I had come to the desert to see about my heart and now I was beginning to open to this intense man with his own giant heart. By the end of our few days together, I started falling in love.

BACK IN BUSINESS

The Ninth Circuit didn't make us wait long this time. During the holiday break in December 2011, just as Patrick and I were leaving an overnight campout spot in Big Basin near Santa Cruz, we received the two decisions. I pulled over to a small, rustic restaurant just off the highway where there was wifi to read them and draft our press release. First, as expected, the court dismissed *Hepting*. As we had hoped, however, it reversed the district court in *Jewel* and sent the case back down for reconsideration. By the time it got there, Judge Walker had retired, and after a small delay, we had a new Judge: Jeffrey White.[47]

We were back in business. About this time, Kevin left EFF, moved to DC, and joined the folks who were now our friends and collaborators at the Center for Democracy and Technology. Luckily, our longtime, outside pro bono counsel, Rick, stepped in to lead the case. Rick took over the leadership of the briefs and ever-growing pile of evidence, and our whole team decided together on strategy. I still wrangled resources, negotiated with the government about process, and helped write and edit most briefs. I still tended to draft most of our introductions.

In summer 2012, we filed cross motions for summary judgment. The government argued that the mountains of evidence we had gathered were still not enough to defeat the state secrets privilege. We maintained that the state secrets didn't apply and instead that the FISA law did, thereby allowing the court to decide if surveillance was legal. Despite losing each time they argued the state secrets privilege, the government persisted. We wanted a clear ruling that vindicated the FISA law paper over the state secrets rock.

As part of our presentation, we once again marshaled all the evidence that had been made public since the initial *New York Times* piece in 2005. We filed a declaration organized by my colleague Kurt Opsahl with 120 exhibits, including news reports, which together demonstrated just how much the public already knew about the mass spying programs. In all, it was multiple boxes of evidence. The hearing was held in December 2012, and after some supplemental briefing, we started another long wait for a decision.

WHERE ARE LAURA AND GLENN?

"Both Laura and Glenn are out of the country for some reason," Trevor Timm announced at the beginning of a Freedom of the Press Foundation board meeting held in the conference room at the EFF offices on Shotwell Street in early June 2013. He was referring to documentary filmmaker Laura Poitras and journalist Glenn Greenwald, two members of the board.

"Can't they just call in?" I asked, a bit annoyed. I was counsel to the organization, and worried we wouldn't have a quorum or the input of two critical voices.

"Apparently not," Trevor shrugged.

The Freedom of the Press Foundation was the brainchild of Trevor, who was still an EFF activist when he created it, although he soon left EFF to become its founding executive director. The organization was born in 2012 out of the nearly complete financial blockade of Wikileaks by major financial institutions like Visa and Mastercard. The blockade prevented people from donating to the organization using their credit cards, which was a major source of their income.

The financial blockade came after Wikileaks began publishing over 250,000 US State Department cables that it received from whistleblower and activist Chelsea Manning. Cables are a key way the State Department still communicates internally. These cables reflected—in both good and embarrassing ways—State Department diplomatic strategies, internal thinking, and even gossip about people and governments around the world.[48] At the time, it was the largest leak of government documents in US history. It created a firestorm of controversy, including about how poorly many of the cables reflected on State Department officials and the potential harm to the US strategic interests from their publication by Wikileaks.

The financial blockade seemed to be the result of intense pressure on the credit card companies by Senator Joseph Lieberman, who was chair of the Senate Homeland Security and Governmental Affairs Committee. The attack on credit card donations, the financial lifeline for so many nonprofits and independent journalists, concerned all of us. It especially enraged Barlow, who at one point wanted EFF to start taking donations on behalf of Wikileaks. I was not a fan of that idea and also knew it would not be something the rest of the EFF board would agree to, but I did spend a few days researching whether we could sue the government or senator for what is called "jawboning." I also talked the idea over with Wikileak's own lawyer, the legendary Michael Ratner of the Center for Constitutional Rights, who I'd worked with a bit on the *Bowoto* human rights case. Jawboning is when the government puts inappropriate pressure on companies to do things the government wants—here, to stop serving Wikileaks. The research didn't look promising, especially since despite the bluster, we didn't have direct evidence that the senator had threatened to use governmental power against the companies in any way if they didn't do what he wanted.

Trevor's idea for the Freedom of the Press Foundation aimed more broadly than just supporting Wikileaks, though, in a clever way. It was to create a nonprofit dedicated to supporting the increasing number of independent journalists that were emerging online, particularly as traditional media shrank. It would do that by running crowdfunding campaigns for a slate of independent media, taking credit card donations for the campaigns, and donating the proceeds to those media. Wikileaks was one of the media beneficiaries, but not the only one.

Trevor's strategy was to demonstrate that Wikileaks was doing the same thing that other journalists do: giving the public useful and important information about what the government is up to. The Freedom of the Press Foundation strategy essentially dared Senator Lieberman or other would-be government censors to censor a slate of media rather than just one outlet. Barlow loved the bigger strategy and signed on to help. I did too. I knew it was important to find funding mechanisms and a fearless voice for the independent journalism that the internet made possible, and I also suspected that Trevor's vision would require some careful lawyering.

The inaugural Freedom of the Press Foundation board of directors was impressive. Along with Barlow, Laura, and Glenn, the board included Daniel Ellsberg, Josh Stearns, Boing Boing blogger Xeni Jardin, and movie star and human rights activist John Cusack. It also included EFF activism director Rainey Reitman, who had immediately jumped in. One of our staff technologists, Micah Lee, was the organization's first chief technology officer and was key to getting the group off the ground.

Ellsberg was an especially critical board member, recruited by Barlow. He had leaked the Pentagon Papers to *The New York Times* and *The Washington Post* in 1971, and that act was one of the pivotal catalysts for ending the Vietnam War.[49] President Nixon had famously called Ellsberg "the most dangerous man in America," and he was still as smart and fearless when he joined the board over forty years later. Ellsberg taught me and the rest of us a tremendous amount about what it's like to be an insider in governmental decision-making, especially around national security and foreign policy issues, and all the ways in which our national approach to governmental secrecy breeds hubris, and ultimately, tragic oversights and mistakes. He was also big fan of EFF's NSA spying cases, which made me proud.

In the end, enough other board members attended the meeting in early June 2013 to allow us to move forward with the day's agenda, and I largely forgot about my moment of frustration with Laura and Glenn for being absent.

THIS IS WHAT IT WOULD LOOK LIKE, RIGHT?

That moment reemerged for me a few days later, though, on June 6. I was sitting in the conference room in EFF's new offices on Eddy Street in San Francisco's Tenderloin district, interviewing a candidate for a human resources position, when Trevor knocked on the conference room's glass door.

"What's going on?" I asked, a bit flustered to be pulled out of the interview.

"You need to come here. This is really important. *The Guardian* just published a leaked order requiring Verizon to turn over all of its telephone records to the NSA."

I made a quick excuse and followed Trevor into his office. He showed me the order. Kevin, who had left EFF for a position at the Center for Democracy and Technology in Washington, DC, the year before, just happened to be visiting that day. I pulled him into the office too.

"This looks like what it would look like, right?" I asked him, referring to the mass telephone records collection that we had alleged in both *Hepting* and *Jewel*.

"I think so," he answered, both of us mulling it over and trying to keep our excitement at bay.

Soon Lee along with Corynne McSherry, Mark Rumold, Kurt Opsahl, and a few other EFF lawyers crowded into Trevor's office as we pored over the news articles. The byline on *The Guardian* article was Glenn Greenwald. Mystery solved. We soon learned that Laura had gone with Glenn to Hong Kong, along with another reporter, to meet a new NSA whistleblower, who gave them the mass telephone records collection order. The whistleblower had approached Laura in part because she knew how to use PGP, the encryption program that had gotten Phil Zimmermann investigated in the 1990s. While difficult to use, PGP was still widely relied on even in the late 2000s. The whistleblower had first approached Glenn, but he couldn't master PGP sufficiently to communicate securely with it.

We were overjoyed. We were right: the government and telecommunications companies had been lying about the mass telephone records program. And we suspected that meant they were lying about the rest of it too.

RED EFF STICKER ON A LAPTOP

A few days later, on June 9, I had just landed at Dulles Airport in Washington, DC, when the phone in my pocket went ding, ding, ding, ding with the sound of incoming texts and voicemails. I was mortified but my hands were full, so I just tried to look apologetic to the other folks waiting to disembark.

Once I got into the terminal, I stepped out of the flow of passengers and looked at my phone. The dings were messages from *The Washington Post, The New York Times, The Guardian, Los Angeles Times, Chicago Tribune,* and on and on. I pulled up the news and there was a photo of a youngish-looking guy sitting behind a laptop with a big red EFF sticker across it. He was the person who had given Glenn and Laura the Verizon order. His name was Edward Snowden.

All the reporters calling and texting wanted to know the same thing: Who was this guy and how did EFF know him? I wanted to know as well.

Before I responded to any of them, I called our membership director, Aaron Jue. Aaron answered immediately, and I asked him to check our membership database to see if this Snowden guy was a donor or otherwise associated with us. Next, I conferenced in Shari, our executive director, who also had access to EFF's member database.

"We don't know him," Aaron assured me. "At least as far as I can tell."

The three of us discussed how our sticker might have ended up on this whistleblower's computer. We knew that our EFF swag was well-known and loved by hackers and geeks of all kinds. Thanks to Hugh, our longtime art director, we have a style that was—and still is—instantly recognizable.

People pick up EFF stickers in many ways. They are available as part of joining EFF online, but we also have them at our tables at technology and security conferences, where people can donate in cash without providing their names. We even knew some folks who regularly pick up a bunch of our stickers and other materials to redistribute at events where our staffers aren't even present. So it wasn't strange that someone who we didn't know had an EFF sticker.

But even if we had known, we wouldn't have shared that information with the press. We care about privacy, and that means we fiercely guard the names of our members. We knew we had supporters who worked at the NSA, Department of Justice, major technology companies, and other entities that we tangled with regularly. We suspected we had many members who wouldn't want their bosses, much less the entire readership of *The New York Times* or *The Washington Post,* to know that they had donated to us. EFF had even gone to court to protect the names of our donors when a patent troll who claimed a patent on podcasting sought to subpoena them. We succeeded in getting the judge to toss out the request on privacy grounds. So while I wanted to know if this guy Snowden was an EFF member, I wasn't about to tell the reporters if he was.

Ultimately we learned that Snowden got our sticker and an EFF black hoodie at an event in Hawaii where none of us were present. It was at a Cryptoparty, where people gather to teach each other how to use encryption and share keys in person to make starting to use tools like PGP a bit easier. Apparently another attendee had brought a bunch of EFF swag. But we knew none of that yet.

We were all a bit panicked. This person had done something incredibly courageous and important, but we knew from past experience that the people who decide to stand up against powerful companies and governments are often themselves not the best standard-bearers for their cause. Our fears ranged widely: Was this a scammer or someone who actually had real information? What were his motives? Had he committed any serious crimes? Just who was he and why did he have an EFF sticker?

Once we had caucused and come up with an answer for them, I called the reporters back.[50] I did my best to reassure them that we were not part of the leaks and didn't have any foreknowledge about them. I avoided the issue of EFF membership as best I could, but I did confirm that I personally didn't know Snowden, which was true.

I'd later learn that it wasn't quite true that no one at EFF knew anything about the leaks. Micah Lee, who was one of EFF's technologists at the time and also served as the chief technical officer of the Freedom of the Press Foundation, had communicated with Snowden and helped to connect him with Laura. Micah had even helped Snowden try to build a website where he considered publishing a manifesto and a petition for supporters to sign. Micah did not tell me (or anyone else at EFF) about this until long afterward.[51] As general counsel to EFF as well as lead counsel in the NSA cases, it was, to put it mildly, something I would have liked to have known. In the end Snowden decided against publishing the website, which was both the right decision and a great relief when Micah finally told me the whole story.

We later discovered that Snowden was a lovely person, who knew what he was doing and acted out of the best of reasons: to make sure that the

US people knew what was being done in their name and counter the flat-out lying by the NSA.

Most important, Snowden was angered by the false testimony of James Clapper to the Senate Intelligence Committee in March 2013. Senator Wyden had famously asked Clapper, "Does the NSA collect any type of data at all on millions or hundreds of millions of Americans?"

"No, sir," Clapper replied. "Not wittingly."

Of course, Snowden knew this was a lie, as we did watching the hearing on C-SPAN from our offices. Later Clapper would say that he hadn't actually lied to Congress because all the congresspersons at the hearing knew the truth already, thanks to the classified briefings they had received. But regardless, Clapper wasn't just talking to Congress in that televised hearing. He was talking to the American people.

DO YOU HAVE STANDING YET?

I wondered if we should offer to become Snowden's lawyers, but quickly rejected the idea. First, it became clear that Snowden's goal was not to be in the spotlight but instead help us stop the spying. We felt it would undermine his goals if we shifted our attention from using the information to win the case to defending him in the criminal case the government was surely going to be bringing against him.

Additionally, as it was with Mark, we knew it would be awkward and potentially impossible for us to represent both Snowden and our clients—AT&T customers whose communications were being swept up by the programs that Snowden had confirmed. In our case, Snowden was a key witness, and it is tricky for a lawyer to represent both a witness and party since their interests can often diverge.

We also saw that Snowden was immediately in good legal hands. Ben Wizner at the ACLU had taken on the representation of Snowden, and we felt that this was a better fit anyway. The ACLU was suing over mass spying too, but it was a much bigger organization, and if necessary, could compartmentalize the representations.

My first call with Ben made clear that Snowden had been watching our cases closely. "He wants me to ask you if you have standing yet," Ben said, with a smile I could hear through the line.

"Well, if we don't now, I'm not sure how we ever will," I answered. "Please give him our heartfelt thanks."

That message made it clear that Ed was not only watching our work but also understood what was going on in the courts. Even though we had Mark's direct evidence and testimony, and tons of newspaper articles and similar information, we continued to struggle with the huge obstacle posed by the government's claims that the state secret privilege should require the case to be immediately dismissed. Snowden reinvigorated us.

With each new revelation, we responded to the press and pushed for more. EFF's Freedom of Information Act work at that time was crucial, and the public pressure led the Obama administration to create a website, unironically named ICOnTheRecord, standing for "Intelligence Community on the Record," but that we joked could be read as "I Con the Record," just as Clapper had tried to. But despite the name, the administration started publishing information and reports about the mass spying. The pressure also helped open up the FISA court, and an EFF case is the first one listed on the public docket initially made available in April 2014.[52]

A couple of years later, I flew to Moscow to meet Snowden in person (fig. 2.6). I got to spend a couple days in a hotel room with one of the only other people in the world as focused as I am on stopping the NSA's mass spying. I felt at home with him immediately; he was one of ours. Ed had a hacker's approach to the world, a huge conscience, and was deeply, deeply smart and thoughtful. If I didn't know better, I might have thought he was one of the crew who came to that first *Bernstein* hearing long ago. But of course, he didn't; he was too young, and instead he had joined the military and become a government agent—a very different path than the hackers who helped me defeat the NSA in the 1990s.

Fortified by trays from room service, we talked about mass spying as well as the information he had found and made public. He helped me understand some of the documents that he had shared and answered some questions about the different vantage point he had from the government's side of the mass spying. His view into it was different from Mark's on AT&T's side, or our telecommunication network experts Brian Reid and J. Scott Marcus. We also talked through how things had likely changed between Mark's documents in 2005 and what Ed had found several years later. Ed confirmed a story I'd been told too: that he had used

Figure 2.6 With Edward Snowden in Russia, courtesy of Parker Higgins.

my PGP key, which was publicly available on EFF's website, as the sample key when he tried, unsuccessfully, to teach Glenn how to encrypt conversations. That encryption connection made me weirdly proud.

FIRST UNITARIAN CHURCH CASE

"David, I have the ultimate lure to get you to come to EFF: let's use the Snowden mass telephone records collection evidence to extend the right to association and assembly." I was sitting in my car in a parking garage near my dentist's office, making the best pitch I could to lure one of the nation's leading First Amendment attorneys, David Greene, into joining EFF.

"You made these leaks happen on purpose just to get me to take the job, didn't you, Cindy," he joked in response. I smiled. I knew we had him. David would mark the fourteenth attorney on our growing team, and he'd take on the role of civil liberties director.

The initial Verizon order published by the press from Snowden confirmed the mass telephone record collection we had been suing over since 2006. This was useful for the *Jewel* case, but it also gave us a chance to spotlight one of the other constitutional problems with the program—one that highlights the need to protect the privacy of metadata under the First Amendment, in addition to the Fourth. The records of our telephone calls, especially collected and analyzed over time, reveal a broad window into our associations. That's why the government does it. It uses who talks to who to map out the associations of its targets.

But this is also why the Constitution has always limited the government's ability to track our associations. In the words of the Supreme Court in the 1950s, when it rejected Alabama's attempts to make the NAACP provide its membership lists, collecting information about the associations of people in the United States "may induce members to withdraw from the association and dissuade others from joining it because of fear of exposure of their beliefs shown through their associations and of the consequences of their exposure."[53] In other words, privacy is important for the First Amendment protected right to hold dissenting views and organize.

In addition to frightening people out of organizing, the government's mass collection and analysis of our telephone records is what lawyers call "overbroad," meaning that it almost inevitably sweeps up a huge number of people who have nothing to do with the issues the government is investigating, but who happen to talk to people who talk to people who the government is targeting. So, for instance, if someone being targeted by the government orders a pizza, everyone else who orders a pizza from that same restaurant is just two "hops" away from a target. After the Snowden leaks, the NSA had admitted that it used the mass telephone records collection to track three "hops" away from all of its targets, which made the overbreadth problem much, much worse.

We had raised these First Amendment arguments in *Hepting* and *Jewel*, but they weren't the centerpiece of either case. Both focused instead on the Fourth Amendment and FISA. Now we wanted to put the First Amendment into the spotlight.

Even before I convinced David to join us, we had started putting together a massive, strange bedfellows' collection of plaintiffs—everyone from the First Unitarian Church of Los Angeles to Calguns, a California gun ownership organization, to People for the American Way, to Students for a Sensible Drug Policy. Our point was that regardless of your political or religious beliefs, everyone who works to make change needs protection from the government tracking their associations. The case, filed on one of David's first days with us, was called *First Unitarian Church of Los Angeles v. NSA*.

One of our longtime pro bono friends, Tom Moore, took the leading role in this one. I had met Tom in the hallway of the Santa Clara county courthouse in 2000, before I had even joined EFF. He and I were both there to see an oral argument in an early EFF case arising out of copyright law. Tom worked at a commercial Palo Alto law firm, but it was clear that his heart was with the hackers and developers who were using the internet to share information and ideas. Like Rick Wiebe and Jim Tyre, Tom became an irreplaceable part of most of our legal cases. Tom and I were generally the ones who wrote the soaring prose that others would sometimes have to gently bring back down to earth. But there's no doubt that he was one of the reasons we developed a reputation for excellence.

Yet as soon as we filed the case, we ran into a brick wall in the form of Judge White. The judge simply refused to hear the case. I have no good explanation for this; judges should not be able to simply veto a case by refusing to decide it, even in the context of national security. Still, that's what ultimately happened, every step of the way the court would find a reason to further delay, leaving us in the position of seeking a preliminary injunction for over a decade. This, to me, is a prime example of how national security warps the judicial process, and with it our ability to actually get legal protection for our rights.

Courts are supposed to be one of the ways that the law becomes real—that rights have remedies and aren't just paper protections. But over time I've seen that cases like *Bernstein*, where national security arguments are carefully evaluated and aren't allowed to become governmental talismans, are not the norm. Far too often national security undermines or transforms judicial processes beyond recognition. In *First Unitarian*, we were denied even a single day in court, and our clients were therefore denied even basic consideration of their rights. While the court hid behind various reasons for delay, in the end I can only ascribe this approach to judicial cowardice. We all deserve better.

A RALLY, VIDEO, AND BLIMP

While the *First Unitarian* case was extremely disappointing, we didn't limit our efforts to the courts after the Snowden revelations came out.

Instead, this became an opportunity for EFF to lead on an issue nationally, using our somewhat new activism team in addition to our lawyers. Trying to make the most out of the intense public outrage spurred by the revelations, I worked closely with EFF's activism director, Rainey Reitman.

Rainey put together a petition asking for the end of the spying, but it was important to me that the petition have real teeth and align with our court strategy. I asked that the petition include three demands:

1. a congressional investigation to shed light on exactly what the NSA was doing.
2. reform of federal surveillance law, specifically section 215 of the Patriot Act, section 702 of the Foreign Intelligence Surveillance Act, and the state secrets privilege
3. that the public officials who were responsible for hiding the mass surveillance be held accountable for their actions[54]

Under Rainey's skillful leadership, we marshaled over a hundred organizations, individuals, and businesses from a wide range of perspectives to join our coalition, including Reddit, Color of Change, Competitive Enterprise Institute, Council on American-Islamic Relations, Free Press, ACLU, Fight for the Future, CREDO Mobile, Demand Progress, Mozilla, and many others.[55] It was the biggest activist-focused group we had ever led.

Our advocacy tools had also increased in sophistication over the years. Every time someone added their name to our petition, we would send a copy of our demands to their representatives in Congress from them. In addition, the coalition set up a dedicated phone number that would connect anyone in the United States to their member of Congress so they could demand an end to mass surveillance. Within just a few weeks, we had over half a million signers onto our campaign—including luminaries like Sir Tim Berners-Lee, the inventor of the World Wide Web, and internationally renowned artist Ai Weiwei.

We decided to host a rally in Washington, DC, on this issue. We chose the anniversary of the Patriot Act being signed into law as our date. To help spread the word about our rally, longtime EFF friend and filmmaker Brian Knappenberger produced a celebrity video about NSA surveillance featuring actors like Maggie Gyllenhaal and John Cusack, director

Figure 2.7 Stop Watching Us protest by S L O W K I N G / licensed under GFDL v1.2 (https://www.gnu.org/licenses/old-licenses/fdl-1.2.html).

Oliver Stone, Representative John Conyers, and a range of whistleblowers, including Daniel Ellsberg, Kirk Wiebe, and Mark Klein. I was in that video too, and it was exciting to see my calls for better oversight of the NSA echoed by such famous voices. The video went viral and shot past one million YouTube views within a few days.

While I wasn't able to attend, the DC rally built even more public attention. We created art that included massive banners with the entire First and Fourth Amendments written out in large print. Those banners and many others were carried by a crowd of thousands through the streets of DC (fig. 2.7), where boxes of our petitions were delivered to members of Congress. A band called YACHT wrote a song about mass surveillance and played it at our rally. The entire day was live streamed over C-SPAN.

We hosted, along with our colleagues at Public Knowledge and others in the coalition, a lobby day where EFF representatives as well as members of our coalition met with members of Congress and their aides to urge them to reform the NSA through a bill called the USA Freedom Act. It was much bigger than our sad attempt to get Congress to pay attention to Mark and reject retroactive immunity five years earlier.

But even with huge momentum, passing national security reforms in Congress is no easy feat. Though we started with strong legislative language that promised to rein in mass surveillance, negotiations in Congress proved difficult as the national security forces fought back, mainly behind the scenes. We were able to fend off many attempts to water down and undermine the reforms, but not all of them. The process dragged on for months, with the EFF activism and legislative teams often working around the clock. We knew that the government had the ability to give secret briefings to members of Congress that we could not counter.

We also knew that we would have a hard fight in the Senate, so we did something EFF had never done before: we created a scorecard for every member of Congress. We graded them on how they had voted in support of our NSA reform provisions. While we didn't cross the line to electioneering, we made it clear who had backed strong reforms and who had only pushed for mediocre reforms. For senators still waiting to vote, we put a "?" as their grade.

Launching our scorecard involved some creative activism too: we flew a blimp over a newish Utah-based NSA data center, which had been built in part to store all the additional data that the NSA was collecting due to the mass surveillance programs (fig. 2.8). EFF didn't have a blimp of our own, but our friends and *First Unitarian* case clients at Greenpeace agreed to let us use their blimp—which they called an airship—in a joint action against NSA spying. Hugh, our art director, designed a gorgeous banner for the side of the blimp, and Brian Knappenberger documented everything for a short video about the flight. In addition to Greenpeace, we were joined by the Tenth Amendment Center, a more libertarian group that was strongly opposed to NSA surveillance. By having groups from across the political spectrum involved in the action, we wanted to show that NSA reform was a strongly bipartisan issue. EFF activist Parker Higgins drove to Utah to fly with our coalition partners over the NSA data center.

The Snowden leaks had pushed the Obama administration to confirm many details about the mass spying programs, including publishing key FISA court rulings since 2008 authorizing pieces of the mass spying. Faced with sustained public pressure and news attention, President Obama empowered

Figure 2.8 Blimp over NSA facility in Utah / licensed under CC BY 4.0 (https://creativecommons.org/licenses/by/4.0).

the Privacy and Civil Liberties Oversight Board, and created President Obama's Review Group on Intelligence and Communications Technology, a five-person panel.[56] These two panels, both handpicked by the president, were allowed to investigate several of the programs and publish important information about them, including a blockbuster Privacy and Civil Liberties Oversight Board report that confirmed that the mass telephone records program had only the most marginal impact on our national security. As it turned out, in each of the cases that the government initially claimed were helped because of the program—about twelve of them—the telephone records collection wasn't useful. The one remaining case didn't even involve a threat inside the United States. It involved some money illegally sent to a banned rebel group in Sudan.

Ultimately the oversight board's report, along with our extensive advocacy campaign and a tremendous ACLU victory in the New York federal courts against the telephone records portion of the spying—before judges who were less afraid than Judge White to actually consider the claims—helped lead Congress in 2014 to dramatically restructure the program.

There's another book to be written about the lobbying for this law. It was messy, and in the end, EFF's lobbying team differed in priorities from many of our otherwise close collaborators. This included the small, progressive telecommunications company CREDO, which caused some complications since, as you'll see in the next section, CREDO was secretly our client during this time. There were hard feelings all around, which is understandable when so much is at stake. Our team at EFF agreed that the final version of the USA FREEDOM Act meant far less change than was necessary. We had even withdrawn our support for it after the ACLU case victory in an effort to press for more, but we were not successful. On the plus side, though, the new law was the first real congressional scaling back of post-9/11 surveillance. It stopped the flat-out mass collection of telephone records of millions of people domestically, and beefed up the FISA court, transparency, and congressional oversight.

Also about that time, we learned that the mass internet records collection we had sued over had been stopped in 2011, reportedly due to "interagency review," but I suspect because of pressure from Senator Wyden and others on the Senate Select Committee on Intelligence.[57]

FIGHTING THE "EMPEROR DOES HAVE CLOTHES" STRATEGY

Yet in the courtroom in our *Jewel v. NSA* case, the government still pretended that the programs were secret—so secret that the state secrets privilege required the courts to stay out. It was maddening.

As the reform efforts and government admissions continued, it gradually became clear that the remaining "secret" the government claimed it needed to protect was not a secret at all: whether AT&T was participating in the Upstream program. There are only two major telecommunications carriers in the United States: AT&T and Verizon. It's a duopoly. The failure of either of the companies to participate would render the program largely, if not entirely, ineffective. And it's no secret that the NSA's goal was to "collect it all." This was even a slogan from one of the internal NSA slides that Snowden revealed in 2013.[58] The government still maintained in court filings, however, that it would harm national security to confirm what everyone knew: that there is no way to run any of the mass surveillance programs it now admitted it was running without involving AT&T and Verizon.

Back in the district court in *Jewel*, the case finally seemed to be on track. In July 2013, just after the Snowden revelations started, Judge White rejected the government's next attempt to dismiss the case under the "state secrets" argument.[59] The judge ruled that the procedures of FISA allowed the case to proceed and not be dismissed, and any properly classified details can be handled inside the case using various procedures to protect them from public disclosure, including FISA section 1806(f). This ruling marked yet another time that the court agreed with us that the case could proceed despite the government's secrecy claims.

We felt vindicated, and in an effort to move the case forward after five years on *Jewel* (plus two on *Hepting*), we decided to focus on the Upstream claim and see if we could bring at least part of the case to a conclusion. We wanted to convince the court that the government tapping into the internet backbone and making copies of all the traffic is a digital version of a general warrant. We prepared a motion for partial summary judgment on whether the Upstream collection violated the Fourth Amendment.[60]

FLUSHING THE EVIDENCE

In March 2014, while we were waiting for that motion to be decided, we learned something that flabbergasted us: the government had been regularly destroying much the information it had collected using the mass surveillance. This was in direct violation of a preservation order issued by the judge way back in 2008, at the beginning of *Jewel*, which itself had extended one we had put into place in 2006 when we started *Hepting*. If this was the case, the government was doing something lawyers call spoliation: destroying evidence that we needed to prove that our clients' communications had been collected in the first place.

We were furious, and the revelation created quite a fire drill. We filed emergency motions and ran to Judge White's courtroom in downtown Oakland multiple times, asking the court to order the government to preserve the evidence. It was a strange position to be in. We didn't think the government should have grabbed communications and records off the internet backbone at all, and here we were asking the court to require the government to keep them. But if they were flushing the evidence, even as they continued to deny that they had ever had it, we wouldn't be able to meet our burden of proof that the surveillance of our clients had actually happened.

Figure 2.9 Editorial cartoon about evidence destruction in NSA spying cases, *Recorder* (San Francisco), March 2014. Diego Radzinsch / © 2025 ALM Global Properties, LLC.

Once caught, the government attorneys shifted their story. They first said that the FISA court had required them to destroy the evidence. Based on this assertion, the local legal newspaper, *The Recorder*, ran an editorial cartoon showing me arguing in front of Judge White while, in the back room, the government flushed papers down a toilet under the watchful eye of the FISA court (fig. 2.9).

That didn't fly. In a nearly unprecedented move, the secret FISA court issued a public ruling saying it had not, in fact, required the government to destroy the records of its collection.

The government next contended that the protective order didn't really apply. That was ridiculous; whether the government was collecting our clients' information was the central question in the case from the beginning. Judge White was not pleased with that argument, and he promptly granted and then confirmed a temporary restraining order in spring 2014 requiring the government to preserve the data it had collected under the challenged programs.[61]

We felt vindicated and hoped this fight would help light a fire under Judge White to move the case forward. One argument that the government made we actually agreed with—that at this point, six years into the *Jewel* case (plus *Hepting* before that), the government had to preserve so much data from its mass collection programs that it was hard to handle and store. The answer, of course, was to let us do the actual fact-finding, require the government to answer straightforward questions about what it was doing, and then move the case to a trial or other final decision. It wasn't to continue to delay and deny while they just flushed the evidence in the back room.

WANT MY OLD JOB AGAIN?

In September 2014, Shari asked me into her office on the first floor of EFF's new offices in the Tenderloin. We were fifty-nine people strong, and the place had started to feel more like a real organization and less like a ragtag team, although we still welcomed characters. At one point, one of our system administrators made a little sticker that said "Keep EFF Weird," and it seemed like our unofficial motto. We had always had a steady stream of legal interns spending a semester or summer with us, so by 2014 we had a large extended community of lawyers who had interned at EFF and were now out in the world.

In late 2013, we moved from the brick building on Shotwell Street into a much bigger, sleet-gray building on Eddy Street that had been the offices of the San Francisco chapter of Planned Parenthood. The chapter, an independent franchise from the national organization, had gone into bankruptcy, apparently quite abruptly. When the realtors showed the building to us for the first time, there were still papers on desks, examining tables in rooms, and lunches in the fridge. It was eerie and a bit creepy, like the place had been frozen in time. We bought it out of bankruptcy and spent about a year remodeling—turning the exam rooms into offices and donating all the medical equipment.

By 2014, we were moved and settled. I entered Shari's office on the first floor completely unaware of how she was about to change my life.

"Do you want my job, again," she said, with a smile.

"Whaaa . . . ," I stammered.

"I'm going to leave EFF. My husband has a new job in Seattle, and we're moving. He moved from DC to allow me to join EFF in San Francisco, so now it's my turn. What do you say?"

"I need to think about it. I already have the best job in the world."

"Yes, but you're ready, and EFF needs you," she said in her always sunny, confident tone.

Once again I thought it through, including by consulting with many friends. At a music festival in the Sierras, I pulled a few people into a friend's RV for a little impromptu pro and con session. I also heard from a couple of EFFers who suspected that Shari was planning to leave. They asked me to step up to the executive director position so that we could keep the organization moving on the path it was on. I knew the job would take me away from the briefs, arguments, and majestic courthouse scenes. But I wanted to support my colleagues and build further on what we had already created.

Ultimately I decided to do it, and we started the process of getting approval from the board and making the necessary adjustments inside the organization so that the transition could formally happen in April 2015. My first decision was to ask my colleague Kurt Opsahl to take my previous role as general counsel as well as serve as deputy director to help me handle the administrative and leadership load. Kurt was the kind of lawyer who could dig deep into any problem, and we trusted each other's judgment. He was as nervous as I was, but he readily agreed to take this leap alongside me.

My second decision was to ask our lead intellectual property lawyer, Corynne McSherry, to take on my old job as the legal director. Corynne had strong writing skills and even stronger instincts about EFF's work. I knew she'd be a great leader of the lawyers and bring some fresh energy to the work. When she gave me her answer the next day, she offered the best vindication of all that we'd done to build up the organization: "I thought about it and realized that when someone asks you to be the legal director of EFF, you say yes."

REVERSAL OF FORTUNE

In the *Jewel* case, despite the flurry around the issue of evidence destruction, there was no fire under Judge White. Instead, he poured cold water on our case in February 2015. He denied our motion for partial summary judgment on the Fourth Amendment claims against the Upstream program and granted the government's motion for summary judgment on the state secrets privilege.[62]

The ruling was confusing and infuriating. While he didn't admit it, Judge White implicitly reversed both his own 2013 ruling and Judge Walker's earlier 2006 rulings that the FISA statute section 1806(f) preempted the state secrets privilege. Judge White now decided that the state secrets privilege *did* prevent us from making any further inquiry into the details of the Upstream process sufficient to allow us to prove that our clients had been individually impacted by the mass spying. He also held that the state secrets privilege would impact future governmental defenses, although he didn't say how nor even say what those defenses might be.

Moreover, he cryptically noted that he had reviewed some classified information submitted by the government and that the operational details of how the program worked that we had presented were "substantially inaccurate." He gave no hint about how those inaccuracies could impact our claims.

During the entire case, all the way back to my first argument before Judge Walker, we had maintained that we didn't need to know most of the operational details about the program. All we needed to know was whether our clients' communications had been accessed by the government. How that occurred, what happened after that, or how the government decided which of them it wanted to keep and which to discard were all legally irrelevant. It was a dragnet from that moment, and dragnets violated both the Fourth Amendment and FISA. That meant that even if we weren't quite right about all the specifics of how the access happened or what happened afterward, that shouldn't block our claims. In fact, we were almost certain that the specifics of how the surveillance happened had changed since Mark knocked on our door nine years earlier, just given the advances in technology. But if the government was still doing the same basic copying and collection of our clients' communications, even if it wasn't ultimately keeping them, the claims should still stand.

In short, the judge pulled a 180-degree turnaround, rejecting multiple decisions by him and Judge Walker since 2006. And he did so without even truly acknowledging it.

The only saving grace was that Judge White did certify his ruling for immediate appellate review. We were hopeful that the Ninth Circuit would quickly reverse him.[63]

DOES THIS MEAN WE WON'T HAVE TO TANGLE WITH YOU ANYMORE?

In spring 2015, I was getting ready to step into the executive director role. I'd put together my team, and the board had agreed.

Also, by this time the internet was deeply ingrained in people's everyday lives. Worldwide more than 2.8 billion people were online, or around 39 percent of the world's population, up from 0.6 percent in 1995.[64] Mobile surpassed even that, with 73 percent penetration globally. Facebook had already peaked, with younger users starting to turn to other social media services. WhatsApp was broadly used, especially around the world, for encrypted, secure messaging. Services like Airbnb and Twitter were very active. The world was starting to worry about data breaches, and China had developed its own set of internet services.

Before I took over as executive director, though, I had an oral argument to do in Washington, DC. EFF had participated as amicus in many of the other cases against the mass surveillance, including several filed after the Snowden revelations. In one case, called *Klayman v. AT&T*, which had been victorious in the district court, I had been granted leave to argue on behalf of EFF and the ACLU in the hearing before the DC Circuit court.[65]

The hallway outside the hearing was packed with lawyers. But in the fray, I saw some of the Justice Department lawyers who were on the other side of the *Jewel* and *Hepting* cases, and who, by now, I knew quite well. They confirmed what I had suspected: that my favorite opposing counsel, Tony, had been promoted and wouldn't be working on the cases any longer. Then they had a question for me: "We heard that you are moving into the executive director role at EFF. Congratulations! Does this mean that you won't be handling the *Jewel* case anymore?"

"Well, no. I won't be as focused on it, but you won't be getting rid of me that easily," I smiled.

"That's too bad," they smiled back. "We were looking forward to not having to tangle with you anymore." I knew they meant it as a compliment. It may have been the best compliment that they could ever have given me.

DISCOVERY ALLOWED BUT THEN THWARTED

In October 2015, we were back at the Ninth Circuit, this time in Pasadena, California. We could tell from the first moment that Rick stood up to argue for us that the court was going to reject our strategy of trying to pull out the easiest part of the case to be decided first. The government contended that an appeal was premature, and sadly, it was clear that our Ninth Circuit judges—McKeon, Hawkins and now Graber—agreed. No amount of pointing out how unfair that was to our clients was going to change their minds.

We saw a glimmer of light at the end of Rick's presentation. Judge McKeon, who had been on the appellate panels hearing our case since *Hepting* in 2007, asked why the case had not progressed since they had last seen it in 2011? Why had there not been any fact-finding or discovery? Why were we still on the starting blocks?

Rick answered, correctly, that Judge White in the district court had forbidden us from actually asking any questions of the government or conducting any of the normal kinds of discovery that happens in other court cases. Judge McKeon seemed puzzled, and we hoped that this, finally, would spur Judge White to get the case moving.

It did.

After eight years and a soft rebuke from the Ninth Circuit, in February 2016, Judge White finally lifted the stay on discovery. Nominally, this should have let us require the NSA to at least confirm that our public evidence was authentic. On the one hand, it was frustrating as a litigator to have to wait eight years to get to do what every other litigation did as a matter of course, usually within two or three months from filing a complaint. On the other hand, this was the first time anyone was allowed to even try to gather factual evidence from the NSA in a case involving the agency's warrantless surveillance. Sometimes you are both discouraged and making history at the same time.

We had to think carefully about how to move forward. We decided to limit our requests to what are called interrogatories and requests for admission—written questions that require written answers—rather than the full panoply of discovery tools like depositions and demands for documents that lawyers can use in ordinary cases. We wanted to make it easy for the court and have a clear record of what we had asked for, tied specifically to the claims in the complaint. We knew that the government would allege that we were trying to use the litigation to bring more information to the public, and that Judge White wouldn't like that. Interrogatories and requests for admission helped protect us while demonstrating that we were only asking for information that was directly needed to confirm the news reports and other widely publicly known information we had gathered.

We shouldn't have needed to get that confirmation or authentication. The government could have simply acknowledged what the whole world knew: that from about 2002, it had been collecting phone records and metadata, and tapping into AT&T's part of the internet backbone on a massive scale that swept up millions of innocent people domestically as well as around the world. From my first conversation with Judge Walker in 2006, through to the Ninth Circuit and beyond, we had maintained that legally, the government's initial collection of our information violated the law. We never needed to show what happened to our communications and records after that initial seizure under the FISA statute or most of the other legal claims we were bringing. We didn't need to know exactly how it was done but instead confirm that it was being done, which just wasn't a secret.

That confirmation wouldn't entirely win the constitutional part of the case, but it should win on some of the FISA claims. Under the Fourth Amendment, there was a requirement that a government's demand for information be "reasonable," and that might have required a bit more context and information about what the government was doing as well as why. But we felt we could meet that standard with the information that had already been publicly revealed by the various whistleblowers and news reports, even without requiring the government to provide any new information.

After all, our goal was to get the court to rule that if you are collecting nearly everyone's communications on the way to finding your suspects or targets, that was always "unreasonable." Or in terms that James Otis and John Adams would understand, that mass collection was a "general warrant" and no more acceptable in the digital world than it was in colonial times.

Before we could even get to that argument, however, we simply wanted the government to confirm facts that had long been known, discussed, and dissected both in the United States and around the world.

To no avail.

The government strategy turned to delay and stonewalling. We were forced to make multiple motions just to get a response to our simple written questions, each tied to an allegation in our complaint. And for reasons I'll never understand, Judge White allowed the government to get away with it.[66] He even allowed it to refuse to confirm or deny things the whole world already knew. We did hear that the government had separately provided some information to the court in a classified form, but we were blocked from even getting an indication of which of our questions that information responded to, so we didn't get anything we could use, even as the judge insisted that *we* still had the burden of proof.[67] We racked our brains trying to find a way to get out of this trap that Judge White had put us in.

Two years later, in 2018, this farce of a discovery process finally came to an end when the judge required us and the government to each file a motion, telling each of us what had to be in it.[68] On our side, the judge required us to demonstrate that our clients had standing—that their specific communications were in fact accessed by the government. We were to do that based on the public record alone, without any governmental confirmation, much less additional information. Separately, Judge White required the government to show why the state secrets privilege would require dismissal of the plaintiffs' claims even if the facts showed that our clients' communications were actually accessed by the government's mass spying.

We felt like we had our hands tied behind our backs. But the way forward was clear: we needed to show the full weight of the public evidence about the mass surveillance regimes, and that based on what was publicly known, at least one communication from one of our clients in *Jewel v. NSA* were among the hundreds of millions of nonsuspected people whose communications and communications records had been accessed in the United States.[69] The presentation included three additional expert witnesses—Professor Matthew Blaze; Brian Reid, who had come to Washington, DC, with us in 2006; and Ashkan Soltani, former chief technologist at the Federal Trade Commission—along with AT&T documents and the other witnesses we first revealed in 2006–Bill Binney, J. Kirk Wiebe, and Thomas Drake.[70]

We marshaled key portions of the now massive number of public admissions by the US government. We even presented the fact that European judges had not been so cowed and had been willing to consider the public facts in a case brought by some of our European allies in an organization called Big Brother Watch.[71] We showed that the program, as publicly admitted, simply had to have included at least one of our clients' communications at the "collect-it-all" stage.[72]

When the government's motion came in, it's main argument was déjà vu all over again: it was a "state secret" whether AT&T was participating in the internet backbone spying. By this point the government had confirmed that the NSA spying programs swept in billions of communications from hundreds of millions of people domestically, and despite the obvious fact that this could only happen if AT&T and Verizon participated, it still claimed that it would somehow harm national security if it said that AT&T was one of the companies participating. Worse, the government took aggressive steps to block the evidence we had that confirmed AT&T's participation.

Because we had been prevented from requiring the government to confirm directly, we had to get creative in order to verify AT&T's role in the mass surveillance. We had a draft NSA inspector general report from 2009 that discussed the mass surveillance program, which was internally called Stellar Wind.[73] Since the government would not confirm or deny the information in the report as authentic—although it obviously was—we asked Snowden, who had leaked the document, to authenticate that the document we were providing to the court was in fact the same one that he came upon during the course of his employment as an NSA contractor. Snowden signed a declaration confirming that he remembered the document because it helped convince him that the NSA had been engaged in illegal surveillance.

Similarly, we had an audit report by the NSA that had been created in response to a secret FISA court order that also confirmed AT&T's participation.[74] That document had been given to *The New York Times* in response to a Freedom of Information Act request. Again, since the government refused, we asked the vice president and deputy general counsel of *The New York Times*, David McCraw, to provide a simple declaration authenticating the report.[75] That's right, the government refused to confirm a document that it had itself supplied a report to *The New York Times* in response to a Freedom of Information Act request. To us that represented a new low in governmental game playing.

But none of that seemed to matter to Judge White. In April 2019, he took the final step in his reversal of his earlier, strong rulings rejecting the idea that national security secrecy should block consideration of whether the government had broken the law or violated the Constitution. He dismissed our remaining claims, stating that it would be impossible to analyze the legality of the mass spying without revealing state secrets.[76] Judge White held that the public evidence was insufficient to prove that our clients were spied on and rejected our efforts to authenticate the key documents without the government needing to agree. This ruling flew in the face of the enormous amount of direct and circumstantial evidence showing that AT&T did participate, and that at least some of our clients' communications were undoubtedly swept up by the NSA dragnet surveillance.[77]

Once again, the judge indicated that he had seen some classified evidence. Perhaps he thought that he had engaged in a rough version of the process that 1806(f) provides, which allows a finding of legality based on a secret review of the government's evidence. But if so, he kept that to himself. He framed his decision about the state secrets privilege only.

The court agreed with the government that anyone seeking to challenge illegal spying is stuck in a catch-22: no one can sue unless the court first determines that their individual communications were subject to the NSA's surveillance.[78] But the court cannot decide whether any particular person's email, web searches, social media, or phone calls were subject to the surveillance unless the government itself admits it. Which, of course, the government will not do.

It was the beginning of the end. Yet it took a long time to get there.

STATE SECRETS PREVAILS

We remained hopeful that the Ninth Circuit would right the course of the case again. In September 2019, we filed our opening brief.[79] We argued that the courts don't have to ignore the government's actions when they involve illegal surveillance on innocent people, especially when everyone else can already see what was happening. Instead, the court must ensure justice for those people who have had their communications subjected to the NSA's mass spying programs in the United States.[80]

In spring 2019, the Ninth Circuit Court of Appeals seemed to send us a lifeline. It was in a case called *Fazaga v. FBI* that arose out of an undercover FBI investigation by a confidential informant who posed as a bodybuilder in order to join a Muslim community in Southern California.[81] The informant's actions were so alarming that the targets themselves called the FBI to report the informant as a potential terrorist. The investigation included extensive electronic surveillance of members of the community. In the decision, the court confirmed our central rock, paper, scissors argument: the state secrets privilege does not apply to cases challenging domestic electronic surveillance for national security because Congress had passed the FISA statute that covered the same issue.[82] At last! We had filed an amicus brief in *Fazaga* on this issue and were overjoyed.

Then in September 2019, we got another boost. This time, in a case called *Husayn* (later called *Abu Zubaydah*), the Ninth Circuit ruled that the government could not claim state secrets over information that was not actually secret.[83] The *Husayn* case arose from the torture of terrorist suspects by contractors to the US government that occurred in a Polish black site. The black site had been acknowledged by the European Court of Human Rights and its existence was also admitted by the former prime minister of Poland. The Ninth Circuit noted, correctly, that since the site was no longer a secret, the state secrets privilege could not be applied to remove that information from the case.

Both cases were headed to the Supreme Court, and we were hopeful that the reasoning of both would be applied to our case. We rushed to ask the appeals court to apply that same reasoning to *Jewel v. NSA*.

But instead, in August 2021, the Ninth Circuit issued a baffling decision. With almost no explanation, it released an unsigned summary decision that rejected our appeal and affirmed the district court's decision applying the state secrets privilege to information that was already publicly known.[84] We had some appellate specialists tell us that the fact that it was unsigned may have been a clue that they were not proud of it, but we'll never know for sure.

We persevered, taking steps to keep our case alive in the hopes that the Supreme Court's decision in *Fazaga* and *Abu Zubaydah* would vindicate us too. We also filed amicus briefs in both of those cases in the Supreme Court.

Our hope didn't last long. In March 2022, the Supreme Court ruled in *Abu Zubaydah* confirming the government's claim that "secret" means whatever facts the government wants to keep out of court by refusing to formally confirm them, regardless of how widely known they are.[85]

Right after came another blow with *Fazaga*.[86] The Supreme Court rejected the central argument we had been making since 2006 that Congress preempted the state secrets privilege when it created a specific process in FISA for handling the government's claims of national security secrecy in cases arising from alleged illegal surveillance. Apparently the FISA paper didn't cover the state secrets privilege rock.

With these decisions, the Supreme Court endorsed one of the core ideas behind the imperial presidency: the unitary executive theory. This doctrine, often pushed by people who are working to make the president more like a king, provides that the executive branch has unilateral authority to use secrecy arguments, no matter how flimsy, to close the courthouse doors for those seeking to vindicate their rights. These people contend that the President can do this even where Congress has passed a law creating an alternative path, as it had in FISA. It's a dangerous elevation of the executive power over both Congress and the judiciary, and it helped set the stage for several of the claims later made by President Trump.

We knew our case would be lost along with those, and sure enough, in June 2022, the Supreme Court formally ended it by refusing to hear our appeal.

NO LEGAL VICTORY, BUT LOTS OF BITES OUT OF NSA SPYING

While we did not prevail in the litigation, the work we did, and the millions of people who raised concerns about the NSA spying over the years, did result in some dramatic changes. Congress stopped the mass telephone records program in 2015 as part of the USA Freedom Act. While the revamped program still (and predictably) ended up collecting and keeping a huge number of telephone records, the random mass collection of everyone's phone records was stopped. The mass internet metadata program was halted in 2011, allegedly due to congressional concerns that it wasn't actually providing any usable intelligence, but public pressure also likely played a role.

The Upstream program changed dramatically too. Until 2017, it had been used to conduct something called "about" searches—which allowed the NSA to search the content of messages to find information "about" selected targets.[87] So if you mentioned bin Laden in an email to a friend in London, that would be swept up, even if neither of you was on the target list. Reportedly due to some technical issues involving threaded messages, this "about" searching power resulted in a huge number of purely domestic communications being collected and kept by the program. Despite multiple promises to fix it, the issue persisted such that even the FISA court started to get exasperated. The FISA court finally held that the flawed collection process violated the Fourth Amendment. Facing court pressure, the NSA decided on its own to stop that part of the collection and destroy what it had gathered rather than seek an appeal. The agency still maintains that it has the authority to restart the collection at any time, though, which is why EFF and others have continued to push Congress to formally outlaw it.

As far as we know, Upstream is still used to sit on the wire—and broadly surveil—millions of people in the United States. That information is available to both the NSA and FBI (plus some other agencies). Thanks to the transparency measures we helped secure in the USA Freedom Act, the government was forced to disclose that between December 2020 and November 2021, the FBI queried the data of potentially more than three million US persons without a warrant.[88] The statute that purports to authorize Upstream, section 702, does at least expire periodically.[89] That has given EFF and our allies periodic windows to try to push for more reform, and we continue to do so.

Of the three programs that we started suing over in 2006, one has been ended entirely, another has been radically changed to prevent wholesale mass data collection, and the third has been cut back significantly, including stopping the collection of the content of communications through "about" searches. Each of these changes happened in different ways and through a combination of pressure points. The FISA court now has a public docket, and there is more transparency in its decisions, along with an "amicus" process that lets the judges hear from an outside voice and not just the government when considering important issues. The US people know a lot more about what their government is doing with their communications.

The next steps remain, however. We won't have digital privacy—and the check on power it provides—until we end all of those programs, and require a full Fourth Amendment warrant for government collection of our communications and metadata. Giving the government the ability to sift through our private communications and map our communications patterns is dangerous enough in ordinary times, and it's critical when our democratic systems are under threat.

3

NATIONAL SECURITY LETTERS: THE ALPHABET CASES

A CALL FROM A TELEPHONE COMPANY

"Remember when you asked us to call you if we got something strange from the government seeking information about our customers?" The question came from the policy director of CREDO, a small, progressive telecommunications company.

"Yeesss," I answered, half an answer and half a question.

"Well, we're calling."

I had been driving from San Francisco to Sacramento in February 2011 to testify at a state legislative hearing when my cell phone rang. It was the policy director, Becky Bond, along with the CEO, Michael Kieschnick, and the general counsel, Jean Parker. They clearly had me on speakerphone as they sat together in a room. CREDO is an interesting company because it provides phone and cell phone service, but was founded to use that business in part to raise money and support for activist causes. It lets its customers vote to give donations to a potential slate of nonprofit organizations and then sends fairly sizable donations to the winners. It also had a policy team, led by Becky, that worked in Congress and elsewhere directly to support progressive causes, including fighting the NSA's surveillance. EFF had received donations from CREDO quite a few times by 2011 and had a cordial relationship.

When I answered the call, I could hear a combination of tension, worry, and excitement in their voices. I had made the remark, offhand, at the end of a lunch presentation I had given in CREDO's San Francisco offices a few months earlier. Many companies had programs to bring in speakers, and we regularly participated as a way to let people know about EFF's work. The presentation was about the problems with the first generation of electronic voting machines, which were security nightmares that had been designed with no way to conduct real recounts or audits. This was another issue that EFF was working on at the time, having been alerted by our friends in the computer science and security communities about the risks caused by these early machines.

I've found that as an impact lawyer, it's always helpful to plant some seeds of possible future cases wherever I go. I have been constantly surprised about the various circuitous routes that my clients have taken to find me. But this was one of the only times I was called out of the blue by a telephone company. And it was a doozy.

They told me that they had been visited by an FBI agent who served them with the papers with the words "national security" on them. Jean, as general counsel, had to go to the front desk to collect the documents personally. The agent had strongly emphasized that the company and Jean were gagged from telling anyone about the visit or the documents they had received. It had been scary and isolating for her, and based on the warnings the agent had sternly given her, she initially feared prosecution if she told anyone else at the company.

The first question they asked me on the phone was whether they had already violated the law by calling me. I asked a few more questions about the documents the agent had left, which sought information about one of their customers who had been identified by a phone number.

As they described the papers, I had to pull off the freeway to settle my breathing. With that call, I had found a client that would let us challenge one of the most troubling changes created by the Patriot Act: National Security Letters (NSLs) and their attendant permanent gag orders. We had struggled against the many kinds of secrecy that the government had used to block accountability to the public since 9/11. Here was a chance to fix one piece of it.

I quickly explained that the FBI had a history of telling recipients of their secret surveillance orders that they couldn't even speak with their outside lawyers about them. But the courts had rejected that argument, and in 2006, Congress had amended the NSL law to make it clear that lawyers could be consulted. I heard in their voices that this made the three people on the phone, who were not used to directly tangling with the FBI, just a bit less nervous.

HAPPY WARRIORS

When I got that call, EFF had thirty-three staffers. We had a two-person activism team, three staff technologists, and a four-person international team along with a dozen US-focused lawyers.

We were in the process of appealing the "generalized grievance" ruling by Judge Walker and the retroactive immunity decision by Congress. We also had lawyers doing Freedom of Information Act work to pry information out of the government and were still pushing back on the excesses of the Patriot Act.

In addition to that more traditional civil liberties work in the courts and the US Congress, we continued to work on protecting free speech and innovation from the overbroad application of copyright law, both in the United States and internationally. At the same time, in 2011, the Arab Spring was occurring, with the internet playing an even bigger role in organizing activism than ever before. Our international team was in the thick of it. We were also working on the problems created by electronic voting machines, the topic I spoke about at CREDO. The organization was steady, and our reach was growing.

NEW BEGINNINGS

That same spring, while I was personally still reeling from my divorce, this was the time when I was also increasingly spending time with Patrick. He was living in Palo Alto, and I was in my Noe Valley flat in San Francisco, so I spent a lot of time driving up and down the 280 freeway.

In July, Patrick and I took our first big trip together, going to Colombia to attend the wedding of two of his former colleagues who had met when they both worked with Patrick. The wedding was in the lush green mountains outside Bogota. We danced until dawn, and then the next few days Patrick took me around the city, where he had lived for a time. We were in that giddy time where even touching our fingertips together caused a tingle. We rode the funicular up to the top of one of the surrounding mountains, Monseratte. We had a drink and took in the view of the sparkling city below. We were still figuring out how we were going to be a couple.

While we had some time for romance, we also both had to work. Patrick was preparing to testify in Guatemala at the genocide trial of the former dictator. I had lugged a large, black legal briefcase with me and was digging through it as I prepared for the Ninth Circuit argument where I was going to try to save the *Hepting* case.

THE CAT THAT BECAME A LION

The NSLs that CREDO called me about remind me of cats. One thing I have come to believe in a lifetime of sharing my home with them: While cats are often cuddly and loving at their small size, if they were the size of lions, they would eat you. That's a bit like what happened with NSLs.

NSLs are a kind of subpoena that secretly and without any court oversight, requires communication providers to turn over information about their customers. Before the Patriot Act, NSLs were narrow, focused tools that could only be issued for tracking spies and other foreign agents. Only a few officials inside the FBI could authorize them. We didn't like NSLs even before the Patriot Act because the FBI could issue them on its own, without any judicial involvement. We knew from a long history that included domestic spying by the FBI under its director J. Edgar Hoover up until today that an FBI without checks on its power could be dangerous. But because NSLs were so limited in what they could be used for, they were a small concern. NSLs before the Patriot Act were more like a mean alley cat than a serious threat to people's privacy in the United States.

With the Patriot Act, Congress turned the NSL cat into a lion. NSLs allowed the FBI to collect any records that were merely "relevant" to "an authorized investigation to protect against international terrorism." This is far broader than just chasing spies. NSLs could be issued by any FBI field office chief and a much wider range of companies, including consumer credit agencies, travel agencies, and service providers far beyond ISPs.

When originally passed in 2001, Patriot Act changes to the NSL statute also failed to include a way to challenge an NSL—something the FBI took to mean that no challenges could ever happen. It took five years for Congress to fix that. But as we'd learn, even years after those reforms, some FBI agents and Department of Justice officials insisted that there was no way to challenge an NSL or accompanying gag order in court, even on constitutional grounds.

The Patriot Act transformed a narrow tool for tracking spies into a broad investigative power for anything the FBI claimed was related to antiterrorism investigations—a term that itself had been broadened by the Patriot Act. FBI agents around the country understood this.

Because of NSLs' ease of use and perpetual secrecy, we had heard from contacts in industry that they were seeing many more of them. Moreover, we heard that a wider range of companies were receiving them. In fact, we were told that these were becoming one of the go-to techniques for an increasing number of investigations across the country. We later learned that the FBI started issuing them in the hundreds of thousands, even though there were less than 550 people convicted of terrorism total in the fifteen years between 2001 and 2016.[1]

One of the most dangerous features of NSLs was that they came with a perpetual gag order on the company to prevent it from telling anyone—its customers, its congressional representatives, or the media—that it had even received them. This combination of powers—to investigate and silence—together allowed the FBI to wield enormous power and operate without meaningful checks, far from the watchful eyes of the judicial branch, much less the public.

All gag orders aren't necessarily bad. A judge might issue a limited gag order when asking a company to provide information about a criminal investigation to avoid tipping off the target. Grand juries generally operate in secrecy for similar reasons. But in both situations, that secrecy ends. NSL gag orders after the Patriot Act were a whole different beast. Without a judge ever approving, the companies that received an NSL were required to hand over information about their customers to the government and *never* allowed to speak about it, even to just confirm that they had received one, two, or even hundreds of NSLs in a single year. If the FBI decided to gag you, you were gagged forever.

We had a strong constitutional argument on our side. While the factual context was quite different, legally we were back in the territory of the *Bernstein* case: the procedural prior restraint doctrine embodied in *Freedman v. Maryland*. This requires that if the government is going to prevent you from speaking, the law needs to have clear rules and a short turnaround time, and require the government to bear the burden of proof in court. The NSL statute had none of those protections. It was legal territory I knew well.

I was beyond excited to hear that we might be able to scale back these NLSs and gags. Yet doing so meant that we were silenced too. The gag order not only gagged the providers but also gagged their counsel. When I took that call from CREDO from the freeway, I had no idea that we would have to keep the name of our clients and nearly everything about the case secret for six years. That secrecy not only complicated our handling of this case but also created problems with our broader advocacy.

NSLs

NSLs were on many people's radar in the first few years after the Patriot Act supercharged them. In 2004 and 2005, the ACLU brought two cases that challenged an earlier version of the NSL statute on behalf of a library and small ISP.[2] The courts had agreed that the statute was unconstitutional. Congress had responded by making small amendments to the statute—including to prevent issuance of NSLs based solely on First Amendment expression—but the broader problems remained.

As part of the reauthorization of the Patriot Act in 2006, Congress had required the Justice Department's inspector general to report on the FBI's use of NSLs. We learned that between 2003 and 2006, the number of NSLs issued increased astronomically to nearly two hundred thousand in a three-year period.[3] This confirmed what our industry friends had told us.

The inspector general revealed other disturbing things too. The telecommunications companies had actually embedded their own employees at the FBI to assist in responding to NSLs. These employees let the FBI flagrantly ignore the law. They would access information about the company's customers without an NSL, and then after the fact, accept "blanket" NSLs to cover their tracks. NSL requests were written on Post-it notes.[4] In three reports issued between 2007 and 2010, the inspector general found that the agency engaged in "systematic and extensive misuse" of NSLs.[5] Some NSLs were still issued based on activities protected by the First Amendment even after Congress had banned that.[6] Other NSLs included requests for "community of interest" or "calling circle" information that, in one instance, allowed the FBI to review the calling records of 10,070 telephone numbers at a single communications provider.[7] Furthermore, the inspector general noted that the FBI completely failed to address the concerns about illegal and inappropriate NSLs, even though those issues were obvious and pervasive.

EFF's own investigations uncovered NSL misuses too. An EFF report based on documents that our team received through a Freedom of Information Act request led to tough questions for the FBI before Congress and helped push for legislative changes.[8] The documents also helped prompt the Senate Judiciary Committee to investigate whether Attorney General Gonzales lied to Congress when he testified in 2005 that there had not been a single incident of abuse of NSLs even though he had received, by that point, numerous reports of abuse.[9]

We had tried to get at the problems with NSLs in 2008 after the government issued one to the Internet Archive.[10] We had worked with the Northern California ACLU to mount a response, but the government quickly backed down.

Then in December 2008, another ACLU case struck a strong blow against NSLs in the Second Circuit on behalf of a small ISP. In the case, which was called *Doe v. Mukasey*, the judges recognized the problems with these secret infinite gag orders. But instead of requiring Congress to fix them, the court suggested narrowing when NSLs could be issued, articulated a new process whereby a recipient could challenge an NSL in court, and set the burden of proof in that process. Then it said that if the Department of Justice followed its suggestions, that would make the NSL statute constitutional.[11]

It's not supposed to work this way. Judges aren't supposed to "fix" the laws that Congress passes by rewriting them to include things that Congress did not include. They aren't supposed to be shadow lawmakers in black robes. If Congress wrote an unconstitutional statute, Congress, not a court, should be the one to fix it.

Worse, the fix the court suggested still didn't fulfill the requirements of *Freedman v. Maryland*. Rather than putting the burden of proof on the government, the *Mukasey* process put the burden on a recipient to challenge the NSLs in court. And the *Mukasey* opinion didn't require the court to rule quickly either. Both of those steps were required by *Freedman*.

While *Mukasey* was a kind of step forward for fixing NSLs, it was still insufficient and definitely the wrong way to address an unconstitutional law. We wanted to get another court to toss out the statute entirely.

That wasn't just because we thought Congress should try again to create a legal prior restraint. It was because we thought tossing the question about NSLs back to Congress would give us a chance to argue that the right way to address the collection of metadata is with a warrant, even in national security cases. We wanted to push for limited gag orders that were tailored to the actual investigation at hand, and not just issued once by FBI officials to silence recipients forever. If the NSL statute was declared unconstitutional, and if we could muster all of those who had been gagged to come forward and talk about their experiences, we could make that bigger case to Congress and possibly actually fix the problems with NSLs.

CASE Q LAUNCHES

To help ensure that CREDO's identity remained secret even inside of EFF, we called the litigation "Case Q." The goal was to have the NSL statute—both the substantive demand portion and gag order—declared unconstitutional, and free our clients and other NSL recipients to tell their stories. That is what lawyers call a facial challenge since it attacks the statute overall and not just in a particular case.

Before we went to court, we tried to see if the government, as in the Internet Archive case, would just back down. My first calls in May 2011 were with the FBI agent and federal prosecutor in the state that issued the NSL.

To put it mildly, the calls did not go well. When I think about government lawyers, especially prosecutors, I often think about a quip that then Texas governor Ann Richards made about President George H. W. Bush, which was apparently taken from legendary Oklahoma coach Barry Switzer: "Born on third base, but thinks he hit a triple."[12]

Why? Because so frequently prosecutors think they are amazing lawyers when the truth is that the field is slanted so sharply in their favor that it's hard for them to lose. Not that there aren't any good lawyers in the government; there are many. But especially less experienced government lawyers often have an outsized view of their skills because they overlook the fact that they have advantages that their opponents like me don't have. This NSL prosecutor seemed to be one of those.

"I represent CREDO, which wants to resist this NSL and its gag," I started.

The prosecutor cut me off: "It can't do that," her voice was sharp and clipped. "National security letters aren't challengeable. No one ever challenges them. Your client needs to comply."

My hackles definitely went up with that. "As you know, the statute allows for legal challenges," I responded, trying not to match her tone but instead to project calm and smoothness. "Our client is a progressive, transparent company that cares about the privacy of its customers. It feels the need to push back here. It wants to make sure the public knows that CREDO fights back against these controversial demands."

"There's nothing controversial about them. Your client should comply because this is a national security letter," she responded, with a predictable emphasis on the words "national security."

The client's usual outside lawyer, a nice guy from a large Bay Area firm, had joined me on the call. Since EFF had been sounding the alarm about NSLs for a long time, we decided in our planning meeting ahead of the call that he would play the softer role.

He now jumped in and noted that CREDO would be willing to respond if the government used one of the other tools at its disposal. A grand jury subpoena or regular FISA order were both ways that the underlying request could have more process protections as well as the involvement of a judge.

But the prosecutor was not interested in discussing other ways and seemed offended that we would even suggest something else. Rather, she just started saying the same thing over and over: this was an NSL and they were never challenged. Her tone was clear that she thought we were out of line to even propose it.

So we filed our lawsuit.

And got a shock.

Immediately after we filed, the government filed its own lawsuit against CREDO, claiming that the company was violating the "sovereign interests" of the United States by seeking judicial review of the NSL. It felt like an aggressive intimidation move, aimed at scaring us into dropping the challenge. I have found few companies—or people—that are not freaked out by being accused in a court of law by their government of harming the United States. Our clients were no exception.

The read-in part of the leadership of the company had to meet several times to determine whether they wanted to push on. They were hampered because due to the gag order, they really couldn't explain what was happening to their board of directors. But they understood that the Patriot Act was a big problem and that the supercharged NSLs were a part of it. Ultimately the company decided that it was not, in fact, hurting the "sovereign interests" of the United States merely by asking a court to look at the law. So it stood firm.

FINDING WHERE THE FIGHT IS

At this point EFF had a well-seasoned team of lawyers. I was always watching for ways these lawyers could grow, including taking the lead on litigation. So when my colleague Matt Zimmerman asked if he could take the helm of the NSL case, I readily agreed. I had recruited Matt from a terrific organization called the First Amendment Project, led by my old friend Jim Wheaton, who also helped us in *Bernstein*. Matt was originally hired to lead our electronic voting advocacy, but he knew his way around the First Amendment too. Matt stepped into the central role, and I stepped back and started playing more of a supporting one—editing briefs and helping think through next steps as Matt skillfully led the team.

Surprised but undaunted by the lawsuit filed in response to our initial filing, we moved quickly to keep the momentum going. We asked the court for a preliminary injunction to lift the gag on our clients while the rest of the case proceeded. The First Amendment case law supports these kinds of requests since stopping speech before it starts (aka a prior restraint) is one of the most serious violations of the Constitution. Moving quickly also signaled to the court that every day that our clients were gagged was important.

To prepare for the oral argument, I followed a process mentioned earlier, gleaned from a presentation by litigation legend (and Mark Klein's lawyer) James Brosnahan that I saw when I was just a new lawyer. I call it: finding where the fight is. The goal was to make sure that Matt was fully prepared to counter the government's arguments and answer any questions the court might ask.

I have yet to find a digital tool that I can use for this process, so I do it longhand. I turn a lawyer's yellow pad on its side, and then draw out a grid horizontally with space for the opening brief, opposing brief, reply brief, and oral argument. I then skip to the argument section of the brief. The format of legal briefs is usually set by a local rule, which don't vary much. They generally require an introduction, and then for longer briefs, a short summary of argument. Next is a recitation of the central facts and then the argument itself. In truth, the argument section is where the rubber meets the road—where the facts that matter are woven into the specific portion of the legal argument they support.

To prepare for the oral argument, I go through the opening brief with as neutral a mind as possible, trying to fairly summarize the key contentions and note the important cases cited on the far-left section of my turned-horizontal legal pad. It's easy to read an opposing brief slanted and only look to poke holes. But it's important to try to read the other side's papers as if you wanted to agree with them. If you do that, and if the lawyers are worth their salt at all, their briefs should scare you.

Only once you've put yourself in the position of a fair-minded judge or the judge's clerk can you marshal the right response for a fair-minded judge. If you're only preaching to the converted, you won't be winning.

On my legal pad, I turn next to the government's opposition brief. Regardless of the order of the arguments in its brief, I line up the arguments the government made next to the ones we made so they appear head-to-head as you look across the legal pad. I stick in any new ones at the end. Then I do the same arrangement for the arguments in the reply brief. By the time this is done, I not only have a good grasp of what everybody argued, I can see where the real fights are—where the three briefs answered each other the most directly. I can also see where arguments were dropped or not really answered. From there, it's easy to decide where you should focus during oral argument and avoid wasting any time in court.

I use this preparation method regardless of whether I'm the one arguing. We had several prep sessions with Matt—some resembling conversations, and others more like a mock argument with some of us playing the role of judge. Overall, we grilled Matt hard and got him ready for what we expected to be a strong argument by the government's attorney.

By then the dismissive local prosecutor who I talked to during the first call was long gone. We were tangling with the main Department of Justice litigators from DC. They handle all serious cases against the government. Our new opposing counsel was a smart and nice guy named Steven Bressler, who had also been opposing counsel in several Freedom of Information Act cases. Steve had the government lawyers' knack for presenting outrageous arguments in reasonable-sounding ways. He played the national security card early and often as well. His presentation style was not flashy, but it was powerful.

FAMILIAR COURTROOM

Walking into the courtroom for our hearing in Case Q, I felt the familiar rush of getting to stand up for what's right, but otherwise it was a stark contrast from my early days in court. I'd been to federal court, and specifically to this courtroom, so many times by then that I had lost count.

That was because our judge was Susan Illston, a highly respected member of the district court. I knew Judge Illston well at this point along with her lead courtroom clerk, who helped keep everything moving smoothly. Judge Illston had been in charge of the *Bowoto v. Chevron* case—the one I'd negotiated with Shari to keep when I joined EFF in 2000.

I especially thought a lot about Judge Illston during my trips to Nigeria. We were certain that we were being surveilled by Chevron and its minions. Stopping at a checkpoint, riding in a boat past villages, or rushing to get to our hotel before dark, I soothed myself by thinking of her in her wood-paneled courtroom in San Francisco. I counted on the fact that a federal judge was watching over the case as one of the reasons that no one would venture to actually hurt me or my colleagues, even in the parts of the Niger Delta that were not all that safe in general, much less for people challenging the giant oil company.

But the time I spent in Nigeria thinking about Judge Illston's protection was overshadowed by the time I spent in her courtroom, or on the phone with her or her courtroom deputy to schedule matters. Chevron brought motion after motion against us, regardless of whether its arguments were good ones. It resisted our discovery demands, requiring us to seek help from Judge Illston for even the most basic requests. The strategy was transparently aimed at exhausting us and draining our meager financial resources. For a while, it seemed like we were in front of Judge Illston on some matter or another every other month or so. As one of the lawyers based in San Francisco, I attended nearly every hearing and handled most of the scheduling too.

Despite Chevron's many attempts to have the case dismissed, Judge Illston decided that it deserved a full jury trial. In October 2008, after a big fight as Chevron tried to block their visas, we brought about a dozen villagers from the Niger Delta to San Francisco to testify. We spent nearly every day of November 2008 in the trial in Judge Illston's courtroom. Our clients and witnesses, dressed in traditional, brightly patterned West African clothing, sat attentively on the dark wooden benches, surrounded by the rest of us in dark Western suits. It was a striking image—a clear visual representation of a local community fighting a Western corporation through the courts. We made quite a stir whenever we passed through security to enter the courthouse.

Ultimately the jury did not side with us in *Bowoto*, which was devastating. Yet our clients told us, repeatedly, that they were buoyed by standing up against the company that had harmed their community. They maintained that the fact that Chevron had to face us in court had made Chevron treat them better in Nigeria.

The upshot was that Judge Illston was a familiar face to me and me to her when we first entered to argue Case Q in November 2011. I knew that she was thoughtful and fair, and not easily bullied or pushed around by powerful lawyers.

HOW IS SAYING "WE GOT A LETTER" A THREAT TO NATIONAL SECURITY?

The first hearing in Case Q was in November 2011, and it was a closed one, meaning no dress-up day for EFF supporters and no press. I sat at the front table near Matt in order to be ready to give him any information he might need. On behalf of the government, Steve started the hearing by making sure we all knew that this was a national security case and even the hearing was to be sealed as confidential.[13] He insisted that the judge affirm that the judge's law clerks—usually law students or recent law graduates—were government employees. The three or four clerks were sitting, as they often do, in the jury box. They were wearing suits and taking notes. It seemed unlikely that Steve had any real fear that our hearing was being infiltrated. I couldn't help but think that this was a not-so-subtle reminder to the judge of the national security context.

Judge Illston immediately wanted our team to explain whether the court-created process described in the *Mukasey* opinion fixed the problems with the NSL statute. The *Mukasey* process required recipients to challenge problematic NSLs in court, but still allowed them to be issued with no judicial oversight. Matt skillfully and clearly noted the difference between what the First Amendment required versus the *Mukasey*-created processes as well as the fact that legal protections had to be in the statute, not just something "suggested" by a court later.

Judge Illston also asked some practical questions of the government focused on the gag order issue. She wanted to know how the government could justify nondisclosure of the simple receipt of an NSL, as opposed to preventing only disclosure of the telephone number or email address of the target.

The question put the government to the hardest part of its argument. Steve first tried to say that the FBI could answer under seal, bringing the secrecy specter up again. But Judge Illston wasn't having it. She asked Matt how many customers our client had. Before he could answer, Jean, the lovely and unflappable general counsel for our client, answered: "One hundred thousand."

This startled everyone, me included. I suspect it even startled Jean.

"May I ask who you are?" Judge Illston asked.

Matt answered: "That's Jean Parker, the general counsel for our client."

"Thank you for that," Judge Illston replied, "but please do let your counsel answer the questions."

"Of course," Jean answered, a bit chagrined, but I suspect a bit proud too.

Judge Illston got back to the point: "One hundred thousand is still a lot."

After more back and forth, it was apparent that this was a big sticking point. Judge Illston said, "I understand the concern about who, but if there's a hundred thousand subscribers . . . how can you say that merely having a company say, 'We got a letter,' is a threat to national security?"

Once again Steve offered a classified declaration or briefing, which Judge Illston declined. I knew we were on the right side of that argument. We left the hearing that November hopeful, but we had a long wait coming.

THE PRICE OF GAGS 1: DODGING THE PRESS

In spring 2012, while we were still waiting for a decision, an investigative reporter named Jennifer Valentino-DeVries at *The Wall Street Journal* started nosing around trying to figure out who our client was. We helped Matt practice talking to Jennifer about the lawsuit generally without accidentally revealing anything about our client's identity.

But Matt got to feel firsthand how frustrating it was to be gagged about a matter of great public importance. We also gained a new understanding about why the First Amendment usually requires prior restraints to be decided quickly by the court.

Jennifer read the redacted court papers for clues, then cross-referenced them with corporate websites and the Federal Communications Commission's records of telecoms. That let her narrow down the possible companies we represented to five. She then contacted each of them to ask if they were the company that had sued. Four of the five outright denied it, leaving our client CREDO as the only one that could neither "confirm or deny," which is what they were supposed to say.

Jennifer rightly deduced that CREDO was our client, but neither we nor CREDO could confirm. At EFF I often say, "We work for tips," by which I mean that part of what we need to do to continue our work is to make sure that the public knows about it. On top of that, we are committed to walking our talk that one of the great benefits of the digital age is that we can share nearly everything about our cases with the public, doing our part to demystify litigation. Indeed, our legal strategy is normally something we want to shout from the rooftops: NSLs violate the First Amendment! We aren't used to having to hide the facts of our cases either, with the exception of our direct communications with our clients and other material protected by the legal privileges. We are definitely not used to having those basic facts speculated about in the nation's leading newspapers and investigated by talented reporters.

Matt handled the journalist's calls well, but he would frequently come into my office to share what she had asked and commiserate about how awkward it was to refuse to answer basic questions. We also knew, though, that a gag order violation had a potential penalty of up to five years in prison for our clients and us lawyers. We worked with CREDO's CEO to issue a nondenial statement that was consistent with the gag, but equally consistent with the advocacy the company had done even before it received its own NSL. It read, "There is a tension between privacy and the legitimate security needs of the country. We think it is best to resolve this through a grand jury or judicial oversight."

On July 17, 2012, Jennifer published her findings in a big *Wall Street Journal* story, including her (correct) conclusion that our client was CREDO. The story included quotes from Matt that merely acknowledged what the public record reflected: that we were counsel to the unnamed NSL recipient.[14]

The months sped by. As we were waiting for Judge Illston to rule, we got a call from a woman who worked for a company called Cloudflare, asking for a meeting. Sitting in our conference room, she told us that the company had been inspired by our work in Case Q. She said that it had recently received two NSLs and wanted to fight them.

Cloudflare operated in a very different part of the internet from CREDO. It was not a telecommunications carrier but instead provided websites with protection, especially against a kind of cyberattack called distributed denial of service. This is a pernicious and easy-to-launch attack that could effectively make a website inaccessible by flooding the host computer with requests. By 2010, the kind of protection that Cloudflare offered was critical for any website with sufficient traffic. Even though it wasn't a traditional ISP or telecommunications company, Cloudflare was (and still is) one of the most important, yet hard-to-see companies keeping the web working.

We were excited to take on another case, and with Matt leading, we started prepping a similar petition to the one we had created for CREDO to have the Cloudflare NSLs set aside. We called the Cloudflare one "Case

Z" internally to keep it separate from our original CREDO Case Q. At this point, in addition to fending off reporters, we had to do some careful work inside EFF to comply with the gag. Our case files were kept in separate physical file cabinets and a separate locked section of our hard drive "shared" database where we kept our digital files. My quarterly reports to the EFF board of directors had to be circumspect; there was no exception to the gag for the nonlawyer board of directors of a nonprofit legal organization. Luckily the EFF board was supportive and understood why we could not tell it more, but it was definitely a strain to act consistently with our duty to keep the board apprised of major work and costs while still handling the cases, which were taking an increasing amount of time by Matt, me, and some of our other senior attorneys.

NO BETTER FEELING

Finally, on March 14, 2013, over a year and a half after the hearing, the judge issued her decision.

Since the case was under seal, we didn't get the opinion in the normal distribution process from the courts, nor did we hear from Bob Egelko, who had so regularly informed me of my victories. Instead it was emailed as an encrypted file from the judge's clerk to our legal secretary, Stephanie. I heard a shout from her office across the hall, and she quickly delivered a printed copy to me and Matt. We gathered around the red couch outside my office to read it, and I could see our smiles getting wider with each page.

Judge Illston agreed with us—and the Second Circuit—that the *Freedman* line of prior restraint cases did apply to NSLs, meaning that the gag orders needed significantly more procedural protections. Judge Illston rejected all the governmental arguments that this was not a prior restraint. She also rejected the ridiculous claim by the government that our clients couldn't ever challenge the NSL statute. Judge Illston noted the obvious: anyone impacted by a statute had to have the ability to challenge its constitutionality.

In applying *Freedman,* Judge Illston agreed with us down the line: the constitutional requirements were not met by voluntary governmental compliance with the suggestions of the Second Circuit court in *Mukasey*. In contrast, Judge Illston wrote,

> The fact that the statute is facially deficient—in not mandating the procedural and substantive protections discussed below—presents too great a risk of potential infringement of First Amendment rights to allow the FBI to side-step constitutional review by relying on its voluntary, nationwide compliance with the Second Circuit's limitations.[15]

Moreover, the court found that the judicial review allowed by the statute was far too narrow. Quoting an earlier opinion, she said, "Under no circumstances should the Judiciary become the handmaiden of the Executive."[16]

This was terrific, but the final section of the opinion was the best. Judge Illston agreed with us that the Second Circuit in the *Mukasey* decision had gone too far in trying to rewrite the statute. She confirmed what we had wanted her to: that the entire statute had to be tossed out and Congress had to try again to write something that would comply with the First Amendment. It wasn't the job of the courts to rewrite statutes and "suggest" procedures to protect the First Amendment. It was Congress's job to do it right.

As I had learned in *Bernstein*, with this opinion Matt got to experience the joy of reading a landmark court decision that agrees with your arguments. It's a mirrorlike experience—as if someone else is channeling the words you wrote and turning them into reality. It's a mix of joy and déjà vu to see the picture you painted in your briefs about how the world ought to work reflected back to you in the form of a ruling. And it's even better when that world will help bring more justice and fairness to lots of people—the clients of course, but in the world of impact litigation, the ultimate winners are all of us. I had a strong sense of passing on that feeling to the next wave of EFF lawyers.

One disappointment was that the decision was put on hold; the court gave the government time to seek an appeal. That meant that despite winning on an argument that quick decisions were needed in prior restraint cases, we were still fully gagged even though two years had passed since we had filed suit.

Judge Illston did reject a couple of our other First Amendment legal theories. As in *Bernstein*, and as lawyers are generally required to do, we had raised all the concerns we had with the law at once because if we had failed to do so, we would have waived them. But for right now we only needed to win on one theory, and we had done it.

We quickly issued a press release. My quote was:

> The First Amendment prevents the government from silencing people and stopping them from criticizing its use of executive surveillance power. The NSL statute has long been a concern of many Americans, and this small step should help restore balance between liberty and security.[17]

We were deep in the midst of preparing for the Cloudflare case when the Case Q opinion came out, but I made sure that our team paused at least for a moment to celebrate. In such instances, I always remember the wise words of my cocounsel in the *Bernstein* case, Bob Corn-Revere. After one of our early interim victories, he said, "Be sure to let yourself enjoy this feeling now. We don't win a lot in this kind of work, so we need to celebrate every single little victory. If we wait for the end of the case in order to let ourselves be happy, we may miss our chance." It's advice I've taken to heart. In fact, we joke at EFF that our job is to declare victory early and often. That's because—given the odds against us—every little step along the way is worthy of celebration.

CASE Z LAUNCHES

Even with the celebration, we managed to file the petition in Case Z that same day. While the government once again affirmatively sued back, and while this predictably rattled the company's leaders, we had prepared them for this possibility. In Case Q, in response to the judge's question, the government had said that these countersuits were part of its interpretation of what the Second Circuit had suggested in *Mukasey*. We thought that was a strange interpretation, but it meant we were able to assure the company leadership that the governments' countersuit wasn't a reflection that the government was claiming that it was being un-American by seeking judicial review of the NSL statute.

Overall, we felt the wind in our sails. In July 2013, before the scheduled hearing on Case Z, the government withdrew one of the two Case Z NSLs, saying it had obtained the requested information by getting a court order under a separate process, just as we had suggested at the beginning of Case Q. Still, the government refused to withdraw the gag order it issued with the NSL, so that part of the fight continued.

Although we had another case pending in Case Z, we thought that losing so clearly in Case Q would lead the government to hesitate before sending another NSL, at least to CREDO. We were wrong.

Just five days after our victory, on March 19, 2013, CREDO received two more NSLs. Once again we were unable to resolve them by talking to the FBI. On April 22, 2013, we petitioned to challenge them too, calling this second CREDO one "Case W." Collectively, we started calling them the "Alphabet Cases."

After our Case Q win, other companies apparently decided that they too could challenge NSLs. On March 29, just a couple of weeks after our big victory, Google brought a challenge to nineteen NSLs, which was also assigned to Judge Illston. We were overjoyed; perhaps our wins were having a ripple effect.

CHANGED COURSE

On May 20, 2013, however, just a few months after Google filed its challenge, Judge Illston changed course. She rejected Google's challenge. A few small things had shifted, but the statute itself was still as unconstitutional in May as it had been in March.

One change that shouldn't have mattered, yet apparently did, was that by May, the government had decided that it would be voluntarily bound by the *Mukasey* compromise. It shouldn't have mattered because Judge Illston had expressly rejected the government's argument that it could avoid the unconstitutionality of the statute by "voluntary binding" to the *Mukasey* decision.

Even more puzzlingly, Judge Illston noted that Google, for its part, didn't address the specifics of any of the NSLs, while the government had presented declarations confirming how each one was relevant to a national security investigation. This seemed strange and unfair. How was Google to know enough about the context of the national security investigations into one or even a dozen of its millions of customers in order to challenge them on the specifics?

While Judge Illston did not expressly reverse her earlier decision and confirmed that the Ninth Circuit would address it "in due course," her dramatic change was still troubling. These May rulings seemed completely inconsistent with the power and logic of the victory she gave us in March.

It got worse. Instead of an anomaly, the Google ruling proved to be prescient. In early August, Judge Illston denied our petitions in Cases W and Z without even allowing us a hearing. She again stated that the government had complied with the *Mukasey* requirements and had made a showing of "good reason" to believe that "some reasonable likelihood of harm to a government investigation" would occur. She also said that the fact that our client hadn't raised specific concerns about the two NSLs at issue was important—again begging the question of how an ISP would know the context behind a national security investigation sufficient to raise a concern.

What had happened?

It's possible that having declared the statute unconstitutional and sent it to the Ninth Circuit, Judge Illston just didn't want to do any more until the Ninth Circuit decided if she was right. That is the most plausible explanation, but not how the Constitution is supposed to work. If your First Amendment rights have been violated, you should win the case—and maybe face a stay pending appeal that would delay your recovery as happened in Case Q. You shouldn't lose the case as had happened to Cases Z and W, pending an appeal of another case.

As we would learn the hard way in the coming years, even a judge who starts out courageous in the face of national security claims, often bends over time. It was frustrating and sad, and made us feel like the judicial processes were indeed becoming what Judge Illston had earlier rejected as "the handmaiden of the Executive [branch]."

THE PRICE OF GAGS 2: ACCUSED OF SPREADING MISINFORMATION

The impact of these decisions wasn't just specific to the companies. Only a month after Judge Illston's ruling against Google, in June 2013, the Snowden revelations started, sparking a raging public debate in Congress and the media about these as well as other tools in the Patriot Act. But we had to keep quiet about the actual impact of NSLs. And now Google had to keep quiet about its experience with NSLs too.

One of Cloudflare's lawyers, Kenneth Carter, was even accused of spreading misinformation by the chief counsel to the House Judiciary Subcommittee on Crime, Terrorism, Homeland Security, and Investigations when he criticized NSLs in a lobbying meeting. The staffer claimed that Cloudflare could never receive an NSL, making Ken look uninformed in front of others in the meeting. Because of the gag order, Ken could not correct her and had to sit quietly instead of stating that in fact, Cloudflare had received several NSLs and was currently fighting them in court.

Similarly, the NSL gag prevented Becky, the vice president and political director for CREDO, from testifying to Congress about CREDO's experience with NSLs during the congressional fight over amendments to the NSL statute in 2014. By then the government had conceded that some changes were needed to the statute, in part because of Judge Illston's powerful decision. Unsurprisingly, though, the government supported only a few of the many changes that were needed and fought back hard against some of the ones we thought were critical.

Becky, who had been on the original call with me in 2011, was in the thick of the congressional fight. She knew that showing up as the company at issue in the litigation would give CREDO's voice more legitimacy and power. As we did, she thought that Congress would be especially concerned that CREDO had been countersued and accused of interfering with the "sovereign interests" of the United States for having sought judicial review of the NSL. Yet predictably, the gag order meant that we could not counter the government's presentations, which featured the FBI's cherry-picked stories of successes along with the continual downplaying of any problems.

The NSL gags also prevented both of our clients from publishing truthful transparency reports. EFF had long pressured companies to issue these reports, describing the type and number of legal processes that they received seeking information about their customers. These reports give us at least a snapshot of what we knew was going on all the time: companies were being required to turn over a lot of their customer's data to the government. Transparency reports are useful for advocacy, but their highest value is to help customers and potential customers evaluate just how frequently companies are turning their information over to law enforcement in both domestic and international situations.

In 2011, we started an annual campaign called "Who Has Your Back" comparing major telecommunications and internet companies on their processes for, as well as commitments to, protecting the privacy of their users. The reports came from a suggestion by then Icelandic parliamentarian Birgitta Jónsdóttir, who we represented in the US courts when prosecutors sought her information from Twitter as part of the grand jury investigation into the original Wikileaks leaks from Chelsea Manning. She noted that Twitter had done a good thing in giving her (and others) notice about the grand jury subpoena and wondered if we could encourage other companies to do the same. Ultimately we decided to rate companies against each other, giving gold stars to those that met certain criteria, including issuing transparency reports, requiring warrants for content, and as Twitter had done, providing notice to users when possible that the government was seeking their information.

The result was that over time, all the major consumer-facing internet companies started doing more of the things that we were rating them about, creating a race to the top. Competition can be a great incentive, and as it turned out, gold stars are a sufficient prize when you get one and your competitor doesn't. We often giggled after getting off the phone with sophisticated and highly paid in-house lawyers negotiating, and even sometimes whining, in an effort to get our gold stars. For a set of public interest lawyers and activists, it was good, clean fun. Noticeably absent from the race were telecommunications giants Verizon and AT&T, which consistently received fewer stars than the internet companies.

Despite our two clients being unable to fully participate due to the NSL gags, the pressure to reduce the bite of the NSL gag orders continued. There were issues in Congress and the public debate, but also before the FISA court. Companies continued to push back on the gag orders, especially as the number of them continued to grow. In January 2014, just as Congress was seriously debating reforms, the Justice Department announced a voluntary agreement to allow companies to begin to report the number of NSLs they had received. It approved disclosures in broad bands: either 0-999, or alternatively, the entire number of all "national security process" it had received (NSLs plus a few other things) in bands starting with 0-249.[18] This represented a tremendous step forward for the large companies, although for clients like our small telecommunications carrier and internet service CREDO, which had received only a few requests and wanted to talk about how these tools were being misused, it was not sufficient.

In the legislative fights, the secrecy hampered EFF too. We couldn't talk with any specificity about NSL gags, which meant that we also couldn't present specific stories about our cases as a part of the broader story of post-9/11 excesses. The gag created internal problems as well. EFF and CREDO ultimately had different views about how much Congress could reasonably be pushed into making overall FISA reforms, and we also differed about what the priorities should be. But the legislative team at EFF couldn't know that CREDO was also our client. There were some clashes along with a lot of uncomfortable conversations about when to compromise and when to keep fighting. This is always the case with big legislation—that's why they say that it's like making sausage—but in this case, it was especially difficult because of the gags.

CASE Q AT THE NINTH CIRCUIT

On October 8, 2014, we were back in front of the Ninth Circuit (fig. 3.1). By then Matt had left EFF. I was busy with *Jewel* and the transition to executive director, which would happen in spring 2015. Another member of our team, Kurt Opsahl, agreed to argue the case. As I had feared, the fact that Judge Illston had both denied all the subsequent NSL challenges and granted all the government's petitions to enforce was raised prominently by the government attorney. Judge Illston's failure to follow the normal course of First Amendment cases was immediately marshaled against us as proof that the courts could "fix" the statute with the *Mukasey* process.

We were hopeful, though. Judge Randy Smith expressly noted how unfair it was that recipients of NSLs had to bear the burden to challenge the gag repeatedly rather than the government lifting it once it was no longer needed. And in a telling admission, the government basically said that it was issuing so many NSLs that it just couldn't keep sufficient track to lift the gags. To me, if you are gagging so many people that you cannot possibly keep track of them sufficiently enough to know when the gag is no longer needed, that's a clear sign that you are going beyond the relatively narrow slice of situations in which national security is really at stake.

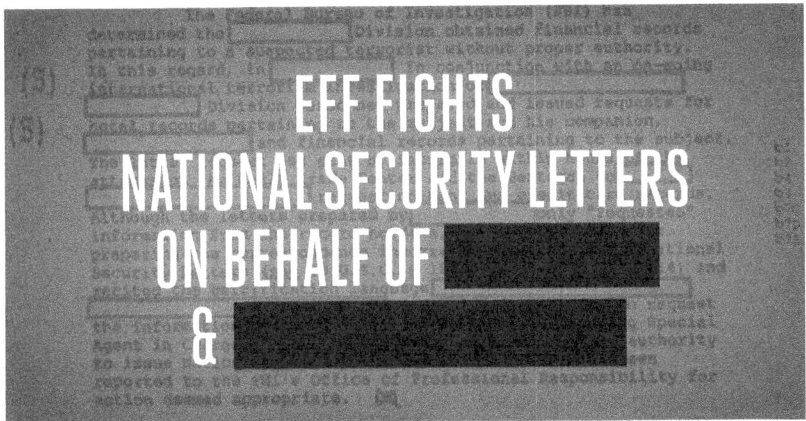

Figure 3.1 EFF banner for national security letters case by Hugh D'Andrade / EFF licensed under CC BY 4.0 (https://creativecommons.org/licenses/by/4.0).

Judge Mary Murguia asked some tough questions of the government attorney too, such as what would happen if the Ninth Circuit said that *Mukasey*'s extra requirements weren't a proper way to fix the statute. When the attorney responded that he hoped the court would give Congress enough time to act, she pointedly noted that it had been six years since the *Mukasey* decision found the constitutional problems and Congress still had not acted.

Overall, the oral argument went well, and Kurt seemed to have captured the attention of the judges about the problems in the government's arguments. We left the courtroom cautiously optimistic.

THE "NEVER GIVE AN INCH" PLAYBOOK

Once again, we weren't the only ones who thought the argument went well for us. Probably seeing the writing on the wall, the government did not seriously object to some changes in the NSL statute as part of the USA FREEDOM Act in June 2015. As I noted above, CREDO was especially frustrated that it couldn't tell its story as a recipient of an NSL to Congress and the public, which likely contributed to the weaker amendments being adopted. Congress did do one big thing that we had been demanding, however. It adopted a version of the previously voluntary *Mukasey* suggestions into actual law. We had come a long way from the initial FBI position that no one could ever even tell their lawyer about an NSL, much less challenge it. But NSL gags still didn't get the full First Amendment protections of other prior restraints.

Because of the new law, the Ninth Circuit sent the case back to Judge Illston for her to review whether the USA FREEDOM Act amendments fixed the problems she had found. Facing another judicial review of its NSL processes by Judge Illston, the government backpedaled even further. In November 2015, the attorney general adopted a formal process—called fittingly, "Termination Procedures for National Security Letter Nondisclosure Requirements"—that required the FBI to rereview the need for gag orders either three years after the start of an investigation or at the close of one.[19] No longer could the FBI issue a single document that gagged recipients forever.

Again, it was progress. Yet our clients didn't want to be gagged for three years just on the FBI's say-so. And while the new procedures were better, they still didn't meet the standards of the First Amendment for prior restraints. We renewed our arguments before Judge Illston, pointing out all the gaps between what the Constitution required and the complicated combination of law and attorney general rules that now applied to NSL gags.

By this point I was used to the government's "never give an inch" playbook. Even after Congress intervened to at least partially fix the problems with the gag orders, and even before the very same judge who had pointed out the problems, the government argued as if it had never even lost. This is especially frustrating to me because unlike counsel for a private party, government lawyers are supposed to be representing "the people." They are not supposed to be just narrowly defending the interests of government agencies as if they were a private client.

All of this to say that I was annoyed but not really surprised that nothing really changed in the government's arguments even after Judge Illston rejected them the first time and Congress significantly changed the law.

Just as before, government counsel argued that the First Amendment protections for prior restraints should not apply at all to NSLs. The Justice Department had to acknowledge the change in the law, of course. But it did so by trumpeting how the new USA FREEDOM Act (that it had strongly opposed) and its new internal rules brought the department "even more clearly" into compliance with the First Amendment. It's a kind of dance: first fighting as if any loss would be catastrophic and then minimizing the losses that do come, even as it seeks credit for making the changes that it was essentially forced into. I continue to find the whole dance fake and frustrating coming from what is, after all, called the Department of Justice.

FREEDMAN CLASSIC AND *FREEDMAN* LIGHT

Unfortunately, once the rules changed to be a bit less unfair to recipients, Judge Illston was done. In March 2016, she ruled that the USA FREEDOM Act had sufficiently addressed the facial constitutional problems with the NSL statute.[20]

I suspect it felt like a middle ground. Judge Illston didn't adopt the government's position that the First Amendment didn't apply to NSLs at all. But she also didn't agree with us that Congress's half measures in the USA Freedom Act still significantly failed to meet the requirements of the prior restraint doctrine. Instead, she held that NSLs weren't "classic" prior restraints and so the half measures were enough.

There is nothing in the First Amendment doctrine that likens it to Coca-Cola—with "classic" and "light" versions. Yet Judge Illston's decision reflected something we were to experience in other cases: the warping impact of national security. Apparently when national security was invoked, people gagged by the government were only deserving of *Freedman* light. Specifically, Judge Illston gave the government a pass on the requirement of prompt judicial review, prompt timing for a court decision, and the degree of deference given to the government. Citing the government's new policy for potentially lifting gag orders after three years as well as the previous agreement allowing companies to disclose wide "bands" of NSL information, the judge determined that the NSL process had been brought sufficiently under control.

Next she had to apply her *Freedman* light ruling to the specific NSLs at hand. For that, we got a mixed decision. For one of the NSLs, our initial case called Case Q, Judge Illston decided that the FBI had failed to provide a sufficient justification for continued gagging of our client. Once again, she stayed the impact of her ruling to let the government have time to appeal if it wanted to.

Perhaps because Judge Illston was right that there was no reasonable justification for an eternal gag for this NSL, the government dropped its appeal of that ruling in November 2016. Finally, six years in, we were able to reveal the client in Case Q as CREDO Mobile.[21] It was a great moment. We issued a press release in which the then CEO, Ray Morris, said, "We were proud to fight these NSLs all these years, and now we are proud to publish the letters and take full part in the ensuing debate."[22]

But we still couldn't reveal the other client, or anything else about the other three NSLs in Cases Z and W.

GOVERNMENT BLINKS AGAIN

We appealed again to the Ninth Circuit, and a year went by while we filed briefs back and forth. The government fought hard—with no hint of what apparently was going on behind the scenes. But just days before the oral argument date in March 2017, it blinked again. We received a notice telling us that the Justice Department had applied the termination procedures required by the USA Freedom Act and partially lifted the NSL gags in the other two cases.[23]

At long last, this allowed us to reveal that our other secret client was Cloudflare. Our main contact there, lawyer Kenneth Carter, had been the one accused of spreading misinformation when he told a congressional staffer that the company could receive an NSL. He felt vindicated, but of course by then the law Cloudflare was lobbying over, the USA FREEDOM Act, had passed and Congress had moved on.

We could also reveal that the client in the 2011 NSL case called Case W, filed just after the statute was declared unconstitutional, was CREDO.

Both clients were ecstatic. We rushed to write a press release that would announce their identities and explain the long fight they had to have before they could reveal themselves. It was the first time that the clients knew who each other were too. This felt extremely gratifying, and I could hear everyone smiling through the phone line as we talked through the strategy together on a conference call.

The last-minute lifting of some portions of the gags by the government meant a scramble as we prepared for oral argument, but it was a good scramble. We knew that the government had blinked at least in part because it calculated that we were likely to win in court. It was too much of a coincidence to believe that national security required a gag up until just two days before the hearing and then, suddenly, didn't. We suspected that the government saw, just as we had, the skepticism the court showed last time when they argued that infinite gags issued solely by the prosecutors were just fine under the Constitution.

EFF: THE NEXT GENERATION

Andrew Crocker was handling the argument for us this time. Andrew represented a new phase of EFF; he had joined EFF fresh out of law school in 2013. The first time we spoke, Andrew told me that he was interested in helping with the NSL cases. I could hear the fight in his voice and immediately recognized someone who felt as strongly as I did that the Constitution applied even in the face of national security claims.

In that first call with Andrew, though, I was a bit hesitant. I was still considering whether EFF's legal team could handle bringing in a brand-new attorney. Despite the fact that I had jumped into internet law while still quite green, I didn't think that was the best way to go. I worried that our cutting-edge docket was too hard to get a handle on while someone was still figuring out the basics of running a lawsuit. While we always had law students as interns, until Andrew, I had only hired people for the EFF legal team who already had multiple years of litigation experience under their belt.

I decided to take a chance, and it turned out to be an excellent decision. It likely was a bit rough for Andrew as we quickly threw him into the deep end of the law with our cases. It helped tremendously that he was a quick study, but also that he had a passion for as well as dedication to both privacy and the First Amendment. By March 2017, he was definitely ready for a showdown on the edge of the law.

In the Ninth Circuit hearing, Andrew argued mightily that the new procedures weren't enough. I watched full of pride. Here was the first EFF lawyer who had started his practice out with us, and he was now arguing one of our marquis cases before the court of appeals.

The government attorney presented well too, however, and had clearly mastered the position of ultimate reasonableness even as he floated a few whoppers. The biggest was his argument that the fact that few companies challenged NSLs somehow meant that they didn't want to. I tried to keep my face straight at that one. It was as if the neighborhood bully claimed that kids actually wanted to give them their lunch money because they never told the teacher.

We had talked to many companies that were flatly scared and intimidated by the prospect of challenging the government on a matter related to national security, regardless of the specifics. This was reinforced by the language and process surrounding the NSL gag orders. The fact that our clients had been affirmatively sued for having challenged the government provided an additional disincentive; most general counsels try to keep their companies as far away from a showdown with the FBI as possible.

Overall, though, the government lawyer marshaled all the changes that we and other advocates had forced onto the NSL process in a skillful way. His basic approach was to embrace them, saying that whatever issues there were had been fixed (never mind that the government had kicked and screamed the whole way) and the statutory scheme was now constitutional. We had a bad feeling coming out of the argument that as with Judge Illston, the Ninth Circuit panel would decide that the law was now "close enough" rather than requiring full First Amendment protection.

We were right to be worried coming out of the oral argument. In July 2017, the Ninth Circuit issued an opinion upholding the amended NSL statute.[24] The decision did apply the toughest First Amendment standards, called strict scrutiny, to the substance of the NSL, but found that they were met. The most egregious part was when the court dismissed the clear requirement that a gag order not be any broader than necessary (what the law calls "narrow tailoring") by saying that it didn't want to "quibble" with the FBI about its processes for issuing and terminating gags, as if our rights were mere annoyances.

But it didn't stop there. What was really wrong was the procedural prior restraint analysis under *Freedman v. Maryland*. This is the requirement that we'd relied on in *Bernstein*: that if the government is going to try to stop speech before it happens, it has to have clear rules, make quick decisions, and bears the burden of proof if challenged in court.

The Ninth Circuit basically held that unilateral gags from the FBI issued with NSLs, despite stopping speech before it happens, just weren't prior restraints. If a government agent stops you from speaking with a piece of paper it issues on its own, you don't get the full protections of the law that you would if that same government agent had denied you a license to have the same effect. This was shocking since for many years after *Freedman*, the prior restraint doctrine had been regularly applied outside traditional licensing schemes. The court seemed to elevate the form of censorship over its substance.

Our clients remained steadfast, and while we were all disappointed, they were nothing but supportive. We were all frustrated, however, since neither of them had taken on this scary and huge fight just for themselves. Still, they had stood up to the government, been painted as unpatriotic for doing so, and had emerged victorious. Their fight had paved a better, if still imperfect, way for others. We hoped that their courage would be contagious.

We filed for rehearing en banc in October 2017, asking for review by a larger panel of judges to overturn the mistakes in what the three-judge panel had done. We rushed to get our papers in and then waited. And waited. And waited. We went from checking in on the status to simply making jokes about how the court had apparently forgotten the core issue in prior restraints: that making a quick decision on a gag was critical. Finally, four and a half years later, in May 2022, the panel issued a small correction to what was essentially a typo in the decision and added a footnote. It kept all of its wrong analysis. We had no idea what took so long.

Long before the en banc decision came out, we knew that despite our victories, there were storm clouds ahead. While the reasons differed, the courts seemed content to let the constitutional civil liberties protections be weakened in national security cases. In the NSL cases, the most glaring part was about time: the courts let our clients be gagged for six years. This meant that our clients were gagged during multiple legislative hearings and sessions in which Congress debated these laws.

MAKING A THOUSAND CUTS

At this point we had won quite a bit of what we had originally set out to do, albeit in a disjointed and unsatisfying way. With all the day-to-day work of strategizing, working with the clients, writing, researching and filing briefs, and preparing for oral arguments as well as efforts in Congress, it required taking a step back to see the progress. But each of our clients could now tell the world, including congressional staff, that they had received NSLs, and been gagged and countersued when they stood up to challenge the government. We had met their first goal of being able to participate in the public debate and use their own experiences as evidence to counter the government's misleading assertions about NSLs. We had increased the procedural protections for those receiving NSLs, including clearing the way to challenge them with standards that were not quite as stacked against them. We had helped create a path for corporate transparency reports that at least gave some information to the public about how often these controversial tools were being used.

We have a saying at EFF: "Total victory for our clients is never enough." We use it to talk about that strange position that impact lawyers like us are frequently in, where their clients are vindicated, yet there is still more to do to get a bigger or broader impact.

The progress also had an unsatisfying narrative; we had a shining initial court victory that we didn't get to confirm on appeal. Instead, we dragged a series of smaller wins out of the muck through a mix of the FBI backing down and Congress creating a series of half measures, all spurred on by our advocacy. Our clients won the right to tell the world that they had gotten an NSL, but we hadn't succeeded in getting the full list of First Amendment protections for the next recipient of an NSL, much less our ultimate goal of getting Congress to require warrants or other judicial approval before the FBI can issue NSLs.

Still, along with a few stalwarts in Congress and a small but mighty coalition of public interest organizations, we had, cut by cut, made significant inroads into the excesses of the Patriot Act. Even with the frustrating, one-sided limitations on what we could do given our nonprofit status, we helped shrink the lion, even if we didn't get it all the way back to the size of a house cat.

We continue to do so to this day. And in some ways, that is the bigger lesson for civil liberties. It's just not like a one-hour TV drama where after fifty minutes the good guys have won, and we get the denouement and then preview of the next episode.

Rather, over time and with lots of paper, we built up the pressure. The ACLU lawsuits set the stage for us in our NSL cases. Our own Freedom of Information Act work kept forcing the government to give up a little more information each time. The inspector general's reports confirmed and added to that. We and our allies were lobbying Congress, along with our clients. Some of the bigger tech companies like Google pushed back as well, both in the public courts and secret FISA ones, even as the telecommunications companies like AT&T and Verizon did not.

Our victory before Judge Illston helped us push for the changes in the USA Freedom Act, and then that law helped push the government to back down and create the "bands" of transparency that allowed companies to at least begin to tell the public about the increased use of this controversial tool. As the smaller victories mounted in these different areas, the press had more to cover (and speculate about), which fed the public's attention. Ultimately, and while largely pretending not to, the government started to cave. It dropped some NSLs. It decided to allow for a little more transparency.

The upshot is that big change isn't always achieved with one sweeping victory. In fact if you look closely, it rarely is. Instead, we win with a thousand tiny cuts. We win by being ready to spring into action when a random comment turns into a phone call turns into a lawsuit.

CONCLUSION

"Would you look at this?" I marveled as Patrick and I walked into the annual EFF awards ceremony. The ornate, Gothic ballroom in San Francisco was filled and buzzing with energy underneath the stained-glass windows and open-beamed, carved-wood ceilings. I brushed my now silver-streaked hair back and thought about whether my mother, who passed in 2015 just a week after I took over as EFF's executive director, would approve of the new dress I wore for the occasion. My father had passed two years after her and I still missed them both.

"I know. Most of these people were not even born when we started the fight for encryption. I suspect they barely remember a world before Snowden, much less the Patriot Act," he answered, reaching for my hand.

Not all the people in that room were that young. Among the mix of business suits, dayglow pink hair, and black T-shirts I could still see and greet many of the folks who had been with us from the time when we were a bunch of misfit lawyers, hackers, and activists gathered outside stately courtrooms. Two declarants in the Bernstein case, Bruce Schneier and Brian Behlendorf, now sat on the EFF board of directors.

But Patrick was right that there were far more people who had joined the cause since then. EFF itself was 120 people strong in 2024, with more lawyers, technologists, and activists than ever before.

This night is special. Our annual awards event is a moment when we come together, both staff and supporters, to reflect on the battles we're facing and celebrate this year's victories. Especially now that we have staff members as far away as Germany, Britain, Japan, Brazil, and Peru, it's a moment when we remind ourselves of why we do this work. It's a moment to celebrate every little victory, as my friend Bob taught me back during the *Bernstein* case.

It's deeply satisfying to see all the ways that the work that we did in the 1990s has shaped the modern digital world. We haven't won every privacy battle, but we've won quite a few. The rollback of the encryption regulations as well as the cutbacks to the NSA spying and NSLs helped protect the privacy and security of millions of people.

But an even broader impact is that these cases, and the principles that we stood up for in them, have become foundational. In *Bernstein*, we helped establish the principle that code is speech, which sets the bar high for attempts to regulate coding or hold the coder responsible for when people misuse the tools they develop. *Bernstein* also helped foster a strong public constituency standing up for encryption that has regularly pushed back on law enforcement demands for access in the United States and around the world.

In the NSA spying cases, we helped shine a light on the fact that metadata can be as powerful, if not more powerful, than the content of our messages for prying into our lives. We haven't won that fight yet, but in a few cases involving cell phone data, the Supreme Court has recognized the power of location data collected over time and started chipping away at the third-party doctrine.

Finally, now and into the future, the primary means of communication and access to information for most people will be through technologies controlled by other people—corporate or otherwise. The central principle of the NSL cases—ensuring that those entities can *tell us* when our information is sought by the government or other third parties—will remain critical.

EFF TODAY

Now over thirty-five years since its founding and twenty-five years since I formally joined, EFF is still working to protect and enhance privacy, and the check on power that privacy provides. As the internet has become more diverse and more vital to people's everyday lives, we have broadened our work as well. The implications of that surveillance for marginalized communities—which have always been disproportionately impacted by government and corporate surveillance—are now central to our work and approach.

The first threats to digital privacy came from the US federal government, but it's no longer the sole province of the NSA and FBI. State, local, and foreign governments all have the ability to engage in mass surveillance. Local police around the United States and world now regularly demand information from the companies that host and carry our communications. On the global scale, data increasingly gets shared with law enforcement across borders.

The threat of government surveillance has gained new urgency since the Supreme Court's decision in *Dobbs v. Jackson Women's Health Organization* and the massive changes under the second Trump administration.[1] By rolling back the constitutional right to an abortion in 2022, the Supreme Court allowed states to impose criminal penalties and create civil lawsuits against those seeking or offering abortion care. Many states are doing so, and are using our digital information to locate and prosecute people. They are also attempting to restrict travel, implicating the location-tracking metadata of our communications.

Even before the *Dobbs* decision, the first Trump administration's willingness to use government to stifle dissent reminded many of the importance of privacy from hostile governments. The second Trump administration has supercharged those concerns, as it seeks to control and troll through governmental databases to identify targets for deportation, firings and retaliation, and in the process, greatly increases security risks to those people whose data is in those databases. So EFF has sued the government to stand up for privacy again.

Corporate surveillance is important to resist in its own right. The massive collection, analysis, and use of our data by tech giants along with the shadowy data broker world cause many problems, including feeding discrimination and injustice as well as maintaining the monopolies of the tech giants and blocking innovation. We desperately need a strong, baseline consumer privacy law in the United States and many places around the world. EFF has long supported this cause, including through lobbying, litigation, public advocacy, and building tools like Privacy Badger that help users limit corporate tracking.

But as the stories I've shared above demonstrate, the government leverages the companies that provide us digital communications services in order to spy on us, with consequences that can include imprisonment and even death. And as the shifts in leadership from Clinton to George W. Bush to Obama to Trump to Biden and then to Trump again demonstrate, people who might not have seemed to need privacy from their government one day, can suddenly, urgently, need it the next. It continues to be critical to protect privacy regardless of whether we're feeling powerful at the moment.

DARK TIME FOR PRIVACY

As proud as I am about what we've accomplished, it's still a dark time for privacy overall. I understand and share the sense of being overwhelmed by the never-ending stream of reports of surveillance, big and small. Even the wins we've gotten are not clean, happily-ever-after wins. The Snowden revelations highlighted that after we prevailed in getting the export regulations reduced in the 1990s, the NSA simply went underground, working to undermine our networks and the key encryption tools that millions of people rely on.[2] We face ongoing efforts to ban or undermine end-to-end encryption both in the United States and abroad, with law enforcement officials trotting out the same old stories about how they are "going dark," even as they have more power to surveil than ever before thanks to technologies like facial recognition systems, ubiquitous camera networks, and the massive spy apparatus and tracking arrayed at the US border.[3]

Even today, over twenty years later, we still do not have a clear picture of what searches the FBI is doing on the NSA's vast collection of information. The FBI refuses to say, and despite dogged efforts by Senator Wyden and others, Congress has refused to force it to give reports of its searches, much less scale back FBI access to the NSA-collected information.[4] Year after year, the inspector general's reports and FISA court reviews of the programs find huge problems in their implementation.[5] The truth is that the government simply cannot simultaneously surveil millions of people consistent with even its own, loose rules, much less consistent with the US Constitution or the privacy protections required by US and international law.

NSLs are still issued, along with gags, in huge numbers with only minimal judicial review, not the full warrant standard. And while we're making inroads, metadata too often remains outside legal, much less constitutional, protections. A federal comprehensive privacy law that would actually protect and empower us still feels a long way off.

Our tools and strategies need an upgrade too. While federal impact litigation has been a powerful tool for a long time, portions of the federal judiciary are more hostile to it these days—using various doctrines to limit who can sue for harms, and in some cases, effectively refusing to recognize privacy harms at all.[6] And as both the NSA spying and NSL stories underscore, the federal courts are increasingly willing to tolerate a national-security-shaped hole in the Constitution. There's a growing need for innovation in our work to protect privacy both inside and outside the courts.

It would be easy to give up. I don't actually think we have a choice, though, but to continue to fight for our privacy. As the *Dobbs* decision, Trump administration's various attacks on privacy, and ongoing hostility to encryption around the globe demonstrate, no one is really safe from the risks of a world without privacy. We just all aren't in the crosshairs all the time. I don't believe there is anyone who, either for themselves or someone they love, is ever completely free of the risks of a surveillance state. So the work must go on.

FLASH WEDDING

"You ready?" my brother said. We were standing, arms intertwined, at the top of my back stairs, looking down onto the garden in the old Mission District Victorian house that Patrick and I had purchased together with Emma, the friend who had moved in with me years ago when my first marriage fell apart. We now regularly hosted live music in that garden, which was lovingly tended by Emma.

Forty-five members of our community stood waiting for us, with two of them serving as officiants standing on a little raised platform we'd rigged up. I was wearing a gold-and-black dress that a Nigerian man in Santa Cruz had made, seemingly just for me. I felt my mother, father, and Harold, all now passed on, present in my bones.

"Yes," I answered, still a little stunned at what we'd pulled off with one week's notice.

"Sally, go ahead." Sally, an eight-year-old, also adopted daughter of one of my friends, expertly held the leash of Lali, our older Bernese mountain dog. Another friend carried the leash of our puppy, Whitney. They led the dogs down through the garden, in between the rows of chairs and up to Patrick, standing in a silver coat and vest. Two of our music festival sing-along friends played guitar and sang a song they'd written as a stand-in for the wedding march. As if on cue, the puppy peed just as he got to Patrick

My brother and I followed into the garden. Patrick pulled a small black container off Lali's collar. It held the rings we'd found just six days before. Less than a month ago, after thirteen and a half years of hinting, Patrick had dropped to one knee and formally asked me to marry him. I had accepted, in that moment feeling the clarity of our connection stretching all the way back to his voice in that first phone call in the 1990s. Patrick may never have fully forgiven me for deciding not to use his declaration in the *Bernstein* case, but he's gotten over it.

The flash in the flash wedding was because my brother could be there after four COVID-filled years apart. I wasn't about to miss this chance, even if it meant many other loved ones couldn't make it. We sent out emails and a spreadsheet, and the community had immediately thrown in to make it happen. Six of the people at the wedding that day had been on that bus to Death Valley with me in the 1990s. More important, those same people had held me together through all the ups and downs since then.

In front of our community, Patrick and I stepped into a new chapter.

THE FIGHT FOR PRIVACY IS EVERGREEN

This work protecting privacy online can feel like a whack-a-mole game at times. It can be heavy and frustrating. But I hope that by sharing this as my personal story, it sounds like it can also be fun and exciting.

Because as I said at the start, I am trying to recruit you.

There's much more to do, both to further fight these entrenched battles and take on the new ones that will appear. Tomorrow's technologies along with future governments and companies will present new versions of the challenge, and as I noted above, we definitely need some new strategies and tactics. Still, if history is any guide, we will have another instance of government or corporate overreach and hubris that will bring the issue of reining in surveillance to center stage again. We need to be ready.

I know I've been lucky that I've had a relatively safe place from which to focus on this work. Many people don't have the luxury of retreating to a music festival to recharge in the midst of a big fight. People who need privacy most are facing immediate problems—prison, deportation, loss of health care and jobs, discrimination, police violence, domestic violence, and war. They face international human rights abuses like disappearances, torture, or death. But I submit that finding a place to recharge and experience joy is one of the ways that human beings find their way through adversity. For me, my community and the music we share together has been critical to sticking with these fights for the long run—now thirty-five years and counting.

As I've talked to and worked with activists around the world, the ones who stay in it for the long haul all have a version of this—a place, even if it's just a mental one, to retreat to and focus on something other than the fight for a little while.

One thing is certain: Just as we needed privacy at the dawn of the internet, future generations will need that right as technology advances. Privacy is a crucial check on power, and it will be even more so in the years to come. The mechanisms of dissent, self-government, and freedom of association require it.

Whether you know your place in the fight for a better world or, like me, are hoping that your place finds you, there's plenty of room at the barricades. We need lawyers, technologists, and activists, but we also need artists, economists, scientists, researchers, writers, analysts, and statisticians like Patrick. I maintain that the people who fight for freedom and justice throw better parties than the forces of repression, but even if parties aren't your thing, there is a community now for digital rights and freedoms that stands together through good times and bad. Come join us.

ABBREVIATIONS

BXA: Bureau of Export Administration. The part of the Commerce Department that regulates exports, which took the lead on cryptography exports. In 2002 it changed its name to the Bureau of Industry and Security or BIS.

CDA: Communications Decency Act. The short name of Title V of the Telecommunications Act of 1996, as specified in Section 501 of the 1996 Act. It was the US Congress's first notable attempt to regulate "indecent" material on the Internet. In the 1997 landmark case *Reno v. ACLU*, the US Supreme Court unanimously struck the act's anti-indecency provisions, although most of its secondary liability protections for internet hosts, called Section 230, remain.

CJ: Commodity Jurisdiction. The initial process to request for a license from the State Department for export of cryptography.

EAR: Export Administration Regulations. The Commerce Department export regulations.

FISA: Foreign Intelligence Surveillance Act. Created in 1978, this law establishes procedures for the surveillance and collection of foreign intelligence on US domestic soil.

FISC: Foreign Intelligence Surveillance Court. US federal court established under the Foreign Intelligence Surveillance Act of 1978 (FISA) to oversee requests for surveillance warrants against foreign spies inside the United States by federal law enforcement and intelligence agencies.

ITAR: International Traffic in Arms Regulations. A set of US Department of State regulations that control the export of defense and military technologies to safeguard national security and further its foreign policy objectives

MDL: Multi-District Litigation. A special federal legal procedure designed to speed the process for handling complex cases with numerous plaintiffs making similar claims, such as air disaster litigation or complex product liability suits.

NSA: National Security Agency. An intelligence agency of the US Department of Defense, under the authority of the director of national intelligence (DNI) responsible for global monitoring, collection, and processing of information and data for global intelligence and counterintelligence purposes.

NSL: National Security Letter. An administrative subpoena issued by the US government to gather information for national security purposes.

SCIF: Sensitive Compartmentalized Information Facility. An enclosed area within a building that is used to process types of classified information.

USML: US Munitions List. A list of articles, services, and related technology designated as defense and space-related by the US federal government, administered by the Department of State.

NOTES

INTRODUCTION

1. Daniel J. Solove, *Understanding Privacy* (Harvard University Press, 2008), 1. See also generally Daniel J. Solove, "Conceptualizing Privacy," *California Law Review* 1087 (2002): 90; Daniel J. Solove, "A Taxonomy of Privacy," *University of Pennsylvania Law Review* 477 (2005): 154.

2. Martin Kaste, "Nebraska Cops Used Facebook Messages to Investigate an Alleged Illegal Abortion," NPR, August 12, 2022, https://www.npr.org/2022/08/12/1117092169/nebraska-cops-used-facebook-messages-to-investigate-an-alleged-illegal-abortion.

3. Nadia Lathan, "Texas Man Drops Lawsuit Against Women He Accused of Helping His Wife Get Abortion Pills," *AP News*, October 11, 2024, sec. U.S. News, https://apnews.com/article/texas-abortion-bans-settlement-4be6bdee1520292d675f678f7053a6ce.

4. Steven Levy, "You Can Now See the Code That Helped End Apartheid," *WIRED*, October 18, 2024, https://archive.is/yK8Jb; Rignam Wangkhang, "Empowering Digital Tibet: An Interview with Activist Lhadon Tethong," IFEX, December 9, 2015, https://ifex.org/empowering-digital-tibet-an-interview-with-activist-lhadon-tethong/; Philip Zimmermann, "PGP 30th Anniversary," accessed November 8, 2024, https://philzimmermann.com/EN/essays/PGP_30th/.

5. Laura Poitras and Glenn Greenwald, "NSA Whistleblower Edward Snowden: 'I Don't Want to Live in a Society That Does These Sort of Things'—Video," *Guardian*, June 9, 2013, sec. US News, https://www.theguardian.com/world/video/2013/jun/09/nsa-whistleblower-edward-snowden-interview-video.

6. Office of the Director of National Intelligence, Senior Advisory Group Panel on Commercially Available Information, *Report to the Director of National Intelligence, 27 January 2022*, https://www.dni.gov/files/ODNI/documents/assessments/ODNI-Declassified-Report-on-CAI-January2022.pdf.

7. Eric Umansky, "How Police Have Undermined the Promise of Body Cameras," *ProPublica*, December 14, 2023, https://www.propublica.org/article/how-police-undermined-promise-body-cameras. In contrast, as we saw in Minneapolis on May 25, 2020, when police officer Derek Chauvin killed George Floyd, camera footage from people with phones has been important to creating increased police accountability. But that's quite different from self-surveillance by the police.

8. Cindy Cohn, "EFF Response to FBI Director Comey's Speech on Encryption," Electronic Frontier Foundation, October 17, 2014, https://www.eff.org/deeplinks/2014/10/eff-response-fbi-director-comeys-speech-encryption.

9. Rafael Bernal, "Trump Administration: Three-Quarters of International Terrorism Convicts Foreign Born," *Hill*, January 16, 2018, https://thehill.com/latino/369126-trump-administration-three-quarters-of-international-terrorism-convicts-foreign-born/.

10. Alina Selyukh, "NSA Staff Used Spy Tools on Spouses, Ex-Lovers: Watchdog," Reuters, September 27, 2013, https://www.reuters.com/article/world/uk/nsa-staff-used-spy-tools-on-spouses-ex-lovers-watchdog-idUSBRE98Q14H/.

11. Polly Sprenger, "Sun on Privacy: 'Get Over It,'" *WIRED*, January 26, 1999, https://www.wired.com/1999/01/sun-on-privacy-get-over-it/.

CHAPTER 1

1. John Markoff, "Data-Secrecy Export Case Dropped by U.S.," *New York Times*, January 12, 1996, sec. Business, https://www.nytimes.com/1996/01/12/business/data-secrecy-export-case-dropped-by-us.html.

2. Suzanne Bearne, "Meet the Female Codebreakers of Bletchley Park," *Guardian*, July 24, 2018, sec. Guardian Careers, https://www.theguardian.com/careers/2018/jul/24/meet-the-female-codebreakers-of-bletchley-park; B. J. Copeland, "Ultra: Allied Intelligence Project," *Britannica*, accessed November 1, 2024, https://www.britannica.com/topic/Ultra-Allied-intelligence-project.

3. Cindy A. Cohn, "The Early Harvest: Domestic Legal Changes Related to the Human Rights Committee and the Covenant on Civil and Political Rights," *Human Rights Quarterly* 13, no. 3 (1991): 295–321, https://doi.org/10.2307/762617; Cindy A. Cohn, "Who's Listening?," *Nordic Journal of International Law* 59, no. 4 (1990): 321–327, https://doi.org/10.1163/157181090X00396.

4. "The WELL," Wikipedia, February 3, 2025, https://en.wikipedia.org/wiki/The_WELL.

5. Cliff Figallo, "The Well: Small Town on the Information Highway System," *Whole Earth Review*, September 1, 1993, https://ia903103.us.archive.org/13/items/CliffFigallo/TheWELLfig1993.html.

6. "Mitchell Kapor," Wikipedia, February 2, 2025, https://en.wikipedia.org/wiki/Mitch_Kapor.

7. Linda Navarro, "A Look Back in Colorado Springs | A Surprising Grateful Dead Connection," *Colorado Springs Gazette*, April 17, 2020, https://gazette.com/arts-entertainment/a-look-back-in-colorado-springs-a-surprising-grateful-dead-connection/article_a7084630-7136-11ea-afb5-035746de9dcd.html.

8. John Perry Barlow, "Crime and Puzzlement," June 8, 1990, https://w2.eff.org/Misc/Publications/John_Perry_Barlow/HTML/crime_and_puzzlement_1.html.

9. John Perry Barlow, "A Not Terribly Brief History of the Electronic Frontier Foundation," November 8, 1990, https://w2.eff.org/Misc/Publications/John_Perry_Barlow/HTML/not_too_brief_history.html.

10. Barlow, "A Not Terribly Brief History of the Electronic Frontier Foundation."

11. Abby Ohlheiser, "The Creator of Godwin's Law Explains Why Some Nazi Comparisons Don't Break His Famous Internet Rule," *Washington Post*, August 14, 2017, https://www.washingtonpost.com/news/the-intersect/wp/2017/08/14/the-creator-of-godwins-law-explains-why-some-nazi-comparisons-dont-break-his-famous-internet-rule/.

12. Qureshi Haseeb, "The Cypherpunks," balajis.com, December 19, 2019, https://nakamoto.com/the-cypherpunks/.

13. "Hash Function," Wikipedia, October 29, 2024, https://en.wikipedia.org/w/index.php?title=Hash_function&oldid=1254008529.

14. Freedman v. Maryland, 380 U.S. 51, 57 (1965).

15. Bernstein v. US Department of State, 922 F. Supp. 1426, 1435 (N.D. Cal. 1996).

16. Bernstein, 922 F. Supp. 1436.

17. Declaration of Dr. Andrew W. Appel in Bernstein v. Department of State, C 95-00582 MHP, July 26, 1996, https://www.eff.org/files/filenode/bernstein/exhibit.d.html.

18. Bernstein v. US Department of State, 974 F. Supp 1288, 1303, 1305 (N.D. Cal 1997).

19. Reno v. ACLU, 521 US 844 (1997).

20. Phillip Elmer De Witt, "Online Erotica: On a Screen Near You," *TIME*, July 3, 1995, https://time.com/archive/6727576/online-erotica-on-a-screen-near-you/.

21. See, for example, Senator Charles Grassley, "Cyberporn," *Congressional Record*, June 26, 1995, S9017–S9023, https://www.congress.gov/congressional-record/volume-141/issue-105/senate-section/article/S9017-2. For a good summary of the history of the Communications Decency Act, including the role of the WELL and EFF's first attorney, Godwin, see Raj Shah, "The Communications Decency Act of 1996," https://www.mit.edu/people/rshah/21H931.major.pdf.

22. John Perry Barlow, "A Declaration of the Independence of Cyberspace," EFF, https://www.eff.org/cyberspace-independence.

23. Peter Swire, "'Going Dark' Versus a 'Golden Age for Surveillance,'" *Center for Democracy and Technology* (blog), November 28, 2011, https://cdt.org/insights/going-dark-versus-a-golden-age-for-surveillance/.

24. Amy Harmon, "The Law Where There Is No Land; A Legal System Built on Precedents Has Few of Them in the Digital World," *New York Times*, March 16, 1998, sec. Business, https://www.nytimes.com/1998/03/16/business/law-where-there-no-land-legal-system-built-precedents-has-few-them-digital-world.html.

25. Bernstein v. US Department of State, 176 F.3d 1132, 1141, 1142, 1146 (9th Cir. 1999).

26. Anthony J. Pennings, "How 'STAR WARS' and the Japanese Artificial Intelligence (AI) Threat Led to the Internet, Part III: NSFNET and the Atari Democrats," January 2, 2011, https://apennings.com/how-it-came-to-rule-the-world/how-%E2%80%9Cstar-wars%E2%80%9D-and-the-japanese-artificial-intelligence-ai-threat-led-to-the-internet-part-iii-nsfnet-and-the-atari-democrats/.

CHAPTER 2

1. Kam C. Wong, "The Making of the USA Patriot Act I: The Legislative Process and Dynamics," *International Journal of the Sociology of Law* 34, no. 3 (September 1, 2006): 179–219, https://doi.org/10.1016/j.ijsl.2006.09.001.

2. Wong, "The Making of the USA Patriot Act I," 180.

3. National Commission on Terrorist Attacks upon the United States, *The 9/11 Commission Report*, July 22, 2004, 79, http://govinfo.library.unt.edu/911/report/911Report.pdf.

4. National Commission on Terrorist Attacks, *9/11 Commission Report*, 258–259, 265.

5. US Department of Justice, Office of the Inspector General, *A Review of the FBI's Handling of Intelligence Information Related to the September 11 Attacks*, June 2006, chap. 1, https://oig.justice.gov/sites/default/files/archive/special/s0606/chapter1.htm.

6. National Commission on Terrorist Attacks, *9/11 Commission Report*, 277.

7. National Commission on Terrorist Attacks, *9/11 Commission Report*, 266; Eric Lichtblau and David E. Sanger, "August '01 Brief Is Said to Warn of Attack Plans," *New York Times*, April 10, 2004, sec. U.S., https://www.nytimes.com/2004/04/10/us/august-01-brief-is-said-to-warn-of-attack-plans.html.

8. National Commission on Terrorist Attacks, *9/11 Commission Report*, 254–255.

9. National Security Agency / Central Security Service, *Transition 2001*, EFF, December 2000, https://www.eff.org/document/nsa-transition-2001.

10. "Privacy Advocates Concerned About Echelon," ACLU, May 1, 2000, https://www.aclu.org/press-releases/privacy-advocates-concerned-about-echelon.

11. "Total Information Awareness," Wikipedia, February 27, 2025, https://en.wikipedia.org/wiki/Total_Information_Awareness.

12. William Tudor, *The Life of James Otis, of Massachusetts: Containing Also, Notices of Some Contemporary Characters and Events from the Year 1760 to 1775* (London: Forgotten Books, 2018), 66.

13. Quoted in Nelson B. Lasson, *The History and Development of the Fourth Amendment to the United States Constitution* (Boston: Da Capo Press, 1970), 59.

14. Payton v. New York, 445 U.S. 573, 583 (1980).

15. Katz v. United States, 389 U.S. 347, 351 (1967).

16. United States v. Warshak, 631 F.3d 266 (6th Cir. 2010).

17. Natasha Lomas, "Stanford Quantifies the Privacy-Stripping Power of Metadata," *TechCrunch* (blog), May 17, 2016, https://techcrunch.com/2016/05/17/stanford-quantifies-the-privacy-stripping-power-of-metadata/.

18. Paul Szoldra, "Leaked NSA Document Says Metadata Collection Is One of Agency's 'Most Useful Tools,'" *Business Insider*, December 7, 2016, https://www.businessinsider.com/nsa-document-metadata-2016-12.

19. David Cole, "We Kill People Based on Metadata," *New York Review* (blog), May 10, 2014, https://www.nybooks.com/online/2014/05/10/we-kill-people-based-metadata/.

20. Alan Rusbridger, "The Snowden Leaks and the Public," *New York Review*, November 21, 2013, https://www.nybooks.com/articles/2013/11/21/snowden-leaks-and-public/.

21. Mary Bruce, "Obama: 'Nobody Is Listening to Your Phone Calls,'" *ABC News*, June 7, 2013, https://abcnews.go.com/blogs/politics/2013/06/obama-nobody-is-listening-to-your-phone-calls/.

22. Congress restored some banking privacy by the Right to Financial Privacy Act of 1978. 12 U.S.C. §§ 3401-3402.

23. "Contacting EFF," Internet Archive, August 15, 2000, https://web.archive.org/web/20000815052750/http://www.eff.org/contact.html#staff; "EFF: About: Staff," Internet Archive, March 5, 2005, https://web.archive.org/web/20050305013103/http://www.eff.org/about/staff/.

24. "History of Gmail," Wikipedia, October 13, 2024, https://en.wikipedia.org/w/index.php?title=History_of_Gmail&oldid=1250880598.

25. Shoshana Zuboff, *The Age of Surveillance Capitalism* (London: Profile Books, 2019).

26. Christopher McFadden, "A Brief History of Facebook and Its Major Milestones," *Interesting Engineering*, March 29, 2023, https://interestingengineering.com/culture/history-of-facebook.

27. "EFF Sues Barney the Dinosaur to Defend Online Free Speech," Electronic Frontier Foundation, August 23, 2006, https://www.eff.org/press/archives/2006/08/23.

28. "DNA Lounge: EFF Benefit: Wil Wheaton vs. Barney Celebrity Wrestling," August 22, 2002, https://www.dnalounge.com/gallery/2002/08-22/024.html.

29. Those machines are called DREs, which stands for Direct Recording Electronic, indicating that the vote is directly recorded into computer memory from the touchscreen.

30. James Risen and Eric Lichtblau, "Bush Lets U.S. Spy on Callers Without Courts," *New York Times*, December 16, 2005, sec. U.S., https://www.nytimes.com/2005/12/16/politics/bush-lets-us-spy-on-callers-without-courts.html.

31. "Internet Backbone," Wikipedia, September 30, 2024, https://en.wikipedia.org/w/index.php?title=Internet_backbone&oldid=1248582613.

32. "Redacted Declaration of J. Scott Marcus," EFF, EFF, April 5, 2006, https://www.eff.org/document/redacted-declaration-j-scott-marcus.

33. Elizabeth Goiten, "Five Myths About Classified Information," Brennan Center for Justice, accessed November 11, 2024, https://www.brennancenter.org/our-work/analysis-opinion/five-myths-about-classified-information.

34. "Court Filings Tell of Internet Spying," *New York Times*, April 7, 2006, sec. U.S., https://www.nytimes.com/2006/04/07/us/nationalspecial3/court-filings-tell-of-internet-spying.html.

35. Peter Spiegel, "Intelligence Committees Hear Wiretapping Details," *Los Angeles Times*, May 18, 2006, sec. Politics, https://www.latimes.com/la-na-nsa18may18-story.html.

36. United States v. Reynolds, 345 U.S. 1 (1953); "*United States v. Reynolds*," Wikipedia, July 17, 2024, https://en.wikipedia.org/w/index.php?title=United_States_v._Reynolds&oldid=1235137914.

37. "Tactical Secrets," *New York Times*, January 25, 2011, sec. Opinion, https://www.nytimes.com/2011/01/25/opinion/25tue2.html.

38. "State Secrets Privilege," Wikipedia, November 2, 2024, https://en.wikipedia.org/w/index.php?title=State_secrets_privilege&oldid=1255035009.

39. Youngstown Sheet & Tube Co. v. Sawyer, 343 U.S. 579 (1952).

40. "50 U.S. Code § 1806—Use of Information," Legal Information Institute, accessed November 11, 2024, https://www.law.cornell.edu/uscode/text/50/1806.

41. Hepting v. AT&T, 439 F.Supp.2d 974 (2006).

42. "Verizon Forced to Hand over Telephone Data—Full Court Ruling," *Guardian*, June 5, 2013, http://www.theguardian.com/world/interactive/2013/jun/06/verizon-telephone-data-court-order.

43. *Hepting*, 439 F.Supp.2d 994.

44. *Hepting*, 439 F.Supp.2d 995.

45. "NSA Spying," EFF, accessed November 11, 2024, https://www.eff.org/nsa-spying.

46. "Three NSA Whistleblowers Back EFF's Lawsuit over Government's Massive Spying Program," EFF, July 2, 2012, https://www.eff.org/press/releases/three-nsa-whistleblowers-back-effs-lawsuit-over-governments-massive-spying-program Electronic; "Thomas Drake Declaration," EFF, 2012, https://www.eff.org/files/filenode/drakedeclaration.pdf; "William Binney Declaration," EFF, 2012, https://www.eff.org/files/filenode/binneydeclaration.pdf; "J. Kirk Wiebe Declaration," EFF, 2012, https://www.eff.org/files/filenode/wiebedeclaration.pdf. Note that J. Kirk Wiebe is no relation to our cocounsel Rick Wiebe.

47. Jewel v. NSA, 673 F.3d 902 (9th Cir. 2011), https://www.eff.org/files/filenode/20111229_9c_jewel_opinion.pdf.

48. Scott Shane and Andrew W. Lehren, "Leaked Cables Offer Raw Look at U.S. Diplomacy," *New York Times*, November 28, 2010, sec. World, https://www.nytimes.com/2010/11/29/world/29cables.html.

49. "Daniel Ellsberg," Wikipedia, November 3, 2024, https://en.wikipedia.org/w/index.php?title=Daniel_Ellsberg&oldid=1255248561.

50. John Schwartz, "The Stickers on Edward Snowden's Laptop," *New York Times*, sec. Lede, 1370889983, https://archive.nytimes.com/thelede.blogs.nytimes.com/2013/06/10/the-stickers-on-edward-snowdens-laptop/.

51. Micah Lee, "Ed Snowden Taught Me to Smuggle Secrets Past Incredible Danger. Now I Teach You," *Intercept*, October 28, 2014, https://theintercept.com/2014/10/28/smuggling-snowden-secrets/.

52. "Public Filings—U.S. Foreign Intelligence Surveillance Court," Foreign Intelligence Surveillance Court, accessed November 1, 2024, https://www.fisc.uscourts.gov/public-filings?page=17.

53. NAACP v. Alabama, 357 U.S. 462–463 (1958).

54. Dara Kerr, "Stop Watching Us Eyes Big Rally Against NSA Surveillance (Q&A)," *CNET*, accessed November 11, 2024, https://www.cnet.com/news/privacy/stop-watching-us-eyes-big-rally-against-nsa-surveillance-q-a/.

55. "Stop Watching Us," October 18, 2014, https://web.archive.org/web/20141018050616/https:/optin.stopwatching.us/.

56. Privacy and Civil Liberties Oversight Board, *Report on the Telephone Records Program Conducted Under Section 215 of the USA PATRIOT Act and on the Operations of the Foreign Intelligence Surveillance Court*, January 23, 2014, https://documents.pclob.gov/prod/Documents/OversightReport/cf0ce183-7935-4b06-bb41-007d1f437412/215-Report_on_the_Telephone_Records_Program%20-%20Completed%20508%20-%2011292022.pdf; Richard Clarke, Michael Morell, Geoffrey Stone, Cass Sunstein, and Peter Swire, "Liberty and Security in a Changing World," White House, December 18, 2013, https://obamawhitehouse.archives.gov/blog/2013/12/18/liberty-and-security-changing-world.

57. Grant Gross, "Report: NSA Collected U.S. Email Records, Internet Use for Years," CSO, accessed November 14, 2024, https://www.csoonline.com/article/539224/privacy-report-nsa-collected-u-s-email-records-internet-use-for-years.html.

58. "Privacy Through Visibility: ScareMail as an Exploit in Computational Surveillance," *NMC Media-N* (blog), November 22, 2014, https://median.newmediacaucus.org/art-infrastructures-information/privacy-through-visibility-scaremail-as-an-exploit-in-computational-surveillance/.

59. "Federal Judge Allows EFF's NSA Mass Spying Case to Proceed," EFF, July 8, 2013, https://www.eff.org/press/releases/federal-judge-allows-effs-nsa-mass-spying-case-proceed.

60. Jewel v. NSA, Plaintiff's Motion for Partial Summary Judgment, No. 4:08-cv-04373-JSW (N.D. Cal. July 25, 2014), https://www.eff.org/files/2014/07/25/jewel_4th_a_mpsj_brief.pdf.

61. Jewel v. NSA, Order Granting Temporary Restraining Order, No. 4:08-cv-04373-JSW (N.D. Cal. March 10, 2014), https://www.eff.org/files/2014/03/11/089_order_granting_tro_3.10.14.pdf; Jewel v. NSA, Order re Emergency Application to Enforce the Court's Temporary Restraining Order, No. 4:08-cv-04373-JSW (N.D. Cal. June 5, 2014), https://www.eff.org/files/2014/06/05/jewel_order.pdf.

62. Jewel v. NSA, Order Denying Plaintiff's Motion for Partial Summary Judgment and Granting Defendant's Motion for Partial Summary Judgment, No. 4:08-cv-04373-JSW (N.D. Cal. February 10, 2015), https://www.eff.org/files/2015/02/10/jewel_order.pdf.

63. Jewel vs. NSA, Judgment on Fourth Amendment Claim, No. 4:08-cv-04373-JSW (N.D. Cal. May 21, 2015), https://www.eff.org/files/2015/05/21/jewel_judgment.pdf.

64. Mary Meeker, "2015 Internet Trends," Kleiner Perkins, May 25, 2015, https://web.archive.org/web/20250214114336/https://www.kleinerperkins.com/perspectives/2015-internet-trends/.

65. "Media Alert: EFF, ACLU to Present Oral Argument in NSA Spying Case on Nov. 4," EFF, October 31, 2014, https://www.eff.org/press/releases/media-alert-eff-aclu-present-oral-argument-nsa-spying-case-nov-4.

66. Jewel v. NSA, Order Regarding Discovery Dispute, No. 4:08-cv-04373-JSW (N.D. Cal. August 28, 2018), https://www.eff.org/files/2023/08/28/412_order_re_discovery_dispute-1.pdf.

67. Jewel v. NSA, Plaintiffs' Motion for Access to Classified Discovery Materials, No. 4:08-cv-04373-JSW (N.D. Cal. May 7, 2018), https://www.eff.org/files/2023/08/29/393_jewel_mtn_for_access_to_classified_discovery_materials_pursuant_to_2712b4_5.7.18.pdf.

68. Jewel v. NSA, Order Requiring Dispositive Motions Briefing, No. 4:08-cv-04373-JSW (N.D. Cal. August 17, 2018), https://www.eff.org/files/2023/08/29/410_order_requiring_dispositive_motions.pdf.

69. "NSA Spying," EFF, accessed November 11, 2024, https://www.eff.org/nsa-spying; "Jewel v. NSA," EFF, July 1, 2011, https://www.eff.org/cases/jewel.

70. Jewel v. NSA, Plaintiffs' Opposition to the Government's Summary Judgment Motion and Plaintiffs' Motion to Proceed to Resolution on the Merits Using the Procedures of Section 1806(f), No. 4:08-cv-04373-JSW (N.D. Cal. September 29, 2018), https://www.eff.org/document/plaintiffs-opposition-governments-summary-judgment-motion-and-plaintiffs-motion-proceed; "About," Ashkan Soltani, accessed November 11, 2024, https://ashkansoltani.org/; "AT&T's Role in Dragnet Surveillance of Millions of Its Customers," EFF, 2007, https://www.eff.org/files/filenode/att/presskit/ATT_onepager.pdf.

71. "Reclaiming Privacy. Defending Freedom," Big Brother Watch, accessed November 11, 2024, https://bigbrotherwatch.org.uk/.

72. "Privacy Through Visibility."

73. "NSA Inspector General Report on Email and Internet Data Collection under Stellar Wind—Full Document," *Guardian*, June 27, 2013, sec. World News, https://www.theguardian.com/nsa-inspector-general-report-document-data-collection.

74. Charlie Savage, "N.S.A. Used Phone Records Program to Seek Iran Operatives," *New York Times*, August 12, 2015, sec. U.S., https://www.nytimes.com/2015/08/13/us/nsa-used-phone-records-program-to-seek-iran-operatives.html.

75. "David McCraw Declaration," EFF, 2018, https://www.eff.org/document/jewel-v-nsa-mccraw-declaration.

76. Aaron Mackey, "Judge Dodges Legality of NSA Mass Spying, Citing Secrecy Claims," EFF, April 26, 2019, https://www.eff.org/deeplinks/2019/04/judge-dodges-legality-nsa-mass-spying-citing-secrecy-claims.

77. "Public Unredacted Klein Declaration," EFF, 2006, https://www.eff.org/document/public-unredacted-klein-declaration; Mort Kondracke, "NSA Data Mining Is Legal, Necessary, Sec. Chertoff Says," *RealClear Politics*, sec. Commentary, January 20, 2006, https://www.realclearpolitics.com/Commentary/com-1_20_06_MK.html; Eric Holder, "Exhibit A—Procedures Used by the National Security Agency for

Targeting Non–United States Persons Reasonably Believed to Be Located Outside the United States to Acquire Foreign Intelligence Information Pursuant to Section 702 of the Foreign Intelligence Surveillance Act of 1978, as Amended," 2009, https://www .documentcloud.org/documents/727943-exhibit-a; Cindy Cohn, "New Witness and New Experts Bolster Our Jewel Case as We Fight Government's Latest Attempt to Derail Lawsuit Challenging Unconstitutional NSA Spying," EFF, October 1, 2018, https://www.eff.org/deeplinks/2018/10/new-witness-and-new-experts-bolster-our -jewel-case-we-fight-governments-latest-0.

78. "Catch-22 (Logic)," Wikipedia, August 20, 2024, https://en.wikipedia.org/w/index .php?title=Catch-22_(logic)&oldid=1241386219.

79. Jewel v. NSA, Appellants' Opening Brief, No. 19-16066 (9th Cir. September 10, 2019), https://www.eff.org/document/jewel-v-nsa-plaintiffs-2019-redacted-opening -brief-9th-cir.

80. "NSA Spying," EFF, accessed November 11, 2024, https://www.eff.org/nsa -spying.

81. Fazaga v. FBI, Opinion, No. 12-56867 (9th Cir. February 28, 2019), https://www.eff .org/document/fazaga-v-fbi-opinion.

82. "The State Secrets Privilege," EFF, December 4, 2012, https://www.eff.org/nsa -spying/state-secrets-privilege.

83. Husayn v. Mitchell, 938 F.3d 1123 (9th Cir. 2019), https://casetext.com/case /husayn-v-mitchell.

84. Jewel v. NSA, Opinion, No. 19-16066 (9th Cir. August 17, 2021), https://www.eff .org/document/jewel-v-nsa-9th-circuit-opinion-august-17-2021.

85. United States v. Abu Zubaydah, 595 U.S. 195 (2022), https://www.supremecourt .gov/opinions/21pdf/20-827_i426.pdf.

86. FBI v. Fazaga, 595 U.S. 344 (2022), https://www.supremecourt.gov/opinions /21pdf/20-828_5ie6.pdf.

87. Charlie Savage, "N.S.A. Halts Collection of Americans' Emails About Foreign Targets," *New York Times*, April 28, 2017, sec. U.S., https://www.nytimes.com/2017 /04/28/us/politics/nsa-surveillance-terrorism-privacy.html.

88. Matthew Guariglia, "New Surveillance Transparency Report Documents an Urgent Need for Change," EFF, May 18, 2022, https://www.eff.org/deeplinks/2022/05 /new-surveillance-transparency-report-documents-urgent-need-change.

89. India McKinney and Cindy Cohn, "Should Congress Close the FBI's Backdoor for Spying on American Communications? Yes," EFF, July 28, 2021, https://www .eff.org/deeplinks/2021/07/should-congress-close-fbis-backdoor-spying-american -communications-yes.

CHAPTER 3

1. Rafael Bernal, "Trump Administration: Three-Quarters of International Terrorism Convicts Foreign Born," *Hill*, January 16, 2018, https://thehill.com/latino/369126

-trump-administration-three-quarters-of-international-terrorism-convicts-foreign-born/.

2. Doe v. Gonzales, 386 F. Supp 2d 66 (D. Conn. 2005); Doe v. Ashcroft, No. 1:04-cv-02614 (S.D.N.Y 2004).

3. Office of the Inspector General, *A Review of the FBI's Use of National Security Letters: Assessment of Corrective Actions and Examination of NSL Usage in 2006*, US Department of Justice, March 2008, https://oig.justice.gov/sites/default/files/legacy/special/s0803b/final.pdf.

4. Jacob Sullum, "Why Use a National Security Letter When You Have Post-It Notes?," *Reason*, January 20, 2010, https://reason.com/2010/01/20/why-use-a-national-security-le/.

5. Office of the Inspector General, *A Review of the Federal Bureau of Investigation's Use of National Security Letters*, US Department of Justice, March 2007, https://www.oversight.gov/sites/default/files/oig-reports/NSL-2007.pdf; Office of the Inspector General, *A Review of the FBI's Use of National Security Letters*; Office of the Inspector General, *A Review of the Federal Bureau of Investigation's Use of Exigent Letters and Other Informal Requests for Telephone Records*, US Department of Justice, January 2010, https://www.oversight.gov/sites/default/files/oig-reports/s1001r.pdf.

6. "18 U.S. Code § 2709—Counterintelligence Access to Telephone Toll and Transactional Records," Legal Information Institute, accessed November 11, 2024, https://www.law.cornell.edu/uscode/text/18/2709.

7. Office of the Inspector General, *A Review of the Federal Bureau of Investigation's Use of Exigent Letters and Other Informal Requests for Telephone Records*, 61.

8. "Report on the Improper Use of an NSL to NC State University," EFF, April 14, 2008, https://www.eff.org/issues/foia/report-nsl-ncstate.

9. Marcia Hofmann, "Senator Cites EFF FOIA Work in Call for Investigation of Attorney General," EFF, August 17, 2007, https://www.eff.org/deeplinks/2007/08/senator-cites-eff-foia-work-call-investigation-attorney-general.

10. "FBI Withdraws Unconstitutional National Security Letter After ACLU and EFF Challenge," EFF, May 7, 2008, https://www.eff.org/press/archives/2008/05/06.

11. John Doe, Inc. v. Mukasey, 549 F.3d 861 (2d Cir. 2008).

12. "The Unknown Barry Switzer," *Chicago Tribune*, December 14, 1986, https://www.chicagotribune.com/1986/12/14/the-unknown-barry-switzer/; "Ann Richards," Wikipedia, October 31, 2024, https://en.wikipedia.org/w/index.php?title=Ann_Richards&oldid=1254490784.

13. In fact, we had to ask the Department of Justice and court to unseal the transcript of this hearing so I could quote from it here. Many thanks to EFF senior staff attorney Aaron Mackey for handling that for me.

14. Jennifer Valentino-DeVries, "Covert FBI Power to Obtain Phone Data Faces Rare Test," *Wall Street Journal*, updated July 18, 2012, https://www.wsj.com/articles/SB10001424052702303567704577519213906388708.

15. In re National Security Letter, 930 F. Supp. 1064, 1074 (N.D. Cal. 2013).

16. United States v. Smith, 899 F. 2d 564 (6th Cir. 1989).

17. "National Security Letters Are Unconstitutional, Federal Judge Rules," EFF, March 15, 2013, https://www.eff.org/press/releases/national-security-letters-are-unconstitutional-federal-judge-rules.

18. The United States' Opposition to the Companies' Motion to Strike the Government's Ex Parte Response to Motions to Disclose Aggregate Data Regarding FISA Orders, No. Misc 13-03, Misc 13-04, Misc 13-05, Misc 13-06, Misc 13-07 (FISA Ct. 2013), https://www.fisc.uscourts.gov/sites/default/files/Misc%2013-03%20Motion-22.pdf.

19. "Termination Procedures for National Security Letter Nondisclosure Requirement," Federal Bureau of Investigation, accessed November 11, 2024, https://www.fbi.gov/file-repository/nsl-ndp-procedures.pdf/view.

20. "Ruling Unsealed: National Security Letters Upheld as Constitutional," EFF, April 21, 2016, https://www.eff.org/press/releases/ruling-unsealed-national-security-letters-upheld-constitutional.

21. "CREDO Confirms It's at Center of Long-Running Legal Fight over NSLs," EFF, November 30, 2016, https://www.eff.org/press/releases/credo-confirms-its-center-long-running-NSL-fight.

22. "CREDO Confirms It's at Center of Long-Running Legal Fight over NSLs."

23. "Government Withdrawal of NSL," EFF, November 29, 2016, https://www.eff.org/document/government-withdrawal-nsl.

24. "Ninth Circuit 2017 NSL Opinion," EFF, July 18, 2017, https://www.eff.org/document/ninth-circuit-2017-nsl-opinion.

CONCLUSION

1. Dobbs v. Jackson Women's Health Organization, 597 U.S. 215 (2022).

2. Joseph Menn, "Exclusive: NSA Infiltrated RSA Security More Deeply than Thought—Study," Reuters, March 31, 2014, sec. World, https://www.reuters.com/article/world/exclusive-nsa-infiltrated-rsa-security-more-deeply-than-thought-study-idUSBREA2U0TY/.

3. Adam Schwartz, "Resisting the Menace of Face Recognition," EFF, October 26, 2021, https://www.eff.org/deeplinks/2021/10/resisting-menace-face-recognition; Nathan Sheard and Adam Schwartz, "The Movement to Ban Government Use of Face Recognition," EFF, May 5, 2022, https://www.eff.org/deeplinks/2022/05/movement-ban-government-use-face-recognition; "EFF Zine on Surveillance Tech at the Southern Border Shines Light on Ever-Growing Spy Network," EFF, May 6, 2024, https://www.eff.org/press/releases/eff-zine-surveillance-tech-southern-border-shines-light-ever-growing-spy-network.

4. Matthew Guariglia, Andrew Crocker, Cindy Cohn, and Brendan Gilligan, "U.S. Senate and Biden Administration Shamefully Renew and Expand FISA Section 702, Ushering in a Two Year Expansion of Unconstitutional Mass Surveillance," EFF,

April 22, 2024, https://www.eff.org/deeplinks/2024/04/us-senate-and-biden-administration-shamefully-renew-and-expand-fisa-section-702-0.

5. Matthew Guariglia, "New Surveillance Transparency Report Documents an Urgent Need for Change," EFF, May 18, 2022, https://www.eff.org/deeplinks/2022/05/new-surveillance-transparency-report-documents-urgent-need-change.

6. "Article III Standing," EPIC, accessed November 15, 2024, https://epic.org/issues/privacy-laws/article-iii-standing/.

INDEX

Note: The letter *f* following a page locator denotes a figure.

Abelson, Hal, 47–48
Abortion, 22
Abu Zubaydah case, 164–165
ACLU v. Reno, 54
Adams, John (founding father), 3
Adams, John (lawyer), 86, 161
Ads, contextual and behavioral, 91
Ai Weiwei, 148
Al-Haramain case, 104–106, 116
American Association for the Advancement of Science, 55
Apache, 49
Appel, Andrew, 48
Ashcroft, John, 58, 130
Association for Computing Machinery, US Public Policy Committee, 55, 77
AT&T, 95–103, 152–153, 191. See also *Hepting v. AT&T*
Authoritarianism, 4

Baker, Stewart, 89
Ball, Patrick, 50–51, 55, 72, 119, 132–133, 135–136, 171–172, 203, 207–208
Bankston, Kevin, 79–80, 85, 87, 95–96, 105, 112, 129, 134–135, 136, 140
Baquet, Dean, 103
Barlow, John Perry, 26–29, 54, 139
Barney the Dinosaur, 91–92
Bauld, Bill, 31, 34, 42–43, 45
Beeson, Ann, 77
Behlendorf, Brian, 49, 203
Berman, Jerry, 123
Berners-Lee, Tim, 56, 148
Bernstein, Daniel, 11, 34–37, 41, 44–45, 47, 52–54, 75–76
Bernstein v. Department of Justice
  beginnings, 31–32, 34
  causes of action, 40
  central argument, 39
  Cohn's contributions, 37
  courtroom described, 44, 119
  courtroom supporters, 1, 56
  decision in favor, 45–46, 186–187, 203
  EFF team, 37–38, 178
  filing, 40–41
  impact case, building the, 36–37
  judge assigned, 41
  media coverage, 41, 119
  mentioned, 173, 199
  motion to dismiss denied, 43–46
  opposing counsel, 90
  purpose, 38–39
  Snuffle program, 35–36
  summary judgment, 46–49, 51–52
Bernstein v. US Department of Commerce
  congressional testimony, 58–59
  en banc review, 67, 75

Bernstein v. US Department of Commerce (cont.)
 expert supporters, 55
 judgment in favor, 65–67
 Ninth Circuit Court of Appeals, 54–58
 summary judgment win, 52–54
Biden (Joe) and administration, 124, 130, 206
Big Brother Watch, 162
Bin Laden, Osama, 82–83
Binney, William (Bill), 129, 162
Bishop, Matthew, 49
Blaze, Matthew, 49, 162
Bond, Becky, 169, 190
Bowoto, Larry, 71–72
Bowoto v. Chevron, 69–72, 94, 115, 138, 180–181
Brennan, William J., 39
Bressler, Steven, 180, 182–183
Brick, Ann, 77, 115
Bright, Melvin, 57, 67
Brosnahan, James (Jim), 101, 107, 113, 178
Bureau of Export Administration (BXA), 211
Burning Man, 135–136
Bush, George H. W., 176
Bush, George W., 80–81, 83, 94, 130, 206

Cameras, police-worn body, 7
Carter, Kenneth, 190, 196
Case Q
 beginnings, 176–177
 Cohn's oral argument preparations, 178–180
 countersuits, 187
 decision in favor, 185–187
 EFF attorneys, 178
 en banc decision, 199
 first hearing, 181–183
 media coverage, 183–185
 mixed decision, 195–196
 Ninth Circuit hearings, 192–195, 197–199
 reversal, 188–189
 secrecy issue, 182–183
Case W, 189, 196
Case Z, 187–189, 196
Censorship, 39–40
Center for Constitutional Rights, 115–116
Center for Democracy and Technology, 123
Central Intelligence Agency (CIA), 81–83
Chevron, Bowoto v., 69–72
Church, Frank, 4–5, 114
Clapper, James, 143
Clinton, Bill, 58, 80, 130, 206
Cloudflare, 186, 190, 196
Coders' Rights Project, x
Cohn, Cindy
 adoption story, 14–15, 21–23, 62–65, 93–94
 characteristics, 76
 childhood, 15–19
 clothing, 1, 40, 56, 94, 119, 135
 community, 20, 25–26, 29, 31, 59–61, 93, 132
 condescension encountered, 41–43
 education, 19–20
 EFF directorship, 155–156, 158–159, 192
 EFF job, 68–69, 71–72
 height, effect of, 44, 73
 on judges, 45
 law career, beginnings, 23–25, 29–30
 at McGlashan and Sarrail, 31, 33–34
 media coverage, 61, 132, 134, 149
 Nigeria trip, 180
 outsider feelings, 15, 17, 19, 22
 personal life, 59–60
 pregnancy, 22
 religion, 17–19

romantic life, 25, 29, 59–60, 68, 92–93, 96, 113, 119, 131–134, 135–136, 171–172, 203, 207–208
Snowden and, 144–145, 145*f*
Unrepresented Nations and People's Organization (UNPO), 30
Colbert, Stephen, 132
Commodity Jurisdiction (CJ), 211
Communications Access for Law Enforcement Act, 122–123
Communications Decency Act (CDA), 54–55, 211
Computer code
commodity jurisdiction requests, 37
export restrictions, 13–14, 36–37, 48–49, 72–76
is language, 46–49, 66
as protected speech, 35–36, 43–45
Contact chaining, 89
Conyers, John, 149
Coppolino, Tony, 41–43, 45, 52, 72–74, 104, 106, 108, 158
Corn-Revere, Bob, 38, 72–74, 187, 203
Corporate surveillance, 205
Cosmo (Newfoundland), 92, 133
CREDO, 152, 169–170, 176, 183–185, 188, 190, 192–193, 196. *See also* Case Q
"Crime and Puzzlement" (Barlow), 27
Crocker, Andrew, 197
Cryptography, 48–51. *See also* Encryption
Cuban, Mark, x
Cusack, John, 139, 148

Dalai Lama, 24, 30
D'Andrade, Hugh, 125, 141, 150
"Declaration of the Independence of Cyberspace" (Barlow), 28, 54
Demberger, James, 49
Diffie, Whitfield, 55
Digital privacy, threats to, 3–4, 205
Dobbs v. Jackson Women's Health Organization, 205, 207
Dodd, Chris, 123, 127
Doe v. Mukasey, 175–176, 182, 186–189, 192–194
Downey, Tom, 124
Drake, Thomas, 129, 162
Dyson, Esther, 77

Eckersley, Peter, 90
Egelko, Bob, 45–46, 53, 185
Eisenberg, Jon, 105, 116
Eisgrau, Adam, 124
Electronic Frontier Foundation (EFF)
annual awards dinner, 203
beginnings, 26–29
blimp over NSA facility, 150, 151*f*
cage matches, 91–92
Communications Access Law Enforcement Act fight, 122–123
congressional member's scorecard, 150
copyright claims work, 92
core issues, 91
in DC, 122–123
expansion, 90–91
funding, 124, 169
furnishings, 90, 103–104
growth, 145, 155–156, 171, 203–204
impact litigation, 76–77
ISP ratings, 191
lobbyists hired, 124
media coverage, 149
next generation, 197–199
office animals, 92–93
open-source law, 77, 109
parody of the NSA eagle, 125*f*
philosophy, 33
public relations, 124–125
Snowden and the, 140–142
split, 123
swag, 140

Electronic Frontier Foundation (EFF) (cont.)
"Who Has Your Back" campaign, 191
work done by, ix–x, 47, 91–92, 171, 204–206
Ellsberg, Daniel, 83, 139, 149
Encryption, 8, 11–14
Encryption software. See also *Bernstein v. Department of Justice*
export restrictions, 13–14, 36–37, 48–49, 72–76
government restrictions on publishing, 11, 13–14
regulation of, 34–36
Epstein, Richard, 58
Erlich, Miles, 101, 107
Export Administration Regulations (EAR), 52–53, 211

Facebook, 91
Fazaga v. FBI, 164–165
Federal Bureau of Investigations (FBI), 82–83
Feinstein, Dianne, 124
Fena, Lori, 77
Figallo, Cliff, 26
Film licensing, 39–40
First Amendment arguments
Hepting v. AT&T, 146
Jewel v. NSA, 146
First Amendment protections, 145–146, 178, 194–195, 198, 200
First Unitarian Church of Los Angeles v. NSA, 146–150
Fletcher, Betty, 57, 64–65, 68, 77
Foreign Intelligence Surveillance Act (FISA), 84, 113–115, 121, 154–155, 211
Foreign Intelligence Surveillance Act (FISA) Amendments Act, 124, 126–128, 130
Foreign Intelligence Surveillance Court (FISC), 211
Fourth Amendment arguments
Hepting v. AT&T, 146
Jewel v. NSA, 146, 160
Fourth Amendment protections, 86–87, 89–90
Fram, Rob, 109, 120
Freedman, Ronald, 39
Freedman v. Maryland, 39–40, 52, 173, 175, 185, 198–199
Freedom of speech, 35–36, 55
Freedom of the Press Foundation, 137–139
Friedman, Jeff, 116

Gag orders, 173–174. *See also* National Security Letter (NSL) gag orders
Gilmore, John, 25–26, 28–29, 31–34, 37–38, 47, 119, 122–123, 132, 135
Godwin, Mike, 28, 34
Godwin's law, 28
Golden Age for Surveillance, 59
Gonzales, Alberto, 117, 175
Google, 188–189
Gore, Al, 58, 73–74
Grateful Dead, 20, 24, 27, 29, 72
Greene, David, 145–146
Green Tortoise bus friends, 60
Greenwald, Glenn, 137, 139, 140–141, 145
Gross, Terry, 136
Grossman, Harvey, 117
Groupthink, 82–83
Gyari, Lody, 30
Gyllenhaal, Maggie, 148

Hackers, 25–26, 34–35
Hackers (Levy), 26
Harmon, Amy, 61
Harris, Leslie, 77
Hash functions, 35–36
Hawkins, Michael, 120–121, 159
Hayden, Michael, 89, 103
Hepting, Tash, 102, 128

Hepting v. AT&T
AT&T replies, 106–108, 110
case dismissed, 136
classified documents question, 104–106
Cohn's responsibilities, 109
counsel, 109, 116–117
decision, 117–119
filing, 102
First Amendment arguments, 146
Fourth Amendment arguments, 146
generalized grievance decision, 131, 134, 171
interlocutory review, 119
Judge Walker, 110–113, 131
media coverage, 103, 107–108
mentioned, 159
motions to dismiss, 113, 117
multidistrict litigation, 115–117
naming, 128
Ninth Circuit hearings, 134–137
opposing counsel, 120
panel of judges, 120–121
preservation of evidence order, 153–155
reconsideration, 128
retroactive immunity decision, 121–122, 127–130, 134, 171
state secrets argument, 111–115, 117–119, 121, 130–131
Higgins, Parker, 150
Hoover, J. Edgar, 172
Human rights, cryptography and, 49–51
Hurricane Katrina, 117
Husayn case, 164

Illston, Susan, 180–186, 188–189, 192, 194–195, 198, 201
Impact litigation, 76–77
International Traffic in Arms Regulations (ITAR), 39, 42, 52–53, 211
Internet
Cohn responsibilities, 77
early years, 27–29, 33, 56, 77
encryption and, 11–13
growth, 56, 158
metadata, 88–89
narratives dominating history of, 10
Internet Archive case, 175–176
Internet backbone, 97–98
Internet Mail Consortium, 55
Internet Service Providers (ISPs), EFF ratings, 191

Jardin, Xeni, 139
Jawboning, 138
Jefferson, Thomas, 3, 59
Jeschke, Rebecca, 132
Jewel, Carolyn, 128
Jewel v. NSA
attempt to dismiss, 153
case dismissed, 166
Cohn responsibilities, 136–137
counsel, 136
delay and stonewalling, 161
filing, 129
First Amendment arguments, 146
Fourth Amendment arguments, 146, 160
judge assigned, 129, 131
mentioned, 192
motion to dismiss, 130–132
naming, 128–129
Ninth Circuit court, 134–137, 159–166
outcomes post-, 166–167
preservation of evidence order, 153–155, 154*f*
reversal of rulings, 157–158
ruling for appellate review, 158
state secrets argument, 153, 157, 164–166
stay on discovery lifted, 159–161
Upstream focus, 153, 157
Jónsdóttir, Birgitta, 191

Jue, Aaron, 141
Junger, Peter, 75
Junger v. Daley, 67, 75

Kapor, Mitch, 26–27, 29, 122
Kathrein, Reed, 116
Katz v. United States, 86–87
Kieschnick, Michael, 169
King, Martin Luther Jr., 114
Klayman v. AT&T, 158
Klein, Mark, 80, 90, 96–99, 101, 102, 104, 106–108, 111, 117, 121, 124–127, 129, 130, 143–144, 149–150, 157, 178
Knappenberger, Brian, 148, 150
Kodiak Bear (Newfoundland), 133

Lali (Bernese mountain dog), 208
Lee, Micah, 139, 141
Lee, Mike, 123
Legislation, privacy, 6
Lemmey, Tara, 77
Lennon, John, 114
Lessig, Larry, 61
Let's Encrypt project, x
Levy, Steven, 26
Lewin, Mr., 18–19
Lieberman, Joseph, 138–139
LOVEINT, 8

Maazel, Ilann, 115
Madison, James, 3, 59
Maell, Linnart, 30
Manning, Chelsea, 138, 191
Marcus, J. Scott, 104, 144
Mayer, Jonathan, 88
McCraw, David, 163
McGlashan, Doug, 34
McIntosh, Scott, 57
McKeon, Margaret, 120, 134, 159
McSherry, Corynne, 102, 140, 156
Menn, Joe, 103
Metadata, 4, 87–90, 145–146
MGM v. Grokster, 94
Mohammed, Khalid Sheikh, 89
Moore, Tom, 147
Morris, Maria, 111, 116
Morris, Ray, 196
Moussaoui, Zacarias, 82
"Mr. Klein Goes to Washington," 126*f*
Multi-District Litigation (MDL), 211
Murakami, Haruki, 93
Murguia, Mary, 193

National Association of Manufacturers, 55
National Computer Security Association, 55
National Security Agency (NSA)
  attempts to limit, 146–152
  eagle parody, 125*f*
  metadata use, 89
  pre-9/11 warnings, 81–83
  Project SHAMROCK, 114
  Upstream program, 128, 157, 166
National Security Agency (NSA) wiretapping case. See also *Hepting v. AT&T*
  congressional support, 123–124, 126–127
  domestic internet backbone surveillance, 98–108, 100*f*, 152
  internet backbone named, 128
  mass domestic surveillance programs, 83–85, 94–95
  mass domestic surveillance programs, fighting, 85–92, 95
  mass domestic telephone records collection, 152
  media coverage, 123, 125
  order for Verizon records, 140–143, 145
  post-9/11, 79–85
National Security Letter (NSL)
  cats compared to, 172
  defined, 212

early challenges, 174–176
First Amendment protections, 194–195, 198, 200
focus, pre- and post-Patriot Act, 172–173
growth, 174
limitations, 170
misuse of, 174–175
power of, 172–174, 176
"Termination Procedures of National Security Letter Nondisclosure Requirements" process, 193
National Security Letter (NSL) gag orders
challenging, 173
effects of, 174, 189–194, 199
lifted, 196–197, 200
Ninth Circuit rulings, 198–199
numbers of, 173
permanency of, 170, 173
post–Patriot Act, 173
National security talisman, 4–5
Nelson, Thomas, 57, 66
Nesson, Charles, 61
Neumann, Peter, 55
Nichols, Carl, 111
Ninth Circuit Court of Appeals described
San Francisco, 56, 134
Seattle, 134
Nixon, Richard, 57, 139
Nonjusticiability doctrine, 43

Obama (Barack) and administration, 89, 124, 127, 130, 144, 150–151, 206
Ogoni Nine, 69–72
Olbermann, Keith, 125
Open-source law, 77, 109
Opsahl, Kurt, 114, 137, 140, 156, 192
Otis, James, 86, 161

Parker, Jean, 169–170, 182
Patel, Marilyn Hall, 1, 41, 44–46, 51–54, 57, 75, 77
Paul, Rand, 123
PGP encryption program, 13, 50, 140, 145
Pickford, Thomas, 82
Poindexter, John, 84
Poitras, Laura, 134, 137, 139, 140–142
Police, power of the, 7–8
Pregerson, Harry, 120, 135
Privacy
meaning of, 2–4
power and, 2–4
present day, 206–207
protections, 9, 87
secrecy vs., 87
security vs., 7, 81
Privacy and Civil Liberties Oversight Board, 151
Privacy Badger, x
Privacy rights, 7
Project SHAMROCK, 114

Ramsey, Izzy, 101, 107
Ratner, Michael, 138
Reid, Brian, 101, 125, 144, 162
Reitman, Rainey, 139, 148
In Re National Security Agency Telecommunications Records Litigation, 117
Reproductive freedom, 3
Richards, Ann, 176
Rivest, Ron, 55
Rowley, Colleen, 82
Rumold, Mark, 140

SAFE Act, 58
Samuelson, Pam, 77
Saro-Wiwa, Ken, 30, 69–70
Sarrail, Karen, 34
Scarlett, Shana, 116
Scarselli, Gino, 67, 75
Schneier, Bruce, 48
Schoen, Seth, 90
Secrecy, privacy vs., 87

Security, privacy vs., 7, 81
Sensitive Compartmentalized Information Facility (SCIF), 212
September 11, 2001 terrorist attacks, 4, 79–85, 152
Shubert case, 115
Simons, Barbara, 55, 77, 92
Smith, Randy, 192
Snowden, Edward, 4, 89, 117, 125, 141–147, 145*f*, 150, 152, 158, 162–163, 189, 203, 206. *See also* Wikileaks
Snuffle program, 35–36
Social media, 91
Sohn, Gigi, 77
Solove, Daniel, 2
Soltani, Ashkan, 162
SOPA/PIPA laws, x
Speech, indecent, 54
State secrets argument
  Hepting v. AT&T, 111–115
  Jewel v. NSA, 153, 157, 164–166
State secrets privilege, 117–119, 121, 130–131
Stearns, Josh, 139
Steele, Shari, 34, 38, 46–47, 52, 68–69, 71, 72–74, 76–77, 79, 141, 155–156, 180
Stone, Oliver, 149
Street-Level Surveillance work, x
Sullivan, Kathleen, 58
Surveillance, 4, 6, 8. *See also* National Security Agency (NSA) wiretapping case
Surveillance capitalism, 91
Swartz, Aaron, x
Swire, Peter, 59
Switzer, Barry, 176

Tenth Amendment Center, 149
Terkel, Studs, 115
Terrorism conviction statistics, 8
Tien, Lee, 37–38, 41, 44, 46, 58, 67–68, 77, 80, 85, 90, 121, 140
Timm, Trevor, 137–138, 140
Torture of terrorist subjects, 164
Total Information Awareness, 84
Totalitarianism, turnkey, 4
Trade secrecy, 87
Trump (Donald) and administrations, 4–5, 165, 205, 206–207
Turing, Alan, 14
Twitter, 191
Tyre, Jim, 109, 147

Unitary executive doctrine, 165
Unrepresented Nations and People's Organization (UNPO), 30
Upstream, 128, 157, 166
USA Freedom Act, 149–152, 166–167, 193–195, 196, 201
USA Patriot Act, 79–82, 189, 200. *See also* National Security Letter (NSL)
USA Patriot Act 2006 reauthorization, 174
US Munitions List (USML), 212
U.S. v. Reynolds, 111–112
U.S. v. Warshak, 87

Valentino-DeVries, Jennifer, 183–184
Vasvari, Ray, 67, 75
Verified Voter Foundation, 92
Verizon, 117–118, 140–143, 145, 191
VOTPCRYP, 49

Walker, Vaughn, 102, 108, 110–115, 117–121, 129–131, 134, 136, 157–158, 160, 171
Walt, Michael van, 24, 30
Weir, Bob, 27
West, Tony, 101, 107, 111, 130
Weston, Burns, 23
Wheaton, Jim, 1, 38, 178
Wheaton, Wil, 92
White, Jeffrey, 136, 147, 151–153, 155, 157–159, 160, 161, 163
Whitney (Bernese mountain dog), 208

"Who Has Your Back" campaign, 191
Whole Earth 'Lectronic Link (WELL), 26–28
Wiebe, J. Kirk, 129, 149, 162
Wiebe, Rick, 96, 136, 147, 159
Wikileaks, 137–143, 191. *See also* Snowden, Edward
Wiretapping, 122–123. *See also* National Security Agency (NSA) wiretapping case
Wizner, Ben, 143
Wozniak, Steve, 28
Writs of assistance, 86
Wyden, Ron, 152, 206

Zimmerman, Matt, 178, 180, 181–186, 192
Zimmermann, Philip, 13, 49–50, 140
Zittrain, Jonathan, 61
Zubaida, Abu, 89
Zuboff, Shoshana, 91
Zuckerberg, Mark, 92

Publisher contact:
The MIT Press
Massachusetts Institute of Technology
77 Massachusetts Avenue, Cambridge, MA 02139
mitpress.mit.edu

EU Authorised Representative:
Easy Access System Europe, Mustamäe tee 50,
10621 Tallinn, Estonia
gpsr.requests@easproject.com

Printed by Integrated Books International,
United States of America